CAMBRIDGE LIBRARY COLLECTION

Books of enduring scholarly value

Cambridge

The city of Cambridge received its royal charter in 1201, having already been home to Britons, Romans and Anglo-Saxons for many centuries. Cambridge University was founded soon afterwards and celebrated its octocentenary in 2009. This series explores the history and influence of Cambridge as a centre of science, learning, and discovery, its contributions to national and global politics and culture, and its inevitable controversies and scandals.

Charters of the Borough of Cambridge

Professor F.W. Maitland was the foremost Victorian scholar on English legal history, and Mary Bateson a Cambridge medieval historian. This 1901 volume was edited for the Corporation of Cambridge and the Cambridge Antiquarian Society. It provides a transcript and translation of the royal charters issued to the borough of Cambridge between the twelfth and the seventeenth centuries. Maitland lays stress on the considerable independence the medieval borough had. It was largely self-governing, royal charters bestowing or confirming liberties rather than regulating the town governance or providing a constitution. However, there were some limitations, chiefly relating to justice, for which royal permission was needed. It was not until the late seventeenth century that royal authority began to tighten its control of borough affairs. The introduction explains the conventions of such charters, and how the reader should interpret the information contained therein. A valuable source of local history with wider significance.

Cambridge University Press has long been a pioneer in the reissuing of out-of-print titles from its own backlist, producing digital reprints of books that are still sought after by scholars and students but could not be reprinted economically using traditional technology. The Cambridge Library Collection extends this activity to a wider range of books which are still of importance to researchers and professionals, either for the source material they contain, or as landmarks in the history of their academic discipline.

Drawing from the world-renowned collections in the Cambridge University Library, and guided by the advice of experts in each subject area, Cambridge University Press is using state-of-the-art scanning machines in its own Printing House to capture the content of each book selected for inclusion. The files are processed to give a consistently clear, crisp image, and the books finished to the high quality standard for which the Press is recognised around the world. The latest print-on-demand technology ensures that the books will remain available indefinitely, and that orders for single or multiple copies can quickly be supplied.

The Cambridge Library Collection will bring back to life books of enduring scholarly value (including out-of-copyright works originally issued by other publishers) across a wide range of disciplines in the humanities and social sciences and in science and technology.

Charters of the
Borough of Cambridge

EDITED BY FREDERIC WILLIAM MAITLAND
AND MARY BATESON

CAMBRIDGE
UNIVERSITY PRESS

CAMBRIDGE UNIVERSITY PRESS

Cambridge, New York, Melbourne, Madrid, Cape Town, Singapore,
São Paolo, Delhi, Dubai, Tokyo, Mexico City

Published in the United States of America by Cambridge University Press, New York

www.cambridge.org
Information on this title: www.cambridge.org/9781108010436

© in this compilation Cambridge University Press 2010

This edition first published 1901
This digitally printed version 2010

ISBN 978-1-108-01043-6 Paperback

THE CHARTERS

OF THE

BOROUGH OF CAMBRIDGE

London: C. J. CLAY AND SONS,
CAMBRIDGE UNIVERSITY PRESS WAREHOUSE,
AVE MARIA LANE.
Glasgow: 50, WELLINGTON STREET.

Leipzig: F. A BROCKHAUS
New York: THE MACMILLAN COMPANY.
Bombay: E. SEYMOUR HALE.

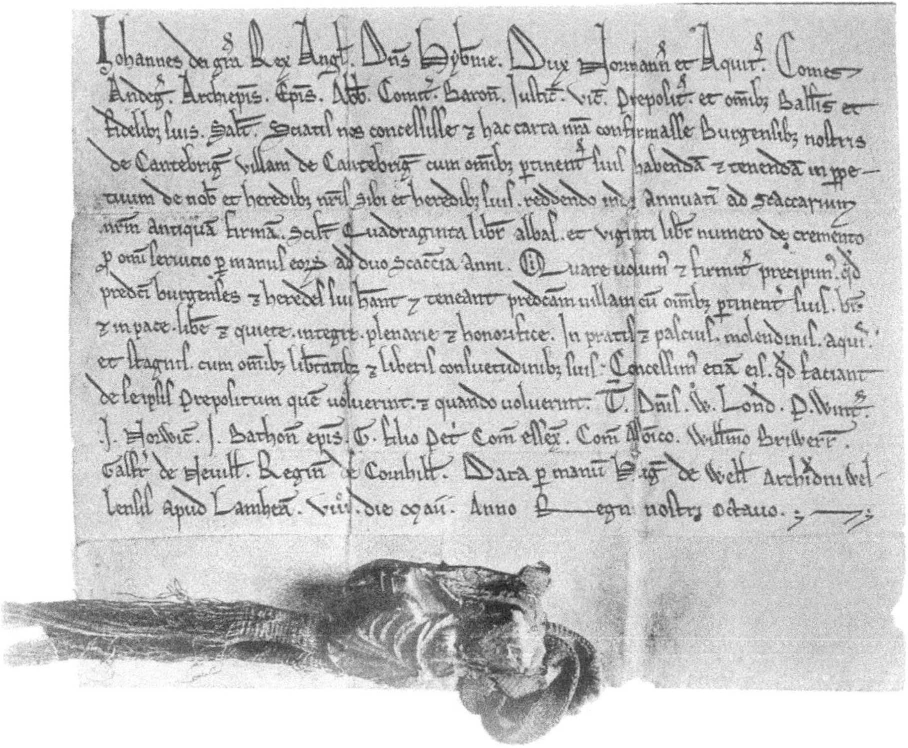

Charter of King John, 8 May, 1207.

THE CHARTERS

OF THE

BOROUGH OF CAMBRIDGE

EDITED FOR

THE COUNCIL OF THE BOROUGH OF CAMBRIDGE

AND THE CAMBRIDGE ANTIQUARIAN SOCIETY

BY

FREDERIC WILLIAM MAITLAND, LL.D., D.C.L.

DOWNING PROFESSOR OF THE LAWS OF ENGLAND

AND

MARY BATESON

ASSOCIATE AND LECTURER OF NEWNHAM COLLEGE

CAMBRIDGE

AT THE UNIVERSITY PRESS

1901

𝕮𝖆𝖒𝖇𝖗𝖎𝖉𝖌𝖊:

PRINTED BY J. AND C. F. CLAY,
AT THE UNIVERSITY PRESS.

TABLE OF CONTENTS.

Table of Contents.

APPENDIX

ILLUSTRATION

Charter of King John, 8 May, 1207, to face Title-page.

Note: The original measures $8\frac{1}{8}$ ins. by $6\frac{7}{8}$ ins.

The publication of the Ancient Charters of the Borough has been undertaken jointly by the Corporation of Cambridge and by the Cambridge Antiquarian Society.

We gratefully acknowledge our indebtedness to the late Mr F. C. WACE, M.A., sometime Mayor, Mr J. E. L. WHITEHEAD, M.A., Town Clerk, and Miss MARY BATESON for their valuable services, and to Dr MAITLAND for his admirable Introduction and general superintendence and revision of the whole work.

H. M. TAYLOR,
Mayor.

J. W. L. GLAISHER,
President of the
Cambridge Antiquarian Society.

CAMBRIDGE,
February 1901.

At a meeting of the Council of the Borough of Cambridge holden at the Guildhall this first day of January in the year of our Lord nineteen hundred and one it was resolved unanimously on the proposition of the Mayor seconded by Mr Alderman Deck "That this Council do hereby, in pursuance of the Honorary Freedom of Boroughs Act, 1885, confer upon FREDERIC WILLIAM MAITLAND, M.A., LL.D., D.C.L., Downing Professor of the Laws of England, the Honorary Freedom of the Borough of Cambridge, in recognition of the care and great ability which he has devoted to the investigation and the illustration of the early annals of this ancient Borough, and of his generosity in placing his erudition at the service of the Council by undertaking gratuitously the editing of the Charters of the Borough, and do hereby admit the said FREDERIC WILLIAM MAITLAND to be an Honorary Freeman of the Borough of Cambridge accordingly."

H. M. TAYLOR,
Mayor.

J. E. L. WHITEHEAD,
Town Clerk.

INTRODUCTION

BY

F. W. MAITLAND.

THE good work of transcribing and translating the royal charters of the town of Cambridge was undertaken some years ago by the late Mr F. C. Wace, M.A., then Mayor of the Borough, and Mr J. E. L. Whitehead, M.A., the Town Clerk. After having been for a while in my hands, it has been brought to completion by Miss Bateson, Associate and Lecturer of Newnham College. Though more than one hand has laboured on this book, I hope that it will not be found unworthy of the Cambridge Antiquarian Society or of the Municipal Corporation which has generously sanctioned and forwarded the publication of these its ancient records.

Cambridge, when it compares itself with other towns, has no reason to be ashamed of its charters. All the kings and queens regnant of England from Henry I to Charles II are represented in the following pages, with the exception of Stephen, Richard I, Edward V, Richard III, and Henry VII, though Edward III and Mary Tudor will appear only in an appendix. The reader will be able to compare a curt writ of Henry I with the artificially contrived cadences that were fashionable in the chancery of Richard II and with the lengthy and wordy, pompous and yet very cautious clauses of the seventeenth century. And beneath all this he may see the growth of an English town.

But to see this he must look somewhat intently. It must be confessed that to a student of institutions the series of

viii   *Introduction.*

charters granted to a borough is apt to be a little disappointing, at least for a moment. He wishes to ask many questions that it will not answer. But, if that be so, it is because he has yet to learn that to answer those questions is not the proper function of the documents which the borough community obtains from the central power. He is interested in constitutions, and he sees in the Cambridge of 1833 (on the eve, that is, of the great Municipal Reformation) a constitution which, if decadent, is elaborate. He sees a mayor, four bailiffs, four councillors, twelve aldermen, four and twenty common councilmen, two treasurers, two coroners, a high steward, a recorder. He sees also a body, a small body, of burgesses. Moreover, he can discover how these various organs and officers of the borough are constituted, what are their duties and what their rights[1]. Then, knowing that these matters had not been fixed by any general law, knowing that the reforming Act of 1835 was the first Act of its kind, he perhaps hopes that as regards each town separately he may see a constitution imposed upon it or manufactured for it by its charters. If that be so, disappointment awaits him. He has yet to learn how autonomous, how self-constituting and self-organizing the borough community had been.

During the Middle Ages the function of the royal charter was not that of 'erecting a corporation' or regulating a corporation which already existed, but that of bestowing 'liberties and franchises' upon a body which, within large limits, was free to give itself a constitution and to alter that constitution from time to time. There were things that it could not do unless it obtained a privilege from the king. It could not, for example, institute coroners, for that would

[1] Appendix to *First Report of the Commissioners appointed to inquire into the Municipal Corporations*, 1835, pt. iv. p. 2185. (I cite this work as *Mun. Corp. Rep.*)

have disturbed the justiciary scheme of the shire of which the borough formed a part. It could not declare that its own officers should do that work of summoning, distraining and arresting which had theretofore been done, even within borough walls, by the sheriff. Nor could it take from the sheriff the power and duty of collecting those rents and tolls which were due to the king. It demanded from the king a certain amount of exemption and immunity. But, this having been acquired, it was very free to give itself a constitution, to develop a conciliar organ, one council or two councils, to define the modes in which burgherhood should be acquired, to adopt the ballot or the open vote, and generally to be as oligarchic or as democratic as it thought fit. And at least from the fourteenth century onwards a large use was made of this liberty. Elaborate constitutions were established and after a few years abolished, and some of our boroughs had revolutions enough to satisfy a South American republic.

It is not uncommonly supposed that this medieval autonomy came to an end in the age of the Tudors, or at all events in the age of the Stewarts; that charters were then granted to the boroughs which imposed rigid and oligarchic constitutions; and that such charters were the outcome of a definite policy on the part of the State. Only to a very small degree is this true of Cambridge. No charter proceeding from any Tudor did anything towards defining the constitution of the burghal community, and yet during the reign of Elizabeth that constitution was being frequently altered at important points by the activity of the burgesses in their Common Halls[1]. The charter of James I (1605) did a very little and that of Charles I (1632) did a little more towards introducing rigidity by drawing a few constitutional

[1] Cooper, *Annals,* ii. 105, 107, 160, 163, 209, 226, 233, 241, 278, 310, 320, 341, 342, 383, 409, 461, 485, 597-8, 612.

outlines, for an outline drawn by charter the burgesses could not destroy by by-law. But it is plain that these instruments were not thrust upon the town by the central power in the State. The charter of James I was obtained by the burgesses after a prolonged and bitter controversy with the University and at the cost of much money. No doubt, in 1685 we at length see royal interference which, however, could soon afterwards be pronounced unlawful and futile. To Charles II the Town had to surrender its power of electing its own officers. The famous suit against the City of London had placed all charters at the royal mercy, for hardly a borough in England could hope to satisfy the king's subservient judges that it had not misused and forfeited its liberties. Still even then, when the king had secured the main matter and had provided by his charter that for the future every borough officer should be 'amovable' by the King in Council, he was for the more part content with the cónstitution that Cambridge had been slowly developing. And, as we know, he failed. After the Revolution of 1688 the charter of 1685 was treated as void; the charter of 1632 was resumed; and, as will be evident to those who study its terms, it was very far from forcing upon Cambridge a constitution that was defined in detail. As a matter of fact, in 1786 a by-law made an important change in the manner in which the mayor was to be elected, and the validity of this change was upheld by the Court of King's Bench[1].

It may also be worthy of observation, for at this point mistakes can be made, that to the very last—that is, until 1835—the constitution of the corporate body at Cambridge was thoroughly democratic. It is true that this body had become very small. In a town with more than twenty thousand inhabitants it consisted of less than two hundred

[1] *Mun. Corp. Rep.* p. 2185; *Newling* v. *Francis*, 3 Term Reports, 189.

men, and a considerable number of them lived elsewhere. But this, let us notice, was the result of the old community's autonomy. That community had been free, too free, to decide the terms upon which it would admit new members, and unfortunately in the eighteenth and perhaps in the seventeenth century that freedom had been misused for unworthy purposes. However, if we look at this little body, this body of burgesses, we see that it is thoroughly democratic. Despite the conciliar organs that it has evolved, despite the twelve aldermen and the four and twenty members of the common council, all the important affairs of the corporation are brought before a general assembly in which all the corporators, all the burgesses, have votes. Possibly it was because the burgensic body was so small that it preserved its democratic shape, but at any rate in Cambridge there never took place that transfer of power to a 'select body' of which we may read elsewhere. To the end the power of the corporation remained in a primary assembly of the burgesses[1].

These brief remarks have been written for the purpose of suggesting to the reader the point of view from which the following documents should be examined. All that he might like to know he will not find in them ; but then the mere fact that the charters are not dictating a constitution is highly important. He will doubtless know where to look for other documents. Cambridge has been very fortunate. Few indeed are the towns of England that can boast so good a book of local history as Cooper's *Annals*. Here we can offer no more than a few words about the royal charters, about the instruments which define the borough's relation to the king ; and we will take them in their chronological order.

I. *Undated Writ of Henry I.* Of the first of the documents that are here printed we have not the original. It is

[1] *Mun. Corp. Rep.* p. 2188.

a writ of Henry I (1100—1135), addressed to Hervey, Bishop of Ely (1109—1131), and attested by an unnamed Chancellor, by Miles of Gloucester, and by Richard Basset, whose names seem to point rather to the latter than to the former half of Henry's reign. A comparatively modern copy of it is found in the Corporation's 'Cross Book.' Apparently the burgesses produced the original before the King's Bench in the days of Richard II (p. 80), and they obtained a confirmation of it in 1548 from Edward VI (p. 76). The fact that it was not included in earlier confirmations will not seem to throw doubt upon its genuineness if its import is considered, since such benefits as it bestows upon the burgesses were of a kind that must in all probability have soon become obsolete or were much more explicitly secured by more modern documents. The brief sentence in it which gave occasion for its production in the time of Richard II and again in the time of Edward VI merely expresses the king's will that men who do wrong in the borough shall 'there do right': that is, shall be tried in Cambridge and not elsewhere. Later documents defined in a far more accurate manner the privilege of being sued at home. Indeed it may be doubted whether Henry I, when he issued this document, supposed that he was conferring a boon upon the townsfolk. The main object of the writ which he sent to the bishop of Ely, who seemingly was acting as the local justiciar, and to the barons of Cambridgeshire, was to make 'his borough of Cambridge' the one 'port' and emporium of the shire. No boat is to be charged or discharged at any hithe in the county except at the hithe of the borough, and the town is to be the one place at which toll is to be taken : we might say in modern terms that the only custom-house is to be there. It has commonly been supposed that the king went so far as to forbid that any carts (*carete*) should be laden except in the borough ; but this seems hardly a possible command. The

important word appears to be, not *carete*, but *carece*, and this might well stand for barges[1]. Indubitably if all traffic by water were thus banned to the hithes of the county town, that town would be a gainer. Still it was toll that the king wanted, and that toll would be paid to the king's officers for the king's use. It is only therefore by a stretch of words that we can give this remarkable writ a place among the borough's Charters of Liberties.

II. *Undated Writ of Henry II.* Our second document is a writ of Henry II (1154—1189) in which he declares that he has granted his town of Cambridge to the burgesses. Here again we have to rely upon a copy in the Cross Book and upon a confirmatory charter granted by Edward VI (p. 74); but we may also gather that the original of this writ was produced before the justices of Richard II (p. 80). Apparently it was then thought to be a writ not of Henry II but of Henry I, and the same opinion seems to have been prevalent in the time of Edward VI. In Richard II's day, so we are told, the burgesses exhibited an undated document which they ascribed to Henry I and which said just what is said by this writ of Henry II. A mistake about such a matter might easily be made in the fourteenth century when not every one remembered that Henry I was neither Duke of Aquitaine nor Count of Anjou. This error, however, seems to be the foundation of the belief, entertained by Mr Cooper, that a grant of the town was made to the burgesses by the first of the Henries though 'neither this grant, nor any copy or enrolment of it is now known to be extant[2].' Such a grant made at so early a day would have given Cambridge a highly exceptional eminence among her sister boroughs and we are

---

[1] See *carrica*, *carica*, in Henschel's Ducange. Also *carrack* in Skeat's Dictionary.

[2] Cooper, *Annals*, i. 22.

inclined to suppose that the burgesses of Richard II's time pardonably confused the Henries and so misled Mr Cooper.

In the year which ended at Michaelmas 1185 the burgesses of Cambridge rendered an account at the Exchequer of three hundred marks of silver and one mark of gold 'that they might have their town at farm and that the sheriff might not meddle therewith[1].' This would seem to be the occasion of the writ or charter that lies before us. Miss Bateson has ascertained by an inspection of the Pipe Rolls that in the next year, that which ended at Michaelmas 1186, the burgesses began to account for the farm of the borough. The writ is tested by Roger Fitz Reinfrid 'apud Keueilli,' a place which is not Kenilworth, but Quevilly near Rouen[2]. The king was in Normandy from April 1185 to April 1186[3].

The king grants the town to the burgesses who thenceforth are to answer at the Exchequer for the 'farm' or rent of the borough which has heretofore been paid by the sheriff. It would be impossible to state in a few words the precise legal effect of this transaction or to deal with all the questions that it raises. As the later history of our town amply shows, learned persons might hold different opinions as to the scope of the few rough words in which a king of the twelfth century spoke of one of his boroughs as a single thing which he could let to farm. Especially was there room for controversy over the question whether he had placed at the burgesses' disposal those bits of waste land which would sooner or later become valuable[4]. However, the main effect of the grant is that the bailiffs or other officers elected by the

---

[1] Madox, *Exchequer*, i. 399; Cooper, *Annals*, i. 28.
[2] We owe this identification to Mr Round, who kindly gave us his help at this point.
[3] Eyton, *Itinerary of Henry II*, pp. 263-7.
[4] I have spoken of this at some length in *Township and Borough*, Univ. Press, 1898.

burgesses will collect those various royal dues which heretofore have been collected by the sheriff—the haw-gavel and land-gavel, that is, the small rents due to the king from houses in the town and arable strips in the fields, also the tolls of the market, the profits of the borough court and of the king's mill—and will thereout pay to the king that 'farm' or rent of the town which the sheriff has formerly paid as part of the 'farm' of his shire. There is a chance that the bailiffs may make a profit; but the main advantage that the townsfolk gain is the exclusion of the sheriff and his subordinates.

It will be observed that this grant of the borough by Henry II is not a grant in perpetuity. It is a grant of the borough in 'farm' but not in 'fee farm.' Probably the king regards it as revocable, though the burgesses have been willing to give him a handsome sum for it.

III. *First Charter of John* (1201). To King John (1199—1215) Cambridge, like many other boroughs, owes her principal charters. The original of that which is dated on the 8th of January 1201 (p. 5) is not known to be extant, but a copy of it stands upon the Charter Roll at the Record Office. We may briefly set forth its contents.

The king grants to the burgesses of Cambridge a gild merchant and declares that all the burgesses of Cambridge of the gild merchant shall be quit of toll and similar dues (passage, lastage, pontage and stallage) in all his lands on both sides of the sea. It seems, however, to be extremely doubtful whether at Cambridge—and the same might be said of some other towns of equal rank—any gild merchant took definite shape and stood apart from the general body of burgesses. Apparently the freedom from toll which King John conceded was conceived to belong to every burgess of Cambridge merely because he was a burgess[1]: in other words,

---

[1] Certainly this was so in later days: *Mun. Corp. Rep.* 2190.

no trace seems as yet to have been found in later documents of any smaller body organized as a gild of merchants which was treated as having an exclusive right to that liberty which had been obtained from the king. It would appear, however, that the mayor and bailiffs, besides holding a court five times a year for suits concerning land, and besides holding a court every Tuesday for personal actions, were prepared to hold 'from day to day and from hour to hour their court of the gild merchant,' to decide disputes between merchant and merchant 'according to the exigence of the complaint.' This we are told in Richard II's day (p. 84). Thus we have a little evidence of a court which did summary justice between merchant and merchant and compelled the defendant to answer so soon as a charge was made against him ; but we do not know that the organization of this court differed in any respect from that of the ordinary borough court. Also we have from the Tudor time a little evidence of an attempt to constitute or reconstitute a gild merchant, of which, however, all burgesses were to be members[1]. This occurs in 1547 exactly at a time when the burgesses were engaged in procuring a confirmation of their most ancient charters, and the suggestion seems allowable that their attention was directed by their legal advisers to the fact that the liberties granted by King John were granted to the burgesses of Cambridge 'of the gild merchant' and to none others[2]. More of the gild merchant cannot here be said ; but John's time was the time when many of the boroughs were busy obtaining charters, when 'common forms' of charter were taking shape in the royal Chancery, and when a gild of merchants really was active and even dominant in some boroughs[3].

---

[1] Gross, *Gild Merchant*, i. 10.

[2] Compare the resolution of 1547 in Cooper, *Annals*, ii. 2 with the two documents of 1548 printed below, pp. 74, 78.

[3] This charter closely resembles one granted to Gloucester in the year 1200.

We may too easily draw the inference that the organization of a town exactly follows the lines which seem to be drawn by its charter. As to the exemption from toll, this was a precious boon worthy of purchase by a good round sum, for the land was full of toll takers. Even until 1835 it was valued by Cambridge burgesses if they dealt in corn, and some of the inhabitants of Cambridge complained of the rules which debarred them from becoming members of the shrunken body which enjoyed this liberty.

Then we see jurisdictional privileges which once were highly prized. The burgesses are not to be impleaded outside the walls of the borough except in respect of 'exterior tenures': that is to say, lands which lie elsewhere. They may decline trial by battle, and instead may defend themselves in pleas of the crown according to the ancient custom of the borough, which probably required an oath sworn with oath-helpers. Their amercements are to be no heavier than such as are sanctioned by the old law of the borough. Again, in suits touching land the ancient custom is to be observed. They are encouraged to make reprisals if the officers of other towns take toll from one who belongs to the gild merchant of Cambridge.

Then their fair in Rogation week—Reach fair—is secured to them. How they had become entitled to a fair held so far outside their town we are not told. They are to be freed from any *geares-gifu*, any year's gift or annual present which the sheriff may have been exacting : such exactions were common and were often called the sheriff's aid or sheriff's welcome. They need not attend those scot-ales which a sheriff is wont to hold : those feasts at which he sells his beer while no one else may sell any.

There follows a general concession of ancient liberties,

Rot. Cart. Joh. p. 56. See Ballard, English Boroughs in the Reign of John, *Eng. Hist. Rev.* xiv. 93.

a declaration that any new customs established in time of war shall be quashed, a grant of royal protection to all traders who visit Cambridge, and a threat that those who trouble the burgesses will incur the penalty, the heavy penalty, of ten pounds.

On the whole this charter secured to Cambridge most of those 'franchises' which the chief boroughs of England enjoyed at the opening of the thirteenth century. Cambridge now starts upon its long career as a royally chartered town.

IV. *Second Charter of John* (1207). In 1207 a final settlement was made of the farm of the borough. The burgesses were to hold the town not only in farm but in fee-farm. They and their heirs were to hold it for ever at a rent of forty pounds of blanched money and twenty pounds of the current coin[1].

To this was added a short clause which said that the burgesses might make of themselves a reeve (*prepositum*) whom they would and when they would. Apparently the borough had up to this time had four bailiffs as its principal officers. It now, following what has become the general fashion, desires to have some one officer at its head. For a short while this officer may have been called the reeve or the alderman; but very soon, and perhaps even in John's reign, the title of mayor, which was rapidly spreading outwards from London, was adopted, and Hervey the son of Eustace the son of Duning appears as mayor of Cambridge[2].

V and VI. *First and Second Charters of Henry III* (1227). In 1227 when Henry III (1216—1272) had attained full age the burgesses obtained from him a confirmation of those liberties which his father had granted to

---

[1] As to the mode of reckoning money see Turner, The Sheriff's Farm, *Transactions of Royal Historical Society*, New Series, xii. 119: 'A sum of money reckoned by tale may be reduced to a sum of blanched money by making a deduction from it of one shilling in the pound.'

[2] Maitland, *Township and Borough*, p. 166.

them.   The two charters of 1227 are copies of John's two
charters.

VII.   *Third Charter of Henry III* (1256).   In 1256
the burgesses went to the king for what may seem to us
a strange concession.   In the Middle Ages the town-com-
munity to which a trader belonged was often conceived
to be under a certain liability for his debts.   A man of
Cambridge will perhaps be arrested in the borough of
Huntingdon because some other man of Cambridge owes
money to a man of Huntingdon.   About the middle of
the thirteenth century a good many boroughs were en-
deavouring to obtain exemption from this rule.   It will be
seen that King Henry III did not grant an absolute
exemption to the townsfolk of Cambridge.   The man of
Cambridge and his goods are to be free from arrest for
the debt owed by another unless that other is solvent and
the Cambridge burgesses in their court have made default
in justice : so if the Cambridge court has 'denied right' to a
man of Huntingdon it will still be imprudent for any
man of Cambridge to visit the neighbouring town.   Not
until 1275 was an end put to this system of intermunicipal
reprisals[1], and long after that the old principle was still
enforced against foreigners.

VIII.   *Fourth Charter of Henry III* (1256).   On the
same occasion, but by another charter, some new and important privileges were acquired by the burgesses.   First
they were to have the highly valued 'return of writs.'   Up
to this time, though they had a court of their own in
which the sheriff did not preside and though he no longer
collected those revenues that had been granted in farm to the
burgesses, he still had much to do in the borough.   It was
for him to execute all the processes of the king's own courts,
the Chancery, Exchequer and Benches, and to do all the

[1] *Stat. West.* I. c. 23.

summoning, distraining and arresting that royal writs commanded. The townsfolk desired to get this work into their own hands so that it might be done by their elected officers. When they have the 'return of writs' the sheriff will still be the person who will be directed by the king's courts to make the requisite summonses, distraints, arrests and so forth; but he will be bound to hand on the writs to the town officers who will execute them. If those officers make default, then the sheriff may be told to disregard the franchise of the town (*quod non omittas propter aliquam libertatem*); still normally all this executive work will be done by the town's own officers. This is a privilege which many boroughs were seeking in the reign of Henry III. At a later time a few took a further step along the same road, and, being made 'counties of themselves,' had sheriffs of their own who were the direct recipients of the writs that flowed from Westminster.

Another right that was granted to the Cambridge burgesses in 1256 was that of entertaining in their court the action which was called in Latin *de vetito namii* and in French *vee de nam*. We know it as the action of replevin. It had been treated as an action which did not fall within the ordinary competence of the communal and seignorial courts, for the distrainor who refused to surrender the distrained goods when security was tendered to him for the prosecution of the claimant's suit was regarded as committing a serious offence against the king.

Thirdly, the townsfolk were to have the right of electing coroners. To be free from the interference of the officers of the shire was the object at which they had been aiming, and by the end of Henry III's reign their exemption was almost complete.

IX. *Charter of Edward I* (1280). From Edward I (1272—1307) they sought no more than a confirmation of

previous charters. In his reign a confirming charter takes the form that is known as an *Inspeximus*. The king says 'We have inspected' such and such charters of our ancestors and we now confirm them : the contents of the documents that are to be confirmed are recited at full length.

X. *Charter of Edward II* (1313). From Edward II (1307—1327) we have a charter granted in 1313. He confirmed charters of his father and grandfather, and the confirmation was followed by a clause which had become usual and which declared that the burgesses were to enjoy the chartered liberties although of such liberties they had made no use in the past. This was a protection against the legal doctrine that franchises are forfeited as well by non-use as by misuse or abuse. A few new privileges were then conceded. The burgesses were to be free from pavage, murage and pickage throughout the king's dominions. Apparently therefore a Cambridge man who went into another town might not only refuse to pay toll and other dues of a similar kind, but could not be compelled to contribute to the paving of the streets or the maintenance of the wall of the town to which he had gone[1]. The right of the burgess to plead and be impleaded only within the borough was declared and defined. The jury which convicts him is to consist of his fellow-townsmen unless either the king or the community of the borough is concerned in the cause. The burgesses may bequeath lands and tenements within the borough as though they were chattels. It is not improbable that long before this in Cambridge, as in other boroughs, the right to give lands by last will had been assumed and was already regarded as sanctioned by custom.

XI. *Letters Patent of Richard II* (1377). The long

---

[1] The old pavages and murages were not direct taxes like modern rates but partook of the nature of tolls. This was at least the common case.

reign of Edward III (1327—1377) is unrepresented. We may suppose that by this time the men of Cambridge had acquired all the privileges that they needed from the king and were busily engaged at home in developing their institutions within those wide limits that were set by the law of the land and by the not illiberal immunities that their ancestors had purchased. On the other hand, from Richard II's time (1377—1399) come some highly important documents. However, the letters patent which were obtained in 1377 at the very beginning of the reign were a mere confirmation of Edward's II's charter. We say ' letters patent ' for, though it is common to speak of all or nearly all the instruments which the kings grant to the towns as ' borough charters,' still there are formal differences between the solemn *carta* and the less solemn *litterae patentes*, and, as usually happens in such cases, the less solemn form gradually prevailed over the more solemn. The reader who is careful of such matters may contrast the long and sometimes very interesting lists of witnesses who attest the execution of a true *carta* with the curt *Teste meipso* which the English king thinks a sufficient authentication of his open letters.

XII. *First Charter of Richard II* (1382). We come to a document which records not an increase but a diminution of those liberties that the community had enjoyed. The story of the Peasants' Revolt in 1381 cannot be told here ; but in consequence of the riots in Cambridge the borough was adjudged to have forfeited its franchises. The effect of such a forfeiture would be not only that the burgesses would lose the precious immunity from toll and other like privileges that had been granted to them, but also that some warden appointed by the king would take the place of their elected mayor and that their farming of the town would come to an end. However, after they had made humble submission, a less extreme punishment was imposed. Their rent was

raised from 101 to 105 marks (in other words from
£67. 6s. 8d. to £70), and at the same time a certain portion
of their liberties was taken from them and bestowed upon the
University. This portion consisted of the guardianship of
the assizes of bread, wine and beer, the guardianship of the
assay and supervision of weights and measures, the jurisdiction over regraters and forestallers, and the jurisdiction over
sellers of unwholesome victuals. Jurisdiction was a source of
revenue, and the result of this change would be that a considerable number of fines and amercements which otherwise
would have been paid to the mayor and bailiffs of the
borough would flow into the coffers of the University. On
these unfavourable terms the liberties of the Town were
restored to the body which we may by this time call the
corporation of the borough : its rent or ' farm ' was increased
and its income was diminished, probably by at least £10, for
this was the sum which the University was annually to pay
for the jurisdictional rights that it was acquiring[1].

The task of reading a Latin charter of this age may
perhaps be lightened if the reader knows that, following a
fashion set by the papal chancery, the scribe of the charter is
often aiming at the production of a certain rhythmical effect.
He wishes to end as many clauses as possible with one or
other of a few admired cadences. The nature of the favourite
cadence may be illustrated by some of the instances that
occur in the document which lies before us. Thus we have—
*graviter impetiti — notorie redundabant — forisfacere non de-
berent — humillime submisissent — integre seisienda.* It is as
though a man writing in English were to strain after such
ends for his sentences as—'university jurisdiction'—'liberal
education'—'all of his faithful lieges'—'to the contrary

[1] For the Peasants' Revolt see Cooper, *Annals*, i. 120 ; Maitland, *Township
and Borough*, p. 192; Powell, *Rising in East Anglia* ; Trevelyan, *England in the
Age of Wycliffe*, c. vi.

B. C.   c

notwithstanding.' It is chiefly in the preambles or narrative parts of documents that this fine writing is found. When the operative part is reached the clerk must attend to business and think less of his style.

XIII. *Second Charter of Richard II* (1385). In 1385 the borough corporation was able, not indeed to recover what it had lost in 1382—for that had been given to the University—but to acquire from the king some new sources of profit. It complained of a diminished income. Not only had the burgesses lost what the masters and scholars had gained, but many burgage houses whence rents (haw-gafol or 'high gable rents') were payable had perished in a recent fire. So the community procured a grant of 'fines, ransoms, amercements and forfeited issues.' These, it will be understood, were not the profits of the borough court. Such profits already formed part of that 'town' which the burgesses held in farm. What they newly acquired in 1385 consisted of pecuniary penalties imposed by the king's own courts, by the King's Bench, the Common Bench, the Exchequer, justices in eyre, justices of assize and gaol delivery, justices of the peace, the steward and marshals of the king's household. Thenceforward if an inhabitant of Cambridge were fined in the King's Bench, the corporation of the town would be able to procure the amount of the fine after it had been paid into the Exchequer. And so with 'forfeited issues.' If in an action in the king's courts a sheriff is commanded to distrain a man of Cambridge in order to compel his appearance, and the sheriff seizes corn or other 'issues' of that man's land, and, owing to continued contumacy, those issues are forfeited, the profit is to come ultimately to the hands of the officers of the town of Cambridge. In addition to this 'the chattels of fugitives, felons and outlaws' were granted to the municipal corporation. Even at the present day a municipal corporation will occasionally be able to make a little profit out of

such clauses as those which are contained in the present charter. Very recently the corporation of Nottingham succeeded in obtaining from the Treasury the proceeds of certain fines that had been imposed upon offenders at Nottingham[1]. In days when felons and outlaws still forfeited their chattels, the revenue of a borough was sometimes materially increased by a lucky windfall.

XIV. *Letters Patent of Richard II* (1394). The charter of 1385 contained a saving clause which excepted out of the grant that was made to the Town 'fines, ransoms, amercements and forfeited issues in cases in which scholars of the University or their servants were parties.' Apparently this gave rise to some difficulties when the burgesses went to the Exchequer to obtain the money to which the charter entitled them. In 1394 those difficulties were to be removed. A certificate from the officers of the University to the effect that a particular fine, amercement or the like did not fall within the exception was to be treated as conclusive at the Exchequer, and without further investigation the Treasurer and Barons were to allow to the burgesses the sum that was in question.

XV, XVI, XVII, XVIII. *Letters Patent of Henry IV, Henry V, and Henry VI* (1399—1461). From the three Lancastrian kings we have nothing but confirmations. Though the confirming documents fill a small space in this book, it should be understood that really they are long. Each *Inspeximus* takes up bodily into itself its immediate predecessor, so that a letter of Henry VI may recite the whole of a letter of Henry V, which may recite the whole of a letter of Henry IV, and so on back to the days of John. Only after reading charters which contain and confirm other charters do we at length reach the few words of confirmation which are being obtained from the reigning king.

---

[1] *In re Nottingham Corporation,* [1897] 2 Q. B. 502.

XIX. *Letters Patent of Edward IV* (1465). This
document of 6 July 1465 might be called an 'exemplification' of a 'private act of parliament' passed in the session
which began on 29 April 1463. The corporation of Cambridge had then presented a petition. It stated that the
town of Cambridge was bound annually to pay to the
king the farm of £70, and had also to pay £8. 10s. to the
Priory of Caldwell and £1 to the Priory of Kenilworth. It
also stated that to every 'dysme and quinzime'—that is to
every national tax which took the form of a 'tenth' on
boroughs and a 'fifteenth' on counties—the inhabitants of
Cambridge had to contribute £46. 12s. 2½d. It also stated
that the corporate revenue did not exceed £40 yearly. It
complained that many houses had been demolished in order
to make room for King's College. It also alleged that
Henry VI 'late King of this realm in deed and not by
right' had by letters patent dated 18 July 1446 reduced
the contribution of the town towards each dysme and
quinzime to £20. It stated that this reduction was to be
effectual although the community of Cambridge might—by
their representatives in parliament, we suppose—be deemed
consenters to the act that imposed the tax, and although that
act contained a clause declaring that exempt places were not
to be excepted. It then said that this deed of the usurping
Lancastrian was void since the Yorkist had 'graciously taken
upon him the crown.' It prayed that Henry's concession
might be confirmed in parliament.

Then we learn that the petition thus presented in the
parliament of 1463 received the royal assent which was
endorsed upon it in the usual form: *Soit fait come il est
desiré.* And now on 6 July 1465 the burgesses obtain an
'exemplification' of this act: in other words a solemnly
authenticated copy of the petition and endorsement, which
copy they will be able to produce if any attempt be

made to exact more than £20 from the inhabitants of Cambridge.

XX and XXI. *Letters Patent of Edward IV* (1466) *and of Henry VIII* (1510). These are mere confirmations.

XXII. *Letters Exemplificatory of Henry VIII* (1530). What is 'exemplified' by this instrument is an extract from the rolls of the court of King's Bench showing how in a then recent case the municipal corporation of Cambridge had asserted and proved its chartered right to the chattels of felons. The extract begins with the record of an inquest held by the two coroners of the borough which tells how Robert Ashwell was slain in Trumpington Street by James Newland, how the murderer fled, and how he had within the liberty of the town of Cambridge goods to the value of twenty marks, which were seized by the mayor and bailiffs. Then we learn that, the indictment having been removed into the King's Bench, the mayor and bailiffs were summoned. They appeared by their attorney, who said on their behalf that they did not understand that the king required an answer from them. This, it may be noted, was the proper and civil phrase for a defendant to use, when he was in effect going to plead that the king was making a baseless claim. Upon this follows a highly interesting plea, which begins with the assertion that Cambridge is a corporate borough by prescription. We may observe that by the time of Henry VIII English lawyers had adopted the notion that a corporation is no natural growth but must have been created by public power. They were, however, willing to admit that corporateness, like other liberties and franchises, could be prescribed for, and, there being no charter which had explicitly created a corporation at Cambridge, the attorney for the borough relied upon prescription. Then he produced the charter of Richard II (No. XIII) which conferred the right to the chattels of felons, fugitives and outlaws. Then he

produced the last of the confirming documents, namely, the letters patent granted by Henry VIII (No. XXI) who was the then reigning king. Then he asserted that the goods of the murderer had been lawfully seized by the mayor and bailiffs, and he ended his plea with the proper offer of verification. To that plea the Attorney-General demurred. And then there was a joinder in demurrer : that is to say, both parties desired the judgment of the court on the question whether the plea was sufficient in law. Upon this follows a judgment for the Town. The mayor and bailiffs may keep the goods of the murderer and ' may go hence without day ': in other words, they are dismissed out of the court without being told that they must appear again. A saving clause for 'the kings right if any' is a common form in such cases. The king is not to be debarred from reasserting his right, if any, upon some future occasion.

From the fact that the Attorney-General demurred we may perhaps infer that the case was treated as being doubtful and important. New ideas about the nature and origin of corporations were making their way into English law, and it may not have been plain that the corporate quality could be claimed on the ground of prescription.

It will be observed that this exemplification does not bear the *Teste meipso* which would stand on letters patent issuing from the Chancery, but was attested by John Fitzjames who was Chief Justice of England. Also the seal seems to be, not the great seal of the realm, but that of the court of King's Bench. An exemplification of a record of a court of law could probably be obtained, not as a favour, but on payment of a fee to the clerk of the court. It was useful to have an authenticated copy of the record of a suit in which the borough had been victorious.

XXIII. *Letters Patent of Edward VI* (1548). A confirmation was obtained from Edward VI of his father's letters

(XXI) which confirmed a long series of earlier instruments. But also for some reason or another the burgesses obtained a confirmation of their two oldest documents, the writs of Henry I and Henry II, and these seem never to have been confirmed before this time. One of them was more and the other but little less than four centuries old.

XXIV. *Letters Exemplificatory of Edward VI* (1548). What are here exemplified are two successful claims of cognizance made in the reign of Richard II, the one in the court of King's Bench, and the other in the court of the King's Household. The rulers of the borough in 1548 must have desired to have in their hands an indisputable proof that in Richard II's days the exclusive right of the borough court to entertain actions arising within the limits of the borough was proved before two high tribunals.

The extract from the rolls of the King's Bench (p. 79) records an action for assault and false imprisonment brought in Richard II's reign by John Longe against William Burton. Thereupon the attorney of the borough appears to claim cognizance of the suit for the borough court (p. 81). A long and interesting assertion follows. It tells us what the men of Cambridge at the end of the fourteenth century thought of the ancient history of the borough and incidentally it throws light upon the courts that they were holding. Their attorney produced the writs of Henry I and Henry II. Apparently that which came from Henry II he ascribed to Henry I (p. 81), but he also seems to have had some confirmatory charter of Henry II, of which we have seen no other trace. Then he showed John's charter. Then he told of the courts that were held: a court held on five stated days in the year for actions touching lands: a court held once a week for personal actions: a court which could be held from day to day if strangers were concerned: a court of the gild merchant which would do justice between merchants not only from day

to day, but from hour to hour : two courts-leet with view of
frankpledge held in spring and autumn (p. 85). Then the
charters of Henry III, Edward II and Richard II were
tendered. Then four cases from the reigns of the then reigning king (Richard II) and of Edward III in which cognizance
had been granted to the borough court were alleged and the
records of the King's Bench were cited (p. 89). Finally a
writ or 'letter close' to the justices which had just been
obtained was produced : in effect it told the justices to allow
the claim of the burgesses. And allowed it was by the usual
words 'Therefore let them have their liberty.' Whereupon
the attorney of the Borough, as in duty bound, appointed a
day for the litigation in the gildhall, and the litigants were
told that, if full and speedy justice were not done to them,
they might return to the King's Bench.

The second record that was exemplified in 1548 came
from the court of the King's Household of Richard II's day
(p. 93). That court being at Cambridge, Thomas Lodeworth
had sued Geoffrey Castur in it for a debt ; but the attorney of
the Town had claimed cognizance of the cause and claimed it
successfully.

XXV. *Letters Patent of Elizabeth* (1589). Not until
1589 did the incorporated burgesses of Cambridge obtain a
secure lordship of Sturbridge Fair, that great fair, 'by far the
largest and most famous fair in all England,' which was held
in the fields of Cambridge. Seemingly their title was of this
sort : A fair had been granted by John to the Lepers'
Hospital which stood in the remotest corner of the territory
of Cambridge where its chapel may be seen to this day. But
that hospital had been founded and endowed by the community of the town and the community claimed to be its
patron. Then we may suppose that, as leprosy became
much rarer than it had been in the twelfth century, and the
hospital was not required, the burgesses began to regard

themselves as entitled to the profits of the fair[1]. It may well be doubted whether to medieval lawyers such a claim on their part would have seemed unreasonable. Elizabeth's charter tells us how Henry VIII attacked their title by an information of *quo waranto*, how they submitted themselves, and how the fair was adjudged to the king[2] (p. 99). Probably their right to the fair was by no means clear, but we cannot argue that they knew that they were in the wrong merely because they declined to plead against King Henry VIII in the fulness of his power. From his daughter they obtained the statement that the fair had been theirs from time immemorial (p. 97) and a grant which would set the question at rest for all time to come. That grant, however, was not obtained until after a prolonged struggle with the University, in the course of which the clauses of the draft charter, or 'book' as it was called, underwent careful criticism and many alterations. We find that the Town had retained the Attorney-General and the University had retained the Solicitor-General. The University was in the act of obtaining letters patent which would secure to her certain jurisdictional rights in the fair. The grant to the Town was dated on the 15th of August, the grant to the University on the 30th. The relation that the two documents were to bear to each other required nice adjustment. The townsfolk were not satisfied by the result and accused their mayor of having betrayed their interests. The University, it will be remembered, had ever since the insurrection of Richard II's time been possessed of that jurisdiction over victuals, weights and measures which the Town had forfeited, and the exercise of jurisdictional rights in Sturbridge Fair had been the occasion of many disputes.

[1] See the History of Sturbridge Fair in vol. v. of *Biblioth. Topograph. Britan.* I think this the most probable account of the matter but am not aware that it has ever been satisfactorily explained.

[2] Cooper, *Annals*, i. 393.

XXVI. *Letters Patent of James I* (1605). Until 1605 the municipal corporation had never been formally 'created' by the king. Already in Henry VIII's reign it had successfully asserted its prescriptive right to be corporate. But in the reign of James I the time had come when it was hardly safe for a body to live without a solemn document wherein the king professedly made it 'a body corporate and politic in deed, fact and name.' Old charters which spoke now of the 'men' and now of the 'burgesses' of the town, now of the mayor and now of the mayor and bailiffs, were apt to occasion difficulty. The greater part of the long and wordy document which was obtained from King James is taken up by the formal creation and erection of a corporation (p. 119), which is to be capable of holding property, of suing and being sued (p. 121), of using a common seal (p. 123), of making by-laws (p. 123), and of acquiring in mortmain lands to the value of £60 a year (p. 127). Then to this corporation are confirmed the rights granted by the king's predecessors, the old rent being still reserved (p. 129). The length and verbosity of the charters of the Stewarts, which are well illustrated by this document and the documents that follow it, are in a great measure due to the extreme severity of the rules of construction which the courts of law had been applying to royal grants. Everything was to be presumed in favour of the kingly grantor. The words by which he purported to confer a right were to mean as little as was possible. The result of this was that the grantees were studious to obtain, and willing to pay for, more and more words. For example, the clause which tells how the king makes the grant 'of our special grace, from our certain knowledge and mere motion' was worth obtaining. It would sometimes, though not always, serve to repel the objection that the king had been 'deceived in his grant' or must not be supposed to have really intended all that he had apparently said.

It will be noticed that even James I did very little in the way of imposing a constitution upon the borough. He established no council to rule the borough. The power to make by-laws was to be exercised by the whole body of the burgesses or the greater part of them, but the mayor was to have a veto (p. 123).

XXVII. *Letters Patent of Charles I* (1632). Except during a brief interval (1685—8) this instrument continued to be for upwards of two centuries 'the governing charter' of the borough. It was so until 1835 when the municipal corporations were reformed. It is a very long document and at first sight may seem to have done far more than really it did. It once more incorporates what was already a corporation both by prescription and the charter of James I (p. 139), and the full flood of words which bestowed capacity to sue and be sued, to hold property, to use a common seal and to make by-laws was let loose once more. It declares that there are to be twelve aldermen and twenty-four members of the common council (p. 143), and in so doing it confers from without a little new rigidity upon the constitution which had been evolved from within. But as to the function of these conciliar bodies it refers to the ancient usage, and nothing was said about qualification, mode of election or tenure of office. Nothing, again, was said about the definition of the general body of burgesses, about the right to burgherhood or the means by which this body might perpetuate itself. We notice also that the power of making by-laws, which is given in large terms, was reposed in this general body assembled in a primary assembly.

The really important clauses of the charter seem to be the following. In the first place much was said of the two treasurers. Apparently it was to be made quite clear that the treasurers were to be able to sue in the borough court for money penalties incurred by infringers of the by-laws (p. 145).

There had been difficulties about this matter. It might be argued that in such a case one and the same person, one and the same corporation, was both plaintiff and judge, besides being the law-maker and the recipient and enjoyer of the exacted money. We may conjecture that all objections on this score were for the future to be carefully precluded. Secondly, it was to be plain that the mayor or a bailiff might appoint a deputy (p. 151). Thirdly, with some exceptions, no one was to exercise in the borough any craft or manual occupation unless he had served for seven years as an apprentice (p. 157). Fourthly,—and perhaps in this clause we may see what the corporation regarded as the main point of the charter —the corporation is to have a very general power of taxing, not merely its own members, but the other inhabitants of the borough (p. 159). Were we to ask whether the king himself had power to lay taxes on his subjects or could give any such power to others, we should ask a question about which in 1632 King Charles and many of his subjects held diametrically opposite opinions. We know how it was finally decided, and that a famous burgess of Cambridge, Oliver Cromwell, took part in the decision.

Then there was a confirmation of ancient liberties (p. 161). The rights of the University were carefully saved (p. 165), and there were elaborate dispensing clauses such as the kings loved and in which they posed as sovereigns who were competent to override both statute and common law (pp. 165—7)[1].

XXVIII. *Letters Patent of Charles II* (1685). On 11 November 1684 the Corporation executed a deed which purported to surrender to the king the right of appointing the

[1] As to these dispensing clauses, which were by no means new under the Stewarts, see Hardy, *Introduction to the Charter Rolls*, pp. xxiv., xxv. The reader can there find an explanation of the reference made in the document that is before us (p. 165) to a statute of 18 Hen. VI.

mayor, aldermen, common councilmen, bailiffs and other officers of the borough. A few weeks afterwards, on 3 January 1685, the present document was sealed. By it the king filled the offices with his nominees, who, however, with some few exceptions, seem to have been the men who were in office at the time of the surrender[1]. The chief point secured by the king in the new charter was that for the future the King in Council would have an absolutely unfettered power of removing all or any of the holders of office, so that all the rulers of the borough would have good reason for dreading his displeasure. Repeated in town after town, this assumption of control over the municipalities would, it need hardly be said, make the king master of parliament. For the rest, we see less change in the constitution of Cambridge than we might have expected. The officers, including the aldermen and councillors, were to be appointed in the manner accustomed within the borough during the last twenty years. This provision would have had the effect of stereotyping some parts of the constitution which in the past had been treated as alterable. But the whole document became a nullity. The surrender of 1684 was never enrolled. At the last moment of his reign the terrified James endeavoured to retrace a few of his many false steps and by a Proclamation declared, in effect, that at Cambridge and other towns which were in a like case the surrendered charters were valid and the substituted charters void[2]. This was on 17 October 1688. On 5 November the deliverer landed.

At this point ends the history of the town of Cambridge, so far as it is written in royal charters. The next interference of national authority with municipal affairs was to be of a far different kind. In 1833 the corporation was called upon to

---

[1] Cooper, *Annals*, iii. 604.

[2] For this proclamation and its legal effect, see *Newling* v. *Francis*, 3 Term Reports, 189: a Cambridge case.

render an account of its stewardship. In 1835 it was reformed.

Appendix I. In an Appendix are printed four documents which have been preserved along with the charters of liberties. Of these, the first shows us the civic corporation bound to pay to the Prior of Caldwell a rent of £8. 10*s*. This rent formed part of the 'third penny' of the borough to which the earl had been entitled[1]. The acquisition by the burgesses of the 'farm' of their town had, at least in some cases, involved not only a settlement with the king, but also a settlement with the earl, for he had been entitled to a third part ('the third penny') of the profits of the borough court.

Appendix II. In 1455 Henry VI grants to the burgesses a piece of land which he had acquired from the Prior of Anglesey, the burgesses having given in exchange another piece of land for the enlargement of the site of King's College. The whereabouts of these plots has been lately explained by the Registrary of the University in his noble History[2].

Appendix III. The practice of giving to burgesses the right to take toll in their town and to be themselves quit of toll both there and elsewhere naturally gave rise to inter-municipal disputes. Sometimes the question whether the men of one town had lawfully become free of toll in another town involved a comparison between the dates of the charters granted to the two towns respectively, and an investigation of the state of affairs which had existed before the charters were sealed. We here see an Award made in 1519 by two arbitrators who are justices of the court of Common Pleas. The matter at stake is the toll demanded in Sturbridge Fair from burgesses of Northampton. An annuity of ten shillings is to be paid by the corporation of Northampton to that of Cambridge, and there is to be a further payment of two pence for

---

[1] Cooper, *Annals*, i. 37, 109.
[2] Clark, *Architectural History*, i. 212; ii. 404.

every cart that leaves the fair laden with 'stuff' of the Northamptoners.

Appendix IV. Our last document shows us Philip and Mary restoring to the corporation certain rents which upon the dissolution of the chantries in the reign of Edward VI had been seized on the part of that protestant king. These rents issuing out of booths in Sturbridge Fair and amounting to £8. 15s. 2d. had been bequeathed to the community by divers benefactors upon trusts which in the language of modern lawyers were partly superstitious and partly charitable. Edward had paid to the burgesses for distribution among the poor an annuity of £6. 10s. 6d., keeping to himself the residue which represented so much as had been devoted to the procurement of masses for the dead. His catholic successors restored the old rents to the corporation, to be held upon the old trusts, which were no longer—though they soon would be once more—unlawful. However, it will be seen that a reason is given for the invalidation of Edward's seizure of the rents, and that this reason has nothing to do with religion. It was said that these rents, since they issued out of customary lands, did not fall within the Act which gave the endowment of chantries to the king.

It is a mistake to suppose that the great Act of 1835 dissolved old corporations and put new corporations in their stead. The Corporation of the Borough of Cambridge whose Council has seen good to provide for the publication of these charters is the selfsame body to which the charters were granted. In 1835 it renewed its youth and at the beginning of another century can look forward to a vigorous life and backward upon a memorable history.

ERRATA.

p. 45, line 3.   For *Quévilly* read *Quevilly*.

p. 53, line 13.   For *private* read *privy*.

pp. 74 and 75.   The date in the margin should be 1548 not 1549.

p. 201, line 25.   For *the private* read *privy*.

CHARTERS

OF THE

BOROUGH OF CAMBRIDGE.

I. Breve Regis Henrici Primi.

A.D. 1120
—1131 [1]Henricus Rex Anglorum Herueio Eliensi Episcopo et omnibus Baronibus suis de Grentebrugeseira salutem. Prohibeo ne aliqua navis applicet ad aliquod litus de Cantebrugeseira nisi ad litus de burgo meo de Cantebruge neque carece onerentur nisi in burgo de Cantebruge neque aliquis capiat alibi theoloneum nisi ibi. Et quicumque in ipso burgo forisfecerit ibidem faciat rectum. Quod si quis aliter fecerit precipio ut sit mihi inde ad rectum coram iusticia mea quando precipio inde placitare. T[estibus :] Cancellario et Milone de Gloecestria [et Ricardo Basset apud Londoniam][2].

II. Breve Regis Henrici Secundi.

A.D. 1161
—1189 [3]Henricus dei gracia Rex Anglie et Dux Normannie et Aquitannie et Comes Andegavie Iusticiariis, Vicecomitibus et omnibus Ministris et Fidelibus suis salutem. Sciatis me tradidisse ad firmam burgensibus meis de Cantebruge villam meam de Cantebruge tenendam de me in capite per eandem firmam quam vicecomites mihi reddere solebant et ut ipsi inde ad scaccarium meum respondeant. Et ideo precipio quod prefatos burgenses et omnia sua custodiatis et manuteneatis sicut mea propria ne quis eis in aliquo iniuriam vel

---

[1] Transcript in Cross Book, f. 47; also Inspeximus of 2 Edw. VI. Original not known to exist.

[2] Not in Cross Book; supplied from the Inspeximus.

[3] Transcript in Cross Book, f. 47; also Inspeximus of 2 Edw. VI. Original not known to exist.

I. Writ of King Henry the First.

[1]Henry King of the English to Hervey Bishop of Ely and A.D. 1120 —1131
all his barons of Cambridgeshire greeting. I forbid that any
boat shall ply at any hithe in Cambridgeshire, save at the
hithe of my borough of Cambridge, nor shall barges be laden,
save in the borough of Cambridge, nor shall any take toll
elsewhere, but only there. And whosoever doth forfeit in
the borough let him there do right. And if any do otherwise,
I command that he be at right thereof before my justice
when I command that there be plea thereof. As witnesses:
the Chancellor and Miles of Gloucester and Richard Basset
at London.

II. Writ of King Henry the Second.

[2]Henry by the grace of God King of England and A.D. 1161 —1189
Duke of Normandy and Aquitaine and Count of Anjou,
to his Justices, Sheriffs and all his Ministers and faithful
People greeting. Know ye that I have delivered at farm
to my burgesses of Cambridge my town of Cambridge to
be holden of me in chief by the same farm which my
sheriffs were wont to render to me, and so that they themselves [the burgesses] do answer therefor at my exchequer.
And therefore I command that ye guard and maintain the
said burgesses and all things to them belonging as though
they were mine own, so that no one may in any wise cause to

---

[1] See Cooper, *Annals*, i. 25.
[2] See Cooper, *Annals*, i. 28.

molestiam faciat aut gravamen. Nolo enim quod ipsi alicui inde respondeant nisi mihi et ad scaccarium meum. Teste : Rogero filio Reinfrido apud Keueilli.

III. CARTA PRIMA REGIS JOHANNIS.

[1]Iohannes dei gracia Rex Anglie etc. Sciatis nos concessisse et presenti carta nostra confirmasse burgensibus nostris de Cantebruge gildam mercatoriam, et quod nullus eorum placitet extra muros burgi de Cantebruge de ullo placito preter placita de tenuris exterioribus, exceptis monetariis et ministris nostris. Concessimus eciam eis quod nullus eorum faciat duellum et quod de placitis ad coronam nostram pertinentibus se possint disracionare secundum antiquam consuetudinem burgi. Hoc eciam eis concessimus quod omnes burgenses de Cantebruge de gilda mercatorum sint quieti de theloneo et passagio et lestagio et pontagio et stallagio in feria et extra et per portus maris Anglie et omnium terrarum nostrarum citra mare et ultra mare, salvis in omnibus libertatibus civitatis Londonie, et quod nullus de misericordia pecunie iudicetur nisi secundum antiquam legem burgi, quam habuerunt temporibus antecessorum nostrorum. Et quod terras suas et vademonia et debita omnia iuste habeant quicumque ca debcat. Et de terris suis et tenuris que infra burgum sunt rectum eis teneatur secundum consuetudinem burgi. Et de omnibus debitis suis que accomodata fuerint apud Cantebruge et de vademoniis ibidem factis, placita apud Canteburge[2] teneantur. Et si quis in tota terra nostra theloneum vel consuetudines ab hominibus de Cantebruge de gilda mercatorum ceperit, postquam ipse a recto defecerit, vicecomes de Cantebruge vel prepositus de Cantebruge namum iude apud Cantebruge capiat, salvis in omnibus libertatibus civitatis Londonie. Insuper eciam ad emenda-

---

[1] From a copy enrolled in Rot. Cart. Joh. A. R. 2, m. 10 as printed in Record Commissioners edition, p. 83. A copy in Cross Book, f. 49. Original not known to exist.

[2] Sic.

them injury or damage or grievance. For I will not that they answer therefor to any but to me and at my exchequer As witness : Roger the son of Reinfrid at Quévilly.

III. First Charter of King John.

[1]John by the grace of God, King of England etc. Know ye that we have granted and by this our present charter have confirmed to our burgesses of Cambridge a gild merchant, and that none of them shall plead without the walls of the borough of Cambridge concerning any plea, unless they be pleas of exterior tenures, except our moneyers and servants. Moreover we have granted to them that none of them shall make [proof by] battle, and that with regard to pleas pertaining to our crown they may deraign themselves according to the ancient custom of the borough. This also we have granted to them, that all the burgesses of Cambridge of the gild of merchants shall be quit of toll and passage and lastage and pontage and stallage, in fair and without, and throughout the ports of the sea of England and of all our lands on this side of the sea and beyond the sea, saving in all things the liberties of the city of London, and that none be adjudged to be in mercy as to his money except according to the ancient law of the borough which they had in the times of our ancestors. And that they may justly have their lands and pledges and all debts, whosoever may owe the same. And that right shall be done to them touching their lands and tenures which are within the borough according to the custom of the borough. And of all their debts which shall have been contracted at Cambridge and of the pledges made there, pleas shall be held at Cambridge. And if any in all our land shall take toll or customs from the men of Cambridge of the gild of merchants and shall have made default in right, then the sheriff of Cambridge or the reeve of Cambridge shall take therefor a distress at Cambridge, saving in all things the liberties of the city of London. Moreover for the amendment

1201
Jan. 8

---

[1] See Cooper, *Annals*, i. 31.

cionem burgi de Cantebruge concessimus eis feriam suam
in septimana Rogacionum cum libertatibus suis sicut eam
habere consueverunt, et quod omnes burgenses de Cantebruge
sint quieti de jherescheve et de scothale si vicecomes noster
vel aliquis alius ballivus scotaliam faciat. Has predictas
consuetudines eis concedimus et omnes alias libertates et
liberas consuetudines quas habuerunt temporibus antecessorum nostrorum quando meliores vel liberiores habuerunt,
et si alique consuetudines iniuste levate fuerint in warra
cassate sint. Et quicunque petierint burgum de Canteburge¹
cum mercato suo, de quocumque loco sint, sive extraney
sive alii, veniant morentur et recedant in salva pace nostra
reddendo rectas consuetudines, et nemo eos disturbet super
hanc cartam nostram. Et prohibemus ne quis inde iniuriam
vel dampnum vel molestiam predictis burgensibus nostris
faciat super forisfacturam nostram decem librarum. Quare
volumus et firmiter precipimus quod predicti burgenses et
heredes eorum hec omnia predicta hereditarie habeant et
teneant de nobis et heredibus nostris, bene et in pace, libere
et quiete, integre et honorifice, sicut superius scriptum est.
Testibus: R[ogero] Sancti Andree Episcopo, G[alfrido] filio
Petri Comite Essexie, R[oberto] Comite Leicestrie, W[illelmo]
Comite Sarrisbirie etc. Data per manum nostram apud
Geytintone, viij die Ianuarii anno regni nostri secundo.

IV. CARTA SECUNDA REGIS JOHANNIS.

1207
May 8

²Iohannes dei gracia Rex Anglie Dominus Hybernie Dux
Normannie et Aquitannie Comes Andegavie Archiepiscopis,
Episcopis, Abbatibus, Comitibus, Baronibus, Iusticiariis, Vicecomitibus, Prepositis, et omnibus Ballivis et Fidelibus suis
salutem. Sciatis nos concessisse et hac carta nostra confirmasse burgensibus nostris de Cantebrige villam de Cantebrige cum omnibus pertinenciis suis habendam et tenendam
in perpetuum de nobis et heredibus nostris sibi et heredibus

---

¹ Sic.
² Original in Borough Archives with a portion of the great seal in green wax
appendant.

of the borough of Cambridge we have granted to them their
fair in Rogation week with its liberties as they were accustomed to have it, and that all the burgesses of Cambridge be
quit of jherescheve and of scotale if our sheriff or any other
bailiff shall make a scotale. These customs aforesaid we have
granted to them and all other liberties and free customs which
they had in the times of our ancestors when they best and
most freely had the same, and if any customs have been
unjustly levied in time of war, they shall be quashed. And
whoever shall seek the borough of Cambridge with their merchandize, whencesoever they be, whether strangers or others,
they may come, stay and return in our sure peace upon rendering right customs, and none shall disturb them upon [pain of
infringing] this our charter. And we forbid that any cause
herein injury or loss or trouble to our burgesses aforesaid
upon pain of our forfeiture of ten pounds. Wherefore we
will and firmly command that the aforesaid burgesses and
their heirs shall have and hold all these things aforesaid in
inheritance of us and our heirs well and peaceably, freely
and quietly, entirely and honourably as is written above. As
witnesses: Roger, Bishop of St Andrews, Geoffrey Fitz Peter
Earl of Essex, Robert Earl of Leicester, William Earl of
Salisbury etc. Given by our hand at Geddington on the
8th day of January in the second year of our reign.

IV. Second Charter of King John.

[1]John by the grace of God King of England Lord of
Ireland Duke of Normandy and Aquitaine and Count of Anjou,
to his Archbishops, Bishops, Abbots, Earls, Barons, Justices,
Sheriffs, Reeves, and all his Bailiffs and faithful People
greeting. Know ye that we have granted, and by this our
charter have confirmed, to our burgesses of Cambridge the
town of Cambridge, with all its appurtenances, to have and to
hold for ever of us and our heirs to them and their heirs,

1207
May 8

---

[1] See Cooper, *Annals*, i. 33.

suis reddendo inde annuatim ad scaccarium nostrum antiquam firmam scilicet quadraginta libras albas et viginti libras
numero de cremento pro omni servicio per manus eorum ad
duo scaccaria anni.   Quare volumus et firmiter precipimus
quod predicti burgenses et heredes sui habeant et teneant predictam villam cum omnibus pertinenciis suis bene et in pace,
libere et quiete, integre, plenarie et honorifice in pratis et
pascuis, molendinis, aquis et stagnis cum omnibus libertatibus
et liberis consuetudinibus suis.   Concessimus eciam eis quod
faciant de se ipsis prepositum quem voluerint et quando
voluerint.   Testibus: Dominis Willelmo Londoniensi, Petro
Wintoniensi, Iohanne Norwicensi, Ioscelino Bathoniensi Episcopis, Galfrido filio Petri Comite Essexie, Comite Alberico,
Willelmo Briwerre, Galfrido de Nevilla, Reginaldo de Cornhille.
Data per manum Hugonis de Welles Archidiaconi Wellensis
apud Lamheam viii° die Maii Anno Regni nostri octavo.

V. CARTA PRIMA REGIS HENRICI TERTII.

1227
April 21
[1] Henricus dei gracia Rex Anglie Dominus Hybernie Dux
Normannie Aquitannie et Comes Andegavie Archiepiscopis,
Episcopis, Abbatibus, Prioribus, Comitibus, Baronibus, Iusticiariis, Forestariis, Vicecomitibus, Prepositis, Ministris, et omnibus Ballivis, et Fidelibus suis salutem.   Sciatis nos concessisse
et presenti carta nostra confirmasse burgensibus nostris de
Cantebrige gildam mercatorum, et quod nullus eorum placitet
extra muros burgi de Cantebrige de ullo placito preter placita
de tenuris exterioribus exceptis monetariis et ministris nostris.
Concessimus eciam eis quod nullus eorum faciat duellum et
quod de placitis ad coronam nostram pertinentibus se possint
disracionare secundum antiquam consuetudinem burgi.   Hoc
eciam eis concessimus quod omnes burgenses de Cantebrige
de gilda mercatorum sint quieti de theloneo et passagio et

---

[1] Original in the Borough Archives with a large portion of the great seal in
green wax appendant.

rendering therefor yearly at our exchequer the ancient farm, to wit forty pounds blanch, and twenty pounds by tale by way of increase, for all services, by their hands at two exchequers in the year. Wherefore we will, and firmly command, that the aforesaid burgesses and their heirs shall have and hold the aforesaid town with all its appurtenances well and peaceably, freely and quietly, entirely, fully and honourably, in meadows and pastures, mills, waters and pools, with all their liberties and free customs. Moreover we have granted unto them that they shall make of themselves a reeve, whom they will and when they will. As witnesses : the lords William Bishop of London, Peter Bishop of Winchester, John Bishop of Norwich, Josceline Bishop of Bath, Geoffrey Fitz Peter Earl of Essex, the Earl Aubrey, William Briwerre, Geoffrey de Nevill, Reginald of Cornhill. Given by the hand of Hugh of Wells, Archdeacon of Wells, at Lambeth, the eighth day of May in the eighth year of our reign.

V. First Charter of King Henry the Third.

[1] Henry by the grace of God King of England Lord of Ireland Duke of Normandy and Aquitaine and Count of Anjou, to his Archbishops, Bishops, Abbots, Priors, Earls, Barons, Justices, Foresters, Sheriffs, Reeves, Ministers and all his Bailiffs and faithful People greeting. Know ye that we have granted and by this our present charter have confirmed to our burgesses of Cambridge a gild merchant, and that none of them shall plead without the Walls of the borough of Cambridge concerning any plea, unless they be pleas of exterior tenures, except our moneyers and servants. Moreover we have granted to them that none of them shall make [proof by] battle, and that with regard to pleas pertaining to our crown they may deraign themselves according to the ancient custom of the borough. This also we have granted to them, that all the burgesses of Cambridge of the gild merchant may be free of toll and passage and lastage and pontage and

1227
April 21

---

[1] See Cooper, *Annals*, i. 40.

lestagio et pontagio et stallagio in feria et extra et per portus maris Anglie et omnium terrarum nostrarum citra mare et ultra mare, salvis in omnibus libertatibus civitatis Londonie. Et quod nullus de misericordia pecunie iudicetur nisi secundum antiquam legem burgi quam habuerunt temporibus antecessorum nostrorum. Et quod terras suas et tenuras et vadimonia et debita omnia iuste habeant quicunque ea debeant. Et de terris suis et tenuris que infra burgum sunt rectum eis teneatur secundum consuetudinem burgi. Et de omnibus debitis suis que accomodata fuerint apud Cantebrige et de vadimoniis ibidem factis placita apud Cantebrige teneantur. Et si quis in tota terra nostra theloneum vel consuetudinem ab hominibus de Cantebrige de gilda mercatorum ceperit postquam ipse a recto defecerit vicecomes de Cantebrige vel prepositus de Cantebrige namum inde apud Cantebrige capiat, salvis in omnibus libertatibus civitatis Londonie. Insuper eciam ad emendandum burgum de Cantebrige concessimus eis feriam suam in septimana Rogacionum cum libertatibus suis sicut eam habere consueverunt. Et quod omnes burgenses de Cantebrige sint quieti de yeresghyve et de scotale si vicecomes noster vel aliquis alius ballivus scotaliam fecerit. Has predictas consuetudines eis concedimus et omnes alias libertates et liberas consuetudines quas habuerunt temporibus antecessorum nostrorum quando meliores vel liberiores habuerunt, et si alique consuetudines iniuste levate fuerint in werra cassate sint. Et quicunque pecierint burgum de Cantebrige cum mercato suo de quocunque loco sint sive extranei sive alii veniant morentur et recedant in salva pace nostra reddendo rectas consuetudines et nemo eos disturbet super hanc cartam nostram. Et prohibemus ne quis inde iniuriam vel dampnum vel molestiam predictis burgensibus nostris faciat super forisfacturam nostram decem librarum. Quare volumus et firmiter precipimus quod predicti burgenses et heredes eorum hec omnia predicta hereditarie habeant et teneant de nobis et heredibus nostris bene et in pace, libere et quiete, integre et honorifice, sicut superius scriptum est et sicut carta domini Iohannis Regis

stallage, in fair and without, and throughout the ports of the sea of England and of all our lands on this side of the sea and beyond the sea, saving in all things the liberties of the city of London. And that none may be adjudged to be in mercy as to his money except according to the ancient law of the borough which they had in the times of our ancestors. And that they may justly have their lands and tenures and pledges and all debts, whosoever may owe the same. And that right shall be done to them touching their lands and tenures within the borough according to the custom of the borough. And of all their debts which shall have been contracted at Cambridge and of the pledges made there, pleas shall be held at Cambridge. And if any in all our land shall take toll or custom from the men of Cambridge of the gild merchant and shall have made default in right, then the sheriff of Cambridge or the reeve of Cambridge shall take therefor a distress at Cambridge, saving in all things the liberties of the city of London. Moreover for the amendment of the borough of Cambridge we have granted to them their fair in Rogation week with its liberties as they were accustomed to have it, and that all the burgesses of Cambridge may be free of yeresghyve and of scotale if our sheriff or any other bailiff shall make a scotale. These customs aforesaid we have granted to them and all other liberties and free customs which they had in the times of our ancestors when they best and most freely had the same, and if any customs have been unjustly levied in time of war, they shall be quashed. And whosoever shall seek the borough of Cambridge with their merchandize, whencesoever they be, whether strangers or others, they may come, stay, and return in our sure peace upon rendering right customs, and none shall disturb them upon [pain of infringing] this our charter. And we forbid that any cause herein injury or loss or trouble to our burgesses aforesaid upon pain of our forfeiture of ten pounds. Wherefore we will and firmly command that the aforesaid burgesses and their heirs shall have and hold all these things aforesaid in inheritance of us and our heirs well and peaceably, freely and

patris nostri quam inde habent racionabiliter testatur. Hiis
testibus: Galfrido Elyensi, Thoma Norwicensi Episcopis,
Huberto de Burgo Comite Kancie Iusticiario nostro, Gilberto
Comite Gloucestrie et Hertfordie, Henrico de Aldithele,
Radulfo filio Nicholai, Nicholao de Molis, Godefrido de
Crawecumbe, et aliis. Data per manum uenerabilis patris
Radulfi Cycestrensis Episcopi Cancellarii nostri apud West-
monasterium vicesimo primo die Aprilis anno regni nostri
undecimo.

VI. CARTA SECUNDA REGIS HENRICI TERTII.

1227
April 21

[1]Henricus dei gracia Rex Anglie Dominus Hybernie Dux
Normannie Aquitannie et Comes Andegavie Archiepiscopis,
Episcopis, Abbatibus, Prioribus, Comitibus, Baronibus, Iusticiariis, Forestariis, Vicecomitibus, Prepositis, Ministris, et
omnibus Ballivis, et Fidelibus suis salutem. Sciatis nos concessisse et hac carta nostra confirmasse burgensibus nostris
de Cantebrige villam de Cantebrige cum omnibus pertinenciis
suis habendam et tenendam inperpetuum de nobis et heredibus nostris sibi et heredibus suis, reddendo inde annuatim
ad scaccarium nostrum antiquam firmam scilicet quadraginta
libras albas et viginti libras numero de cremento pro omni
servicio per manus eorum ad duo scaccaria anni   Quare
volumus et firmiter precipimus quod predicti burgenses et
heredes sui habeant et teneant predictam villam cum omnibus
pertinenciis suis bene et in pace libere et quiete integre
plenarie et honorifice in pratis et pascuis, molendinis, aquis et
stagnis cum omnibus libertatibus et liberis consuetudinibus
suis. Concessimus eciam eis quod faciant de se ipsis prepositum quem voluerint et quando voluerint sicut carta
domini Iohannis Regis patris nostri quam inde habent racionabiliter testatur. Hiis testibus: Galfrido Elyensi, Thoma
Norwicensi Episcopis, Huberto de Burgo Comite Kancie

---

[1] Original in Borough Archives with a portion of the great seal in green wax
appendant.

quietly, entirely and honourably as is written above and as the charter of the lord King John our father, which they have thereof, reasonably testifies. As witnesses : Geoffrey Bishop of Ely, Thomas Bishop of Norwich, Hubert de Burgh Earl of Kent our Justiciar, Gilbert Earl of Gloucester and Hertford, Henry of Audley, Ralph Fitz Nicholas, Nicholas de Molis, Godfrey of Crowcombe and others. Given by the hand of the reverend father Ralph Bishop of Chichester our Chancellor at Westminster on the twenty-first day of April in the eleventh year of our reign.

VI. SECOND CHARTER OF KING HENRY THE THIRD.

[1]Henry by the grace of God King of England Lord of Ireland Duke of Normandy and Aquitaine and Earl of Anjou, to his Archbishops, Bishops, Abbots, Priors, Earls, Barons, Justices, Foresters, Sheriffs, Reeves, Ministers and all his Bailiffs and faithful People greeting. Know ye that we have granted and by this our charter have confirmed to our burgesses of Cambridge the town of Cambridge with all its appurtenances to have and to hold for ever of us and our heirs to them and their heirs, rendering therefor yearly at our exchequer the ancient farm, namely forty pounds blanch, and twenty pounds by tale by way of increase, for all services, by their hands at two exchequers in the year. Wherefore we will and firmly command that the aforesaid burgesses and their heirs may have and hold the aforesaid town with all its appurtenances well and peaceably, freely and quietly, entirely, fully and honourably, in meadows and pastures, mills, waters and pools with all their liberties and free customs. Moreover we have granted unto them that they shall make from among themselves a reeve, whom they will and when they will, according as the charter of the lord King John our father, which they have thereof, reasonably testifies. As witnesses: Geoffrey Bishop of Ely, Thomas Bishop of Norwich, Hubert de Burgh

1227
April 21

---

[1] See Cooper, *Annals,* i. 40.

Iusticiario nostro, Gilberto Comite Gloucestrie et Hertfordie, Henrico de Aldithele, Radulfo filio Nicholai, Nicholao de Molis, Godefrido de Crawecumbe, et aliis. Data per manum venerabilis patris Radulfi Cycestrensi Episcopi Cancellarii nostri apud Westmonasterium vicesimo primo die Aprilis anno regni nostri undecimo.

VII. CARTA TERTIA REGIS HENRICI TERTII.

1256
April 11

[1]Henricus dei gracia Rex Anglie Dominus Hibernie Dux Normannie Aquitannie et Comes Andegavie Archiepiscopis, Episcopis, Abbatibus, Prioribus, Comitibus, Baronibus, Iusticiariis, Vicecomitibus, Prepositis, Ministris, et omnibus Ballivis, et Fidelibus suis salutem. Sciatis nos concessisse et hac carta nostra confirmasse dilectis burgensibus nostris de Cantebrugia quod ipsi inperpetuum per totam terram et potestatem nostram hanc habeant libertatem videlicet quod ipsi vel eorum bona quocumque locorum in potestate nostra inventa non arestentur pro aliquo debito de quo fideiussores aut principales debitores non extiterint, nisi forte ipsi debitores de eorum sint communa et potestate habentes unde de debitis suis in toto vel in parte satisfacere possint et dicti burgenses creditoribus eorundem debitorům in iusticia defuerint et de hoc racionabiliter constare possit. Quare volumus et firmiter precipimus pro nobis et heredibus nostris quod predicti burgenses inperpetuum habeant libertatem prescriptam sicut predictum est. Et prohibemus super forisfacturam nostram decem librarum ne quis eos contra libertatem illam in aliquo vexare, molestare vel inquietare presumat. Hiis testibus : Guidone de Lezignano fratre nostro, Johanne Priore de Novo Burgo, Henrico de Bathonia, magistro Simone de Wautone, Willelmo de Grey, Willelmo Maudut, Artaldo de Sancto Romano, magistro Johanne Manselle, Philippo de Bocland,

---

[1] Original in Borough Archives with a large portion of great seal in green wax appendant.

Earl of Kent our Justiciar, Gilbert Earl of Gloucester and Hertford, Henry of Audley, Ralph Fitz Nicholas, Nicholas de Molis, Godfrey of Crowcombe and others. Given by the hand of the reverend father Ralph Bishop of Chichester our Chancellor at Westminster on the twenty-first day of April in the eleventh year of our reign.

VII. THIRD CHARTER OF KING HENRY THE THIRD.

[1]Henry by the grace of God King of England Lord of Ireland Duke of Normandy and Aquitaine and Count of Anjou, to his Archbishops, Bishops, Abbots, Priors, Earls, Barons, Justices, Sheriffs, Reeves, Ministers and all his Bailiffs and faithful People greeting. Know ye that we have granted and by this our charter have confirmed to our beloved burgesses of Cambridge that they may for ever throughout the whole of our land and dominion have this franchise, namely that they themselves or their goods, wheresoever found in our dominion, shall not be arrested for any debt of which they shall not be the sureties or principal debtors, unless perchance the debtors shall be of their commonalty and power and shall have whereout to make satisfaction for their debts in whole or in part and the said burgesses shall have made default in justice to the creditors of the same debts and this be reasonably proven. Wherefore we will and firmly command for ourselves and our heirs that the aforesaid burgesses may for ever hold the above written franchise as aforesaid. And we forbid upon pain of our forfeiture of ten pounds that any one presume to vex, molest or disturb them in anything contrary to that franchise. As witnesses: Guy de Lusignan our brother, John Prior of Newburgh, Henry of Bath, Master Simon of Walton, William de Grey, William Mauduit, Artald de Sancto Romano, Master John Mansel, Philip of Buckland,

1256
April 11

---

[1] See Cooper, *Annals*, i. p. 46.

Willelmo Gernun et aliis. Data per manum nostram apud Westmonasterium undecimo die Aprilis anno regni nostri quadragesimo.

VIII. Carta Quarta Regis Henrici Tertii.

1256
April 11

[1]Henricus dei gracia Rex Anglie Dominus Hibernie Dux Normannie Aquitannie et Comes Andegavie Archiepiscopis, Episcopis, Abbatibus, Prioribus, Comitibus, Baronibus, Iusticiariis, Vicecomitibus, Prepositis, Ministris, et omnibus Ballivis, et Fidelibus suis salutem. Sciatis nos concessisse et hac carta nostra confirmasse dilectis burgensibus nostris de Cantebrugia quod ipsi inperpetuum habeant returnum omnium brevium nostrorum villam nostram Cantebrugie et libertatem eiusdem ville tangencium et quod per manus suas proprias respondere possint ad scaccarium nostrum de omnibus demandis et summonicionibus eiusdem scaccarii ipsos burgenses contingentibus. Et quod decetero placitare possint infra villam predictam omnia placita libertatem suam tangencia tam de vetito namio quam de aliis placitis suis que sine iusticiariis nostris placitari possunt, ita quod nullus vicecomes aut alius ballivus noster intromittat se de aliquibus ad libertates suas spectantibus nisi per defectum predictorum burgensium vel ballivorum suorum eiusdem ville. Et quod iidem burgenses de se ipsis eligere possint et creare coronatores in villa predicta ad atachiamenta placitorum corone nostre infra predictam villam Cantebrugie emergencium facienda usque ad adventum iusticiariorum nostrorum sicut alibi ad coronatores nostros pertinet. Quare volumus et firmiter precipimus pro nobis et heredibus nostris quod predicti burgenses inperpetuum habeant omnes libertates prescriptas sicut predictum est. Et prohibemus super forisfacturam nostram decem librarum ne quis eos contra libertates et concessiones huiusmodi vexare, molestare vel inquietare presumat. Hiis testibus: Guidone de Lezignano fratre nostro, Iohanne Priore

---

[1] Two originals in Borough Archives. They are duplicate except in the date. That not used as the foundation of our text is dated April 12. Each has a portion of the great seal in green wax appendant.

William Gernun and others. Given by our hand at Westminster the eleventh day of April in the fortieth year of our reign.

VIII. FOURTH CHARTER OF KING HENRY THE THIRD.

[1]Henry by the grace of God King of England Lord of Ireland Duke of Normandy and Aquitaine and Count of Anjou, to his Archbishops, Bishops, Abbots, Priors, Earls, Barons, Justices, Sheriffs, Reeves, Ministers and all his Bailiffs and faithful People greeting. Know ye that we have granted and by this our charter have confirmed to our beloved burgesses of Cambridge that they shall for ever have the return of all our writs touching our town of Cambridge and the liberty of the same town, and that they may have power by their own hands to answer at our Exchequer to all demands and summonses of the same Exchequer concerning them the aforesaid burgesses. And that henceforth they may be able to plead within the town aforesaid all pleas touching their liberty as well for *vee de nam* [replevin] as other their pleas which can be pleaded without our justices, so that no sheriff or other our bailiff may meddle in any things relating to their liberties, save by default of the aforesaid burgesses or their bailiffs of the said town. And that the said burgesses may elect and create from among themselves coroners in the town aforesaid for making the attachment of pleas of our crown arising within the aforesaid town of Cambridge until the coming of our justices as belongs to our coroners elsewhere. Wherefore we will and firmly command for ourselves and our heirs that the aforesaid burgesses may for ever have all the before written liberties as aforesaid. And we forbid upon pain of our forfeiture of ten pounds that any presume to vex, molest or disturb them contrary to these liberties and grants. As witnesses: Guy de Lusignan our brother, John Prior of

1256
April 11

---

[1] See Cooper, *Annals*, i. p. 46.

de Novo Burgo, Henrico de Bathonia, magistro Simone de Wautone, Willelmo de[1] Grey, Willelmo Maudut, Artaldo de Sancto Romano, magistro Iohanne Manselle, Philippo de Boclande, Petro Everard, Willelmo Gernun et aliis.   Data per manum nostram apud Westmonasterium undecimo die Aprilis anno regni nostri quadragesimo.

IX. CARTA REGIS EDWARDI PRIMI.

[2]Edwardus dei gracia Rex Anglie Dominus Hibernie et Dux Aquitannie Archiepiscopis Episcopis, Abbatibus, Prioribus, Comitibus, Baronibus, Iusticiariis, Vicecomitibus, Prepositis, Ministris et omnibus Ballivis et Fidelibus suis salutem.   Inspeximus cartam quam celebris memorie dominus Henricus dudum Rex Anglie pater noster fecit burgensibus de Cantebrigia in hec verba : Henricus dei gracia &c.

> Here follows a copy of the Charter granted by Henry III. in the 11th year of his reign and on the 21st April 1227 hereinbefore printed and numbered V.   The present Charter then proceeds as follows :—

Inspeximus eciam cartam quam prefatus pater noster fecit predictis burgensibus in hec verba : Henricus dei gracia &c.

> Here follows a copy of the Charter granted by Henry III. in the 40th year of his reign and on the 11th April 1256 hereinbefore printed and numbered VIII.   The present Charter then proceeds as follows :—

Nos autem donaciones et concessiones predictas ratas habentes et gratas eas pro nobis et heredibus nostris quantum in nobis est concedimus et confirmamus sicut carte predicte racionabiliter testantur.   Hiis testibus : venerabilibus patribus Roberto Bathoniensi et Wellensi et Thoma Menevensi Episcopis, Edmundo fratre nostro, Willelmo de Valencia avunculo nostro, Johanne de Vescy, Roberto Tybotot, Antonio Beke Archidiacono Dunolmensi, Hugone filio Otonis, Roberto filio

---

[1] *de* repeated.

[2] Two originals (duplicate) in Borough Archives.   In one a space is left blank for the initial letter.

Newburgh, Henry of Bath, Master Simon of Walton, William de Grey, William Mauduit, Artald de Sancto Romano, Master John Mansel, Philip of Buckland, Peter Everard, William Gernun and others. Given by our hand at Westminster the eleventh day of April in the fortieth year of our reign.

IX. CHARTER OF KING EDWARD THE FIRST.

[1] Edward by the grace of God King of England Lord of Ireland and Duke of Aquitaine, to his Archbishops, Bishops, Abbots, Priors, Earls, Barons, Justices, Sheriffs, Reeves, Ministers and all his Bailiffs and faithful People greeting. We have inspected a charter which our father lord Henry of famous memory late King of England made to the burgesses of Cambridge in these words: Henry by the grace of God &c.

1280
Nov. 24

> Here follows a copy of the Charter granted by Henry III. in the 11th year of his reign and on the 21st April 1227 hereinbefore translated and numbered V. The present Charter then proceeds as follows :—

We have inspected also a charter which our father aforesaid made to the aforesaid burgesses in these words : Henry by the grace of God &c.

> Here follows a copy of the Charter granted by Henry III. in the 40th year of his reign and on the 11th April 1256 hereinbefore translated and numbered VIII. The present Charter then proceeds as follows :—

Now we ratifying and according the gifts and grants aforesaid do grant and confirm the same for ourselves and our heirs so far as in us lies as the aforesaid charters reasonably testify. As witnesses : the reverend fathers Robert Bishop of Bath and Wells and Thomas Bishop of St David's, Edmund our brother, William de Valence our uncle, John de Vescy, Robert Tybotot, Antony Beke Archdeacon of Durham, Hugo Fitz Otes, Robert Fitz John, Richard de

[1] See Cooper, *Annals*, i. 60.

Iohannis, Ricardo de Bosco, Galfrido de Pycheforde, Eustachio de Hacche, Elya de Hauville, Petro de Huntingfeld, Iohanne de Bykenore, et aliis. Data per manum nostram apud Westmonasterium vicesimo quarto die Novembris anno regni nostri nono.

X. Carta Regis Edwardi Secundi.

1313
Nov. 27

[1]Edwardus dei gracia Rex Anglie, Dominus Hibernie, et Dux Aquitannie, Archiepiscopis, Episcopis, Abbatibus, Prioribus, Comitibus, Baronibus, Iusticiariis, Vicecomitibus, Prepositis, Ministris, et omnibus Ballivis, et Fidelibus suis salutem. Inspeximus cartam quam dominus Henricus quondam Rex Anglie avus noster fecit burgensibus de Cantebrige in hec verba : Henricus dei gracia &c.

Here follows a copy of the Charter granted by Henry III. in the 11th year of his reign and on the 21st of April 1227 hereinbefore printed and numbered VI. The present Charter then proceeds as follows :—

Inspeximus etiam cartam confirmacionis quam dominus Edwardus quondam Rex Anglie pater noster fecit eisdem burgensibus in hec verba : Edwardus dei gratia &c.

Here follows a copy of the Charter of Inspeximus granted by Edward I. in the 9th year of his reign and on the 24th November 1280 hereinbefore printed and numbered IX. The present Charter then proceeds as follows :—

Nos autem donaciones concessiones et confirmaciones predictas ratas habentes et gratas eas pro nobis et heredibus nostris quantum in nobis est prefatis burgensibus et eorum heredibus ac successoribus concedimus et confirmamus sicut carte predicte racionabiliter testantur. Preterea volentes eisdem burgensibus graciam facere ampliorem concessimus eis pro nobis et heredibus nostris quod licet ipsi aliqua vel aliquibus libertatum et quietanciarum predictarum hactenus

---

[1] Original in Borough Archives. Initial letter adorned with grotesques. A small portion of the great seal appendant. Contemporary note at foot: *Examinata per R. de Haliwell et W. de Clyf. dupplicata.* A duplicate in Borough Archives with a larger portion of the seal, but with a space left blank for the initial E. This duplicate has at the end a note : *per finem centum marcarum.*

Bois, Geoffrey of Pitchford, Eustace of Hatch, Elias of
Hautville, Peter of Huntingfield, John of Bicknor and others.
Given by our hand at Westminster on the 24th day of
November in the ninth year of our reign.

X. Charter of King Edward the Second.

[1] Edward by the grace of God King of England Lord of
Ireland and Duke of Aquitaine, to his Archbishops, Bishops,
Abbots, Priors, Earls, Barons, Justices, Sheriffs, Reeves,
Ministers and all his Bailiffs and faithful People greeting.
We have inspected a charter which Lord Henry formerly
King of England our grandfather made to the burgesses of
Cambridge in these words: Henry by the grace of God &c.

1313
Nov. 27

> Here follows a copy of the Charter granted by Henry III.
> in the 11th year of his reign and on the 21st of April 1227
> hereinbefore translated and numbered VI. The present Charter
> then proceeds as follows :—

We have inspected also a charter of confirmation which
Lord Edward formerly King of England our father made to
the same burgesses in these words: Edward by the grace
of God &c.

> Here follows a copy of the Charter of Inspeximus granted
> by Edward I. in the 9th year of his reign and on the 24th
> November 1280 hereinbefore translated and numbered IX. The
> present Charter then proceeds as follows :—

Now we ratifying and according the gifts, grants and
confirmations aforesaid, do grant and confirm the same for
ourselves and our heirs so far as in us lies to the aforesaid
burgesses and their heirs and successors as the aforesaid
charters reasonably testify. Moreover, being willing to do an
ampler favour to the same burgesses, we have granted to them
for ourselves and our heirs that, although they may not hitherto
have fully used the beforementioned liberties and quittances

---

[1] See Cooper, *Annals*, i. 73.

plene usi non fuerint ipsi nichilominus et heredes ac successores sui predicti libertatibus et quietanciis predictis et
earum qualibet decetero absque inquietacione vel impedimento nostri vel heredum nostrorum aut ministrorum nostrorum quorumcumque racionabiliter gaudeant et utantur.
Et insuper concessimus eis pro nobis et heredibus nostris
quod ipsi et heredes ac successores sui predicti de pavagio
muragio et picagio infra regnum et potestatem nostram
imperpetuum sint quieti. Et quod terras et tenementa sua
infra eundem burgum et suburbium eiusdem existencia tanquam catalla sua in ultima voluntate sua legare possint
quibuscumque et cuicumque voluerint dum tamen ad manum
mortuam non deveniant. Et quod de transgressionibus seu
contractibus in eisdem burgo et suburbio factis non placitent
nec implacitentur extra burgum illum nisi res ipsa tangat nos
vel heredes nostros et quod super transgressionibus et contractibus illis aut aliis factis intrinsecis per forinsecos minime
convincantur set solummodo per comburgenses suos nisi factum
illud tangat nos vel heredes nostros aut comunitatem burgi
predicti, ita tamen quod magistris et scolaribus universitatis
eiusdem ville super aliquibus libertatibus eis per progenitores
nostros quondam Reges Anglie concessis per concessiones
nostras supradictas nullatenus preiudicetur. Hiis testibus:
venerabilibus patribus Iohanne Norwycensi et Iohanne Bar-
thoniensi et Wellensi Episcopis, Gilberto de Clare Comite
Gloucestrie et Hertfordie, Adomaro de Vallencia Comite
Pembrochie, Hugone le Despenser, Radulfo filio Willelmi,
Bartholomeo de Badelesmere et aliis. Data per manum
nostram apud Westmonasterium vicesimo septimo die Novembris anno regni nostri septimo.

XI. LITTERE PATENTES REGIS RICARDI SECUNDI.

1377
Dec. 8   [1]Ricardus dei gracia Rex Anglie et Francie et Dominus
Hibernie omnibus ad quos presentes littere pervenerint salutem.
Inspeximus cartam domini Edwardi quondam Regis Anglie

---

[1] From an Inspeximus of Henry VI.   An original is not known to be extant.

or some of them, they nevertheless and their heirs and successors beforementioned may henceforth reasonably enjoy and use the liberties and quittances beforementioned and every of them without let or hindrance by us or our heirs or any of our ministers whomsoever. And moreover we have granted to them for ourselves and our heirs that they and their heirs and successors beforementioned shall be for ever free from pavage, murage and pickage within our realm and dominion. And that they may by last will bequeath their lands and tenements within the borough and the suburb thereof as if the same were their chattels to whatsoever persons or person they may wish, provided the same shall not come into mortmain. And that concerning trespasses or contracts made in the same borough and suburb they may not sue or be sued outside that borough unless the matter concerns us or our heirs. And that touching those trespasses and contracts or other internal affairs they shall not be convicted by strangers but only by their fellow-burgesses, unless the matter concerns us or our heirs or the commonalty of the aforesaid borough. But so nevertheless that by our grants abovementioned no manner of prejudice be done to the masters and scholars of the university of the same town in any of the liberties granted to them by our progenitors formerly Kings of England. As witnesses : the venerable fathers John Bishop of Norwich and John Bishop of Bath and Wells, Gilbert de Clare Earl of Gloucester and Hertford, Aymer de Valence Earl of Pembroke, Hugh le Despenser, Ralph Fitz William, Bartholomew of Badlesmere and others. Given by our hand at Westminster on the twenty-seventh day of November in the seventh year of our reign.

XI. LETTERS PATENT OF KING RICHARD THE SECOND.

[1]Richard by the grace of God King of England and France and Lord of Ireland to all to whom the present letters shall come greeting. We have inspected the charter of the lord Edward formerly King of England, our great-grandfather,

1377
Dec. 8

[1] See Cooper, *Annals*, i. 116.

proavi nostri burgensibus ville de Cantebriggia factam in hec
verba : Edwardus dei gracia etc.

Here follows a copy of the Charter granted by Edward II.
in the 7th year of his reign and on the 27th of November 1313
hereinbefore printed and numbered X. The present instrument
then proceeds as follows :—

Nos autem donaciones, concessiones, confirmaciones, libertates et quietancias predictas ratas habentes et gratas, eas pro
nobis et heredibus nostris quantum in nobis est acceptamus,
approbamus, ratificamus et tenore presencium eisdem burgensibus et eorum heredibus ac successoribus concedimus et
confirmamus prout carta predicta racionabiliter testatur, et
prout iidem burgenses libertatibus et quietanciis predictis
semper hactenus a tempore concessionis et confeccionis carte
predicte racionabiliter uti et gaudere consueverunt.   In cuius
rei testimonium has litteras nostras fieri fecimus patentes.
Teste me ipso apud Westmonasterium octavo die Decembris
anno regni nostri primo.

XII.   Carta Prima Regis Ricardi Secundi.

1382
May 1

[1][R]icardus dei gracia [R]ex Anglie et Francie et [D]omi-
nus Hibernie Archiepiscopis, Episcopis, Abbatibus, Prioribus,
Ducibus, Comitibus, Baronibus, Militibus, Iusticiariis, Vicecomitibus, Prepositis, Ballivis, Ministris et aliis Fidelibus suis
salutem.   Sciatis quod cum maior ballivi et comunitas ville
nostre Cantebrigie coram nobis in ultimo parliamento nostro
accusati fuissent et graviter impetiti de eo quod ipsi nuper
contra nos ac honorem nostrum et ligeancie sue debitum
nequiter insurrexisse ac varios defectus et excessus notabiles
et enormes ac mala quamplurima tempore huiusmodi insurreccionis perperam commisisse debuissent, que non solum in
nostre regie maiestatis dedecus et offensam verum eciam in
quorundam fidelium ligeorum nostrorum dampnum gravis-
simum ac iacturam, ut dicebatur, notorie redundabant: Super

---

[1] Original in Borough Archives with a portion of the great seal in green wax
appendant.   Space left for the initial.

made to the burgesses of the town of Cambridge in these words : Edward by the grace of God &c.

> Here follows a copy of the Charter granted by Edward II.
> in the 7th year of his reign and on the 27th of November 1313
> hereinbefore translated and numbered X. The present in-
> strument then proceeds as follows :—

Now we ratifying and according the said gifts, grants, confirmations, liberties and quittances aforesaid, do for our-selves and our heirs, so far as in us lies, accept, approve, ratify and by the tenour of these presents grant and confirm the same to the said burgesses and their heirs and successors in such wise as the aforesaid charter reasonably testifies, and as the said burgesses have always hitherto been wont reason-ably to use and enjoy the aforesaid liberties and quittances from the time of the grant and making of the aforesaid charter. In witness whereof we have caused these our letters to be made patent. As witness myself at Westminster on the eighth day of December in the first year of our reign.

XII. FIRST CHARTER OF KING RICHARD THE SECOND.

[1]Richard by the grace of God King of England and France and Lord of Ireland to his Archbishops, Bishops, Abbots, Priors, Dukes, Earls, Barons, Knights, Justices, Sheriffs, Reeves, Bailiffs, Ministers and other faithful People greeting. Know ye that whereas the mayor, bailiffs and com-monalty of our town of Cambridge were accused and gravely impeached before us in our last parliament, for that they of late wickedly revolted against us and our honour and their debt of allegiance, and in the time of the said insurrection were said to have wilfully committed divers notable and enormous defaults and excesses and very many wrongs, which, it was said, notoriously redounded not only to the disgrace and contempt of our royal majesty but also to the most grievous damage and loss of some of our faithful lieges : Whereas thereupon

1382
May 1

---

[1] See Cooper, *Annals,* i. 125.

quo prefatis maiore et ballivis in propriis personis suis ac
dicta comunitate per duos comburgenses suos coram nobis in
eodem parliamento nostro iuxta formam cuiusdam brevis
nostri eis inde directi comparentibus et super premissis
allocutis ac responso per ipsos ibidem proposito dies eis
per nos fuisset prefixus et assignatus ad respondendum
finaliter, et ad proponendum et allegandum inter alia pro
se ipsis, si quid haberent seu dicere scirent in forma iuris,
quare libertates et privilegia eis per cartas progenitorum
nostrorum quondam regum Anglie data et concessa et per
nos confirmata racione defectuum et excessuum predictorum
et maxime occasione dicte insurreccionis forisfacere non de-
berent: Prefatique maior, ballivi et comunitas habentes sufficientis temporis spacium super premissis deliberandi et nichil
effectuale coram nobis in parliamento illo e contrario pro
se ipsis proponere seu allegare scientes tandem se quoad
libertates et privilegia sua predicta cessantibus et omissis
excusacionibus quibuscunque in hac parte disposicioni et
ordinacioni nostris humilime submisissent: Ac nos dicta libertates et privilegia pro defectu sufficientis responsionis, con-
siderata eciam suorum qualitate delictorum, de assensu
eiusdem parliamenti in manum nostram tanquam forisfacta
decreverimus integre seisienda: Subsequenterque consideratis
et debite ponderatis defectubus et excessubus supradictis
super quibus dicti maior et ballivi et comunitas fuerant ut
premittitur impetiti et ut ipsi ac omnes alii in regno nostro
magis caveant in futuro erga nos et heredes nostros consimilia
perpetrare 'ac efficacius et solicicius studeant in fide et
obediencia nostris fideliter permanere, et ut huiusmodi defectus et excessus pena non careant: Volentes quedam
privilegia dicte comunitati auferre pro perpetuo et per ea
universitatem Cantebrigie, que est mater et propagatrix
scienciarum et doctrine erga quam viscera nostra intime sunt
commota, que eciam universitas multa et varia infra breve
dispendia et pressuras sustinuit, exaltare ordinavimus et per
cartam nostram confirmavimus pro nobis et heredibus nostris
quod cancellarius universitatis Cantebrigie et successores sui

the aforesaid mayor and bailiffs appearing in their proper persons and the said commonalty by two of their fellow-burgesses before us in our said parliament according to the form of a certain writ directed to them in that behalf, and ·being charged with the premisses, and an answer having been propounded by them there, a day was fixed and assigned to them by us for replying finally and for pro-pounding and alleging on their behalf amongst other things what, if aught, they might or could say in form of law by way of showing cause why they should not forfeit, by reason of the said defaults and excesses and especially of the said insurrection, the liberties and privileges given and granted to them by the charters of our progenitors formerly Kings of England and by us confirmed : And whereas the aforesaid mayor and bailiffs and commonalty, having a sufficient space of time to deliberate on the matters aforesaid, and not being able to propound on their behalf or allege anything effectual to the contrary, before us in the said parliament, at length most humbly submitted themselves in the matter of the liberties and privileges aforesaid, to our disposition and ordinance, all excuses in this behalf being stayed and abandoned : And whereas we, for the default of sufficient answer, and in consideration of the quality of their evil deeds, decreed by the assent of the said parliament that the said liberties and privileges should wholly be seized into our hands as forfeited : And whereas, having thereafter con-sidered and duly weighed the defaults and excesses aforesaid of which the said mayor and bailiffs and commonalty were impeached as is aforesaid, and to the end that they and all others in our kingdom may for the future dread to commit the like against us and our heirs and may the more effi-caciously and anxiously study faithfully to remain in our faith and obedience, and in order that defects and excesses of this kind may not lack punishment : We (willing to take away certain privileges from the said commonalty for ever and thereby to exalt the university of Cambridge who is the mother and propagatrix of sciences and learning, towards

et eorum vices gerentes soli et in solidum habeant custodiam
assise panis vini et cervisie, ac cognicionem et punicionem
eiusdem, ac eciam custodiam assise et assaie ac supervisum
mensurarum et ponderum in dicta villa Cantebrigie et suburbiis eiusdem, necnon potestatem inquirendi et cognoscendi
de forstallatoribus, regratariis, carnibus et piscibus tam putridis,
viciosis et aliis incompetentibus quam aliis super hiis punicionem debitam faciendi ac gubernacionem correccionem et
punicionem premissorum et aliorum victualium quorumcumque, simul cum finibus forisfacturis et amerciamentis inde
provenientibus, pro quadam firma decem librarum nobis et
heredibus nostris inde annuatim reddenda imperpetuum prout
in eadem carta plenius continetur: Et quia iam posito in
ipsorum maioris ballivorum et comunitatis libera eleccione
ex precepto nostro si ipsi residua libertates et privilegia in
manum nostram taliter existencia pro quodam annuo incremento ultra antiquam firmam, quam ipsi pro villa et omnibus
libertatibus et privilegiis per ipsos prius optentis nobis reddere
solebant, recipere et rehabere voluerint necne, iidem maior
ballivi et comunitas restitucionem residuorum libertatum et
privilegiorum predictorum cum incremento quatuor marcarum
nobis et heredibus nostris pro eisdem imperpetuum ultra
antiquam firmam suam predictam reddendo humiliter et
instancius sibi fieri postularunt et suum ad hoc voluntarium
prebebant assensum: Ac considerantes bonum gestum quem
ipsi erga nos et progenitores nostros antea habuerunt, volentesque propterea ad graciam cum eisdem maiore et ballivis
et comunitate ne ipsi totalem amissionem suarum defleant
libertatum, non obstante decreto aut forisfactura predictis,
ex pietate regia peragendam misericorditer inclinari, de avisamento et deliberacione prelatorum procerum et magnatum
nobis in dicto parliamento nostro assistencium, concessimus
dictis maiori et ballivis ac burgensibus dicte ville nostre et
hac carta nostra confirmavimus villam nostram predictam
cum omnibus pertinenciis suis: Habendam et tenendam sibi
heredibus et successoribus suis burgensibus eiusdem ville de
nobis et heredibus nostris imperpetuum una cum omnibus et

whom our bowels are moved within us, which university moreover has of late day sustained many and various expenses and extortions) have ordained and by our charter have confirmed for us and our heirs that the chancellor of the university of Cambridge and his successors and their vice-gerents jointly and singly shall have the guardianship of the assize of bread, wine and beer and cognizance and punishment of the same, and also the guardianship of the assize and assay and supervision of measures and weights in the said town of Cambridge and the suburbs of the same, and the power of inquiring and taking cognizance of forestallers, regraters, flesh, fish (as well bad, stale and otherwise improper as of other), and of inflicting due punishment for these matters, and the government, correction and punishment of the aforesaid and of all other victuals whatsoever, together with the fines, forfeitures and amercements thence arising, for a certain rent of ten pounds to us and our heirs thence annually to be paid for ever, as in the same charter is more fully contained: And whereas by our command it was placed in the free choice of the said mayor, bailiffs and commonalty whether or no they wished to take back and repossess the remaining liberties and privileges, these being in our hand, for some annual increment beyond the ancient farm which they were used to render to us for the town and all the liberties and privileges formerly obtained by them, and the said mayor, bailiffs and commonalty humbly and earnestly begged that a restitution might be made to them of the remaining liberties and privileges aforesaid with an increment of four marks to be paid to us and our heirs for the same for ever over and above their aforesaid farm, and gave to this their voluntary assent: Now we (considering the good bearing which they beforetimes had towards us and our progenitors and wishing therefore of our royal pity mercifully to incline towards favour to be shown to the said mayor, bailiffs and commonalty, so that they may not have to deplore a total loss of their liberties, and notwithstanding the decree or forfeiture aforesaid), with the advice and de-

singulis privilegiis, quietanciis, immunitatibus, liberis consuetudinibus, donacionibus, concessionibus, feriis ac aliis liber
'tatibus quibuscumque sibi per cartas dictorum progenitorum
nostrorum et confirmacionem nostram predictam concessis,
adeo plene et integre sicut ea ante impeticionem submissionem et decretum predicta racionabiliter habuerunt et
tenuerunt, et eadem privilegia quietancias immunitates,
liberas consuetudines, donaciones, concessiones, ferias et alias
libertates predictas sibi heredibus et successoribus suis predictis imperpetuum iuxta formam cartarum et confirmacionis
nostre predictarum habenda restituimus eisdem : Salvis dumtaxat et exceptis libertatibus cancellario dicte universitatis
Cantebrigie et successoribus suis per cartam nostram predictam concessis ut est dictum, nolentes quod iidem maior
ballivi et burgenses seu eorum aliquis se de eisdem ex nunc
sub gravi indignacione nostra intromittant seu intromittat set
quod dicto cancellario pro tempore existenti ac eius commissariis sive vicem gerenti inde auxilientur et intendant
secundum formam dicte carte : Reddendo nobis et heredibus
nostris annuatim antiquam firmam dicte ville, videlicet
centum et unam marcas et ulterius predictas quatuor marcas
de novo incremento ad festa Pasche et Sancti Michaelis per
equales porciones imperpetuum : Quare volumus et firmiter
precipimus pro nobis et heredibus nostris quod iidem maior
ballivi et burgenses dictam villam Cantebrigie cum omnibus
suis pertinenciis ac eciam privilegiis, quietanciis, immunitatibus,
liberis consuetudinibus, donacionibus, concessionibus, feriis ac
aliis libertatibus predictis habeant et teneant sibi heredibus et
successoribus suis predictis de nobis et heredibus nostris
imperpetuum adeo plene et integre sicut ea ante impeticionem,
submissionem et decretum predicta juxta tenorem cartarum
et confirmacionis nostre predictarum racionabiliter habuerunt
et tenuerunt, salvis dumtaxat et exceptis libertatibus cancellario dicte universitatis Cantebrigie et successoribus suis predictis per cartam nostram predictam concessis sicut predictum
est, nolentes quod iidem maior ballivi et burgenses seu eorum
aliquis se de eisdem exnunc sub gravi indignacione nostra

liberation of the prelates, nobles and magnates assisting us in our said parliament, have granted to the said mayor and bailiffs and burgesses of our said town and by this our charter have confirmed our said town with all its appurtenances: To have and to hold to them their heirs and successors burgesses of the said town, of us and our heirs for ever, together with all and singular the privileges, quittances, immunities, free customs, gifts, grants, fairs and other liberties whatsoever granted to them by the charters of our said progenitors and by our confirmation aforesaid, as fully and entirely as they reasonably had and held them before the impeachment, submission and decree aforesaid, and we restore to them the same privileges, quittances, immunities, free customs, gifts, grants, fairs and other liberties aforesaid to be had by them their heirs and successors aforesaid for ever according to the form of the charters and of our confirmation aforesaid : Save only and except, as has been said, the liberties granted to the chancellor of the said university of Cambridge and to his successors by our charter aforesaid, our will being that the said mayor, bailiffs and burgesses or any of them shall not from henceforth meddle therewith upon pain of our grievous displeasure, but that they shall be aiding and intendant therein to the said chancellor for the time being and his commissaries or vicegerent according to the form of the said charter : Rendering to us and our heirs yearly the ancient farm of the said town, to wit, one hundred and one marks and further the aforesaid four marks of new increment, at the feasts of Easter and of Saint Michael, by equal portions for ever : Wherefore we will and firmly command for us and our heirs that the said mayor, bailiffs and burgesses shall have and hold the said town of Cambridge with all its appurtenances, and also the privileges, quittances, immunities, free customs, gifts, grants, fairs and other liberties aforesaid, to them, their heirs and successors aforesaid, of us and our heirs for ever, as fully and entirely as they reasonably had and held the same before the impeachment, submission and decree aforesaid, according to the tenour of the charters and

intromittant seu intromittat set quod dicto cancellario ac eius commissario inde auxilientur et intendant secundum formam dicte carte, reddendo nobis et heredibus nostris annuatim centum et unam marcas ac dictas quatuor marcas ut de novo incremento imperpetuum sicut predictum est. Hiis testibus venerabilibus patribus Willelmo Archiepiscopo Cantuariensi tocius Anglie Primate, Willelmo Wyntoniensi et Radulpho Sarisbiriensi Episcopis, Iohanne Rege Castelle et Legionis Duce Lancastrie, Thoma Comite Bukyngham avunculis nostris carissimis, Ricardo Arundell, Thoma Warrewico Comitibus, Ricardo Lescrope Cancellario, Hugone de Segrave Thesaurario nostris, Albredo de Veer Camerario nostro, Iohanne de Monte Acuto Senescallo Hospicii nostri et aliis. Data per manum nostram apud Westmonasterium primo die Maii anno regni nostri quinto.

per ipsum Regem et consilium

MUSKHAM.

XIII. CARTA SECUNDA REGIS RICARDI SECUNDI.

1385
Dec. 9

[1]Ricardus dei gracia Rex Anglie et Francie et Dominus Hibernie Archiepiscopis, Episcopis, Abbatibus, Prioribus, Ducibus, Comitibus, Baronibus, Iusticiariis, Vicecomitibus, Prepositis, Ballivis, Ministris, et aliis Fidelibus suis salutem. Sciatis quod cum plures libertates et franchesie dilectorum burgensium nostrorum ville nostre Cantebrigie una cum pluribus commoditatibus et proficuis unde magna pars firme sue levari consuevit eis nuper ablate et scolaribus universitatis ibidem concesse fuissent et dicta nichilominus eorum firma exaltata et granditer augmentata: Et insuper iam tarde magna pars

---

[1] Original in Borough Archives. Great seal in green wax nearly perfect.

of our confirmation aforesaid (save only and except the liberties to the chancellor of the said university of Cambridge and to his successors aforesaid granted by our charter aforesaid as has been said before, it being our will that the said mayor, bailiffs and burgesses or any of them shall not from henceforth meddle therewith upon pain of our grievous displeasure, but they shall be aiding and intendant therein to the said chancellor and his commissary according to the form of the said charter), rendering to us and our heirs yearly for ever one hundred and one marks and the said four marks by way of new increment as is aforesaid. As witnesses : the venerable fathers William Archbishop of Canterbury Primate of all England, William Bishop of Winchester, Ralph Bishop of Salisbury, John King of Castile and Leon Duke of Lancaster, Thomas Earl of Buckingham, our dearest uncles, Richard Earl of Arundel, Thomas Earl of Warwick, Richard Le Scrope our Chancellor, Hugh de Segrave our Treasurer, Aubrey de Vere our Chamberlain, John de Montacute the Steward of our Household and others. Given by our hand at Westminster on the first day of May in the fifth year of our reign.

By the King himself and council

MUSKHAM.

XIII. SECOND CHARTER OF KING RICHARD THE SECOND.

[1]Richard by the grace of God King of England and France and Lord of Ireland to his Archbishops, Bishops, Abbots, Priors, Dukes, Earls, Barons, Justices, Sheriffs, Reeves, Bailiffs, Ministers and other his faithful People greeting. Know ye that whereas many liberties and franchises of our beloved burgesses of our town of Cambridge together with many advantages and profits, whence a great part of their farm was wont to be raised, have lately been taken away from them and granted to the scholars of the university there, and their said farm nevertheless has been increased and greatly augmented: And moreover now of late a great part of the

1385
Dec. 9

---

[1] See Cooper, *Annals,* i. 130.

B. C. 3

ville predicte videlicet centum burgagia et plura magna et
parva simul cum omnibus bonis et catallis in eisdem burgagiis
existentibus unde magna pars dicte firme levari et solvi
debuit per duo subita ignis infortunia combusta fuissent et
penitus devastata, eoque pretextu nonnulli burgensium qui
dicta burgagia inhabitabant de villa predicta recesserunt
aliique burgenses eiusdem ville nisi succursum pariter et
auxilium de dampnis et deperditis huiusmodi cicius habeant
villam illam proponant relinquere desolatam : Nos igitur
super premissis pie compacientes ac volentes indempnitati
nostre in hac parte prospicere et relevacioni et emendacioni
ville nostre predicte ac status burgensium nostrorum eiusdem
ville in salvacionem et continuacionem firme nostre predicte
manus apponere adiutrices, de gracia nostra speciali et ad
requisicionem burgensium nostrorum predictorum concessimus pro nobis et heredibus nostris et hac carta nostra
confirmavimus eisdem burgensibus, quod ipsi et heredes ac
successores sui burgenses eiusdem ville imperpetuum habeant
omnia fines redempciones et amerciamenta ac exitus forisfactos omnium hominum tam residencium infra eandem
villam et libertatem eiusdem quam aliorum quorumcumque
quos in eadem villa, occasione alicuius placiti vel querele
liberum tenementum in eisdem villa et libertate tangencium,
seu occasione alicuius debiti vel transgressionis contractus seu
querele alterius rei infra easdem villam et libertatem emergencium, tam coram iusticiariis nostris et heredum nostrorum
ad placita coram nobis tenenda assignatis, et iusticiariis
nostris de banco, ac coram thesaurario et baronibus nostris
et heredum nostrorum de scaccario, ac coram iusticiariis
nostris ad assisas capiendas, inquisiciones faciendas, gaolas
deliberandas, et ad pacem nostram conservandam, ac iusticiariis ad inquirendum de artificibus laboratoribus et aliis
operariis necnon de ponderibus et mensuris, ac iusticiariis
itinerantibus et quibuscumque aliis iusticiariis nostris, quam
coram senescallo et marescallis ac clerico mercati hospicii
nostri, ac coram escaetoribus vicecomitibus et aliis officiariis
et ministris nostris quibuscumque amerciari vel exitus foris-

town aforesaid namely one hundred burgages and more, great and small, together with all goods and chattels being within the same burgages, whence a great part of the said farm was leviable and payable, has, by two sudden calamities of fire, been burnt and completely devastated, and on that account certain of the burgesses who used to inhabit the said burgages have departed from the said town, and other burgesses of the same town, unless they quickly have succour and aid in such their damages and losses, also propose to leave the town desolate : We therefore being pitifully compassionate in the matters aforesaid, and wishing to provide for our indemnity in this behalf, and to apply helping hands to the relief and amendment of our town aforesaid and of the estate of our burgesses of the same town in the salvation and continuance of our farm aforesaid, of our special grace and at the request of our said burgesses have granted for us and our heirs and by this our charter have confirmed to the same burgesses that they and their heirs and successors, burgesses of the same town, shall for ever have all fines, ransoms, and amercements and forfeited issues of all men, as well of residents within the same town and the liberty thereof, as of all others who in the same town may happen to be amerced or to forfeit issues, by occasion of any plea or plaint touching any free tenement in the same town and liberty, or by occasion of any debt, trespass, contract or plaint of any other matter arising within the same town and liberty, as well before the Justices of ourselves and our heirs assigned to hold pleas before us, and our Justices of the Bench, and before the Treasurer and Barons of the Exchequer of ourselves or our heirs, and before our Justices for holding assizes, taking inquisitions, delivering gaols and for preserving our peace, and the Justices for inquiring about artificers, labourers, and other workmen and about weights and measures, and Justices in eyre and other our Justices, as also before the Steward and Marshals and Clerk of the Market of our Household, and before the Escheators, Sheriffs and all other our officers and ministers whomsoever. And that they shall have all manner

facere contigerit. Et quod habeant omnimoda catalla felonum
ac fugitivorum ac utlagatorum de omnibus tam de tenentibus
et residentibus infra villam et libertatem predictas quam de
extraneis et aliis quibuscumque que infra villam et libertatem
predictas inveniri contigerit: Ita quod liceat eisdem burgensibus huiusmodi fines redempciones et amerciamenta et
exitus forisfactos statim cum adiudicata fuerint per ballivos
seu deputatos suos colligere et levare, et de huiusmodi catallis
felonum et fugitivorum in seisinam se ponere, et ea ad usum
eorumdem burgensium in auxilium firme sue predicte retinere
possint, absque impedimento nostri vel heredum nostrorum,
iusticiariorum, escaetorum, vicecomitum aut aliorum ballivorum seu ministrorum nostrorum vel heredum nostrorum
quorumcumque, et absque compoto vel alio raciocinio inde
nobis vel heredibus nostris seu ministris nostris quibuscumque
reddendo imperpetuum : Salvis semper cancellario magistris
et scolaribus universitatis nostre ville predicte et successoribus suis finibus forisfacturis amerciamentis et aliis proficuis ac libertatibus et privilegiis quibuscumque eis et
predecessoribus suis per nos et progenitores nostros quondam
reges Anglie concessis: Salvis eciam et exceptis huiusmodi
finibus redempcionibus amerciamentis exitibus forisfactis et
catallis in casibus quando scolares dicte universitatis vel
servientes sui partes existunt: Quare volumus et firmiter
precipimus pro nobis et heredibus nostris quod predicti
burgenses heredes ac successores sui omnia huiusmodi fines
redempciones amerciamenta et exitus forisfactos, ac eciam
omnimoda huiusmodi catalla felonum fugitivorum et utlagatorum in forma predicta habeant et percipiant et libertatibus illis plene gaudeant et utantur imperpetuum : Salvis
semper ut premittitur cancellario magistris et scolaribus
universitatis predicte et successoribus suis finibus forisfacturis
amerciamentis et aliis proficuis ac libertatibus et privilegiis
quibuscumque eis et predecessoribus suis per nos et progenitores nostros predictos concessis: Salvis eciam et exceptis
huiusmodi finibus redempcionibus amerciamentis exitibus
forisfactis et catallis in casibus quando scolares dicte uni-

of chattels of felons and fugitives and outlaws, from all, as well of tenants and residents within the town and liberty aforesaid, as of strangers and all others, which [chattels] shall happen to be found within the town and liberty aforesaid : So that it may be lawful for the same burgesses to collect and levy all such fines, ransoms and amercements and forfeited issues as soon as they may have been adjudged, by their bailiffs or deputies, and of such chattels of felons and fugitives they may put themselves in seisin and retain the same to the use of the said burgesses in aid of their farm aforesaid, and without hindrance by us or our heirs or the Justices, Escheators, Sheriffs or other bailiffs or ministers of us or of our heirs, and this for ever, without rendering therefor account or other reckoning to us or our heirs or any our ministers : Saving always to the chancellor, masters and scholars of our university of the town aforesaid and to their successors, the fines, forfeitures, amercements and other profits and liberties and privileges whatsoever granted to them and their pre-decessors by us and our progenitors formerly Kings of England : Save also and except all such fines, ransoms, amercements and forfeited issues and chattels in cases in which scholars of the said university or their servants are parties : Wherefore we will and firmly command for our-selves and our heirs that the aforesaid burgesses, their heirs and successors, shall have and take all such fines, ransoms, amercements and forfeited issues, and also all manner such chattels of felons, fugitives and outlaws in the form aforesaid, and shall fully enjoy and use these liberties for ever : Save always as is before said to the chancellor, masters and scholars of the university aforesaid and to their successors the fines, forfeitures, amercements and other profits and liberties and privileges whatsoever granted to them and to their predecessors by us and our progenitors aforesaid : Save also and except such fines, ransoms, amercements and for-feited issues and chattels in cases in which scholars of the said university or their servants are parties as is aforesaid. As witnesses : the venerable fathers William Archbishop

versitatis vel servientes sui partes existunt sicut predictum est. Hiis testibus : venerabilibus patribus Willelmo Archiepiscopo Cantuariensi tocius Anglie primate, Roberto Londoniensi, Willelmo Wyntoniensi Episcopis, Iohanne Rege Castelle et Legionis Duce Lancastrie, Edmundo Eboraci, et Thoma Gloucestrie Ducibus avunculis nostris carissimis, Ricardo Arundell, Hugone Staffordie, Michaele de la Pole Suffolcie Cancellario nostro Comitibus, Hugone Segrave Thesaurario nostro, Iohanne de Monte Acuto Senescallo Hospicii nostri et aliis. Data per manum nostram apud Westmonasterium nono die Decembris anno regni nostri nono.

per breve de privato Sigillo

SCARLE.

[1] Irrotulata in memorandis scaccarii inter recorda de termino Sancte Trinitatis anno decimo Regis Ricardi secundi ex parte Rememoratoris Thesaurarii.

XIV.   LITTERE PATENTES REGIS RICARDI SECUNDI.

1394
Feb. 28

[2][R]icardus dei gracia [R]ex Anglie et Francie et Dominus Hibernie omnibus ad quos presentes littere pervenerint salutem. Sciatis quod cum nos nuper considerantes dampna et deperdita que ville nostre Cantebrigie ac burgensibus nostris eiusdem ville tam per ablacionem libertatum et franchesiarum suarum quam per diversa et subita ignis infortunia evenerunt, de gracia nostra speciali in relevacionem et emendacionem ville nostre predicte ac status burgensium nostrorum predictorum necnon salvacionem et continuacionem firme nostre eiusdem ville concesserimus pro nobis et heredibus nostris et carta nostra confirmaverimus eisdem burgensibus quod ipsi et heredes ac successores sui burgenses eiusdem ville imperpetuum habeant omnia fines redempciones et amerciamenta ac exitus forisfactos omnium hominum tam residencium infra eandem villam et libertatem eiusdem quam aliorum quorumcumque quos in eadem villa occasione alicuius placiti

[1] An endorsement on the charter.

[2] Original in the Borough Archives with a part of the great seal in green wax appendant.

of Canterbury Primate of all England, Robert Bishop of
London, William Bishop of Winchester, John King of Castile
and Leon Duke of Lancaster, Edmund Duke of York and
Thomas Duke of Gloucester our dearest uncles, Richard Earl
of Arundel, Hugh Earl of Stafford, Michael De La Pole Earl
of Suffolk our Chancellor, Hugh Segrave our Treasurer, John
de Montacute the Steward of our Household and others.
Given by our hand at Westminster on the ninth day of
December in the ninth year of our reign.

By writ of privy seal

SCARLE.

Enrolled in the Memoranda of the Exchequer among the
records of the Trinity Term in the 10th year of King Richard
the Second on behalf of the Remembrancer of the Treasurer.

XIV. LETTERS PATENT OF KING RICHARD THE SECOND.

[1]Richard by the grace of God King of England and
France and Lord of Ireland to all to whom the present
letters shall come greeting. Know ye that whereas lately we,
considering the damages and losses which have happened
to our town of Cambridge and to our burgesses of the same
town, as well by the taking away of their liberties and
franchises, as by divers and sudden misfortunes by fire, of our
special grace for the relief and amendment of our town
aforesaid and of the estate of our burgesses aforesaid, and
also the salvation and continuance of our farm of the same
town, granted for ourselves and our heirs and by our charter
confirmed to the said burgesses that they and their heirs and
successors, burgesses of the said town, should have for ever
all fines, ransoms and amercements and forfeited issues of
all men, as well of residents within the same town and the

1394
Feb. 28

---

[1] See Cooper, *Annals,* i. 142.

vel querele liberum tenementum in eisdem villa et libertate tangencium, seu occasione alicuius debiti vel transgressionis contractus seu querele alterius rei infra easdem villam et libertatem emergencium tam coram iusticiariis nostris et heredum nostrorum ad placita coram nobis tenenda assignatis, et iusticiariis nostris de banco, ac coram thesaurario et baronibus nostris et heredum nostrorum de scaccario, ac coram iusticiariis nostris ad assisas capiendas, inquisiciones faciendas, gaolas deliberandas et ad pacem nostram confirmandam, ac iusticiariis ad inquirendum de artificibus laboratoribus et aliis operariis necnon de ponderibus et mensuris, ac iusticiariis itinerantibus, et quibuscunque aliis iusticiariis nostris, quam coram senescallo et marescallis ac clerico mercati hospicii nostri ac coram escaetoribus, vicecomitibus et aliis officiariis et ministris nostris quibuscumque fines facere vel amerciari aut exitus forisfacere contigerit, et quod habeant omnimoda catalla felonum et fugitivorum ac utlagatorum de omnibus, tam de tenentibus et residentibus infra villam et libertatem predictas, quam de extraneis et aliis quibuscumque, que infra villam et libertatem predictas inveniri contigerit[1], ita quod liceat eisdem burgensibus huiusmodi fines, redempciones, amerciamenta et exitus forisfactos statim cum adiudicata fuerint, per ballivos seu deputatos suos colligere et levare, et de huiusmodi catallis felonum et fugitivorum in seisinam se ponere, et ea ad usum eorumdem burgensium in auxilium firme sue predicte retinere possint, absque impedimento nostri vel heredum nostrorum, iusticiariorum, escaetorum, vicecomitum aut aliorum ballivorum seu ministrorum nostrorum, vel heredum nostrorum, quorumcunque, et absque compoto vel alio raciocinio inde nobis vel heredibus nostris seu ministris nostris quibuscumque reddendo imperpetuum : Salvis semper cancellario et magistris et scolaribus universitatis nostre ville predicte et successoribus suis, finibus, forisfacturis, amerciamentis et aliis proficuis ac libertatibus et privilegiis quibuscumque eis et predecessoribus suis per nos et progenitores nostros quondam Reges Anglie

---

[1] corr. *contigerint.*

liberty of the same, as of all others who in the same town by
reason of any plea or plaint touching a free tenement in the said
town and its liberty, or by reason of any debt or breach of
contract or plaint of any other matter arising within the said
town and its liberty, should chance to make fines or to be
amerced or to forfeit issues, as well before the Justices of
ourselves and our heirs assigned to hold pleas before ourselves, and our Justices of the Bench, and the Treasurer and
Barons of the Exchequer of ourselves and of our heirs, and
before our Justices for taking assizes, making inquisitions,
for gaol delivery and for confirming our peace, and the
Justices for inquiring about artificers, labourers and other
workmen, also about weights and measures, and Justices in
eyre, and all other our Justices, as also before the Steward
and Marshals and Clerk of the Market of our Household, and
before Escheators, Sheriffs and all other our officers and
servants, and that they [the said burgesses] should have all
manner of chattels of felons and of fugitives and of outlaws
from all men, as well from tenants and residents within the
town and liberty aforesaid, as from strangers and all others
whomsoever, which [chattels] may chance to be found within
the town and liberty aforesaid, so that it may be lawful for
the said burgesses to collect and levy by their bailiffs or
deputies such fines, ransoms, amercements and forfeited issues,
so soon as they shall have been adjudged, and of such
chattels of felons and of fugitives may put themselves in
seisin, and retain the same to the use of the said burgesses in
aid of their farm aforesaid, without hindrance from us or our
heirs, or the Justices, Escheators, Sheriffs or of any other
bailiffs or ministers of us or of our heirs, and this for ever,
without rendering account or other reckoning therefor to
us or to our heirs or any our ministers: Save always to the
chancellor and masters and scholars of our university of the
town aforesaid and to their successors the fines, forfeitures,
amercements and other profits and liberties and privileges
whatsoever granted to them and their predecessors by us and
our progenitors formerly Kings of England: Save also and

concessis : Salvis eciam et exceptis huiusmodi finibus, redempcionibus, amerciamentis, exitibus forisfactis et catallis
in casibus quando scolares dicte universitatis vel servientes
sui partes existunt, prout in carta nostra predicta plenius
continetur : Iamque predicti burgenses nobis supplicaverint
ut cum ipsi super allocacione et percepcione huiusmodi
finium, redempcionum, amerciamentorum, exituum forisfac-
factorum ac catallorum felonum, fugitivorum et utlagatorum
sibi per nos sic concessorum, pretextu excepcionum predictarum in dicta carta nostra contentarum multipliciter
impediti et retardati existant, velimus eis de remedio in
hac parte graciose providere : Nos volentes ipsos burgenses
plenum et integrum beneficium et effectum concessionis
nostre predicte habere et reportare, de gracia nostra speciali
et de assensu consilii nostri in presenti parliamento nostro,
volumus et concedimus pro nobis et heredibus nostris prefatis
burgensibus et successoribus suis quod, quandocumque et
quocienscumque vicecomes Cantebrigie pro tempore existens
retornum brevium, summonicionum seu aliorum mandatorum
nostrorum maiori et ballivis ville predicte pro huiusmodi
finibus, redempcionibus, amerciamentis, exitibus et catallis ad
opus nostrum infra villam predictam et libertatem eiusdem
levandis aliquo tempore futuro fecerit, et iidem burgenses
et successores sui burgenses ville predicte huiusmodi fines,
redempciones, amerciamenta, exitus et catalla infra villam
et libertatem predictas emergencia ad opus suum proprium
virtute carte nostre predicte super compotum vicecomitis
comitatus predicti prout moris est clamaverint, cancellarius
universitatis eiusdem ville qui pro tempore fuerit vel ejus
vicem gerens in casu illo et in omnibus aliis casibus et
processubus huiusmodi fines, redempciones, amerciamenta,
exitus et catalla in quibuscumque curiis et placeis nostris
tangentibus sive concernentibus thesaurario et baronibus
nostris et heredum nostrorum de scaccario, quociens et
quando per ipsos maiorem et ballivos aut eorum aliquem
fuerit requisitus, absque aliqua difficultate seu domigerio,
certificet sub sigillo officii sui, si scolares dicte universitatis

except such fines, ransoms, amercements, forfeited issues and chattels in cases in which scholars of the said university or their servants are parties, as in our charter aforesaid is more fully contained : And whereas now the aforesaid burgesses have besought us that, whereas they, in the collection and receipt of such fines, ransoms, amercements, forfeited issues and the chattels of felons, fugitives and outlaws, so granted to them by us, are much hindered and retarded by pretext of the aforesaid exceptions in our said charter contained, we would be pleased graciously to provide a remedy for them in this behalf : Now we, willing that the said burgesses should have and obtain the full and complete benefit and effect of our grant aforesaid, do, of our special grace and with the assent of our council in our present parliament, will and grant for ourselves and our heirs to the aforesaid burgesses and their successors that, when and as often as the sheriff of Cambridge for the time being shall in time to come make a return of our writs, summonses or other commands to the mayor and bailiffs of the town aforesaid, for levying to our use within the said town or the liberty thereof any such fines, ransoms, amercements, issues and chattels, and the said burgesses and their successors, burgesses of the town aforesaid, shall by virtue of our said charter claim to their own proper use, upon the account of the sheriff of the said county, as the usual course is, any such fines, ransoms, amercements, issues and chattels arising in the town and liberty aforesaid, then the chancellor for the time being of the university of the said town or his vicegerent, in that case and in all other cases and processes in any of the courts or places belonging to us or concerning us, shall certify such fines, ransoms, amercements, issues and chattels, when and so often as it shall be required by the said mayor and bailiffs or any of them, without any difficulty or danger, under the seal of his office, to the Treasurer and Barons of the Exchequer of us and our heirs, whether or no the scholars of the said university or their servants are parties in such fines, ransoms, amercements, issues and chattels : And that the said Treasurer and Barons

vel servientes sui in huiusmodi finibus, redempcionibus, amerciamentis, exitibus et catallis partes fuerint necne. Et quod iidem thesaurarius et barones de omnibus et singulis huiusmodi finibus, redempcionibus, amerciamentis, exitibus et catallis de quibus eis per huiusmodi certificacionem dicti cancellarii vel ejus vicem gerentis successivis temporibus faciendam constare poterit scolares dicte universitatis aut servientes suos partes non existere, plenam allocacionem eisdem burgensibus iuxta tenorem carte nostre predicte, absque aliqua alia verificacione, inquisicione seu informacione in hac parte facienda vel habenda faciant indilate: ipsosque burgenses omnia huiusmodi fines, redempciones, amerciamenta, exitus et catalla iuxta tenorem eiusdem carte ac certificacionem huiusmodi habere et percipere ac eis pacifice gaudere permittant imperpetuum. Volumus insuper et concedimus quod predicti burgenses de omnibus huiusmodi finibus, redempcionibus, amerciamentis, exitibus et catallis citra datam carte nostre predicte factis vel emersis, de quibus nobis nondum est satisfactum, plenam allocacionem iuxta tenorem carte nostre predicte per huiusmodi certificacionem cancellarii dicte universitatis in scaccarium nostrum in hac parte faciendam, absque alia inquisicione vel verificacione inde capienda vel facienda, habeant et optineant de gracia nostra speciali pariter et favore. In cuius rei testimonium has litteras nostras fieri fecimus patentes. Teste me ipso apud Westmonasterium vicesimo octavo die Februarii anno regni nostri decimo septimo.

per peticionem in parliamento

SCARLE.

[1] Irrotulate in memorandis scaccarii inter recorda de termino Sancte Trinitatis anno decimo septimo Regis Ricardi secundi ex parte Rememoratoris Thesaurarii.

[1] An endorsement.

of all and singular such fines, ransoms, amercements, issues and chattels, in which, as by any such certificate hereafter made of the said chancellor or of his vicegerent, it shall be apparent to them that the scholars of the said university or their servants are not parties, shall without delay make full allowance to the said burgesses according to the tenour of our charter aforesaid, without any other verification, inquisition or information to be made or had in this behalf, and shall permit the said burgesses to have, receive and peaceably enjoy all such fines, ransoms, amercements, issues and chattels, according to the tenour of the said charter and such certificate, for ever. Moreover we will and grant that the aforesaid burgesses of all such fines, ransoms, amercements, issues and chattels as have been made or arisen since the date of our charter aforesaid and for which satisfaction has not as yet been made to us, shall, of our special grace and favour, have and obtain a full allowance, according to the tenour of our charter aforesaid by such certificate of the chancellor of the said university to be made in our Exchequer on this behalf, without any other inquisition or verification to be taken or made for the same. In witness whereof we have caused these our letters to be made patent. As witness myself at Westminster the twenty-eighth day of February in the seventeenth year of our reign.

by petition in parliament

SCARLE.

Enrolled in the Memoranda of the Exchequer amongst the Records of Trinity Term in the 17th year of King Richard the Second on behalf of the Treasurer's Remembrancer.

XV. LITTERE PATENTES REGIS HENRICI QUARTI.

1405
Feb. 19

[1][H]enricus dei gracia [R]ex [A]nglie et Francie et [D]ominus Hibernie omnibus ad quos presentes littere pervenerint salutem. [I]nspeximus cartam domini Ricardi nuper Regis Anglie secundi post conquestum factam in hec verba : [R]icardus dei gracia &c.

> Here follows a copy of the Charter granted by Richard II. in the 9th year of his reign and on the 9th December 1385 hereinbefore printed and numbered XIII. The present instrument then proceeds as follows :—

Inspeximus eciam litteras patentes eiusdem domini Ricardi nuper Regis similiter factas in hec verba : [R]icardus dei gracia &c.

> Here follows a copy of the Letters Patent of Richard II. dated in the 17th year of his reign and on the 28th February 1394 hereinbefore printed and numbered XIV. The present instrument then proceeds as follows :—

[N]os autem donaciones concessiones et voluntates predictas ratas habentes et gratas, eas pro nobis et heredibus nostris quantum in nobis est acceptamus approbamus et dilectis nobis nunc burgensibus ville predicte ac heredibus et successoribus suis de gracia nostra speciali concedimus et confirmamus prout carta et littere predicte racionabiliter testantur, et prout iidem burgenses et successores sui huiusmodi fines redempciones amerciamenta et exitus forisfactos ac eciam catalla felonum fugitivorum et utlagatorum necnon certificacionem et allocacionem in forma predicta a tempore confeccionis carte et litterarum predictarum habuerunt, ac libertatibus predictis seu earum aliqua a tempore predicto semper hactenus uti et gaudere consueverunt : Salvis semper cancellario magistris et scolaribus universitatis nostre ville predicte et successoribus suis finibus forisfacturis amerciamentis et

---

[1] Original in the Borough Archives with a portion of the great seal in green wax appendant.

XV. LETTERS PATENT OF KING HENRY THE FOURTH.

[1]Henry by the grace of God King of England and France Lord of Ireland, to all to whom the present letters shall come greeting. We have inspected the charter of the lord Richard, formerly King of England, the second since the conquest, made in these words: Richard by the grace of God &c.

> Here follows a copy of the Charter granted by Richard II. in the 9th year of his reign and on the 9th December 1385 hereinbefore translated and numbered XIII. The present instrument then proceeds as follows :—

We have inspected also the letters patent of the same Lord Richard formerly King similarly made in these words : Richard by the grace of God &c.

> Here follows a copy of the Letters Patent of Richard II. dated in the 17th year of his reign and on the 28th February 1394 hereinbefore translated and numbered XIV. The present instrument then proceeds as follows :—

Now we therefore, ratifying and according the said gifts, grants and injunctions, do for ourselves and our heirs, so far as in us lies, accept and approve, and to our beloved the now burgesses of the aforesaid town and to their heirs and successors do, of our special grace, grant and confirm the same, in such wise as the charter and letters aforesaid reasonably testify, and in such wise as the same burgesses and their successors have had such fines, ransoms, amercements and forfeited issues and also the chattels of felons, fugitives and outlaws, and certificate and allowance in the form aforesaid, from the time of the making of the charter and letters aforesaid, and have always hitherto been wont to use and enjoy the aforesaid liberties or any of them from the time aforesaid : Save always to the chancellor, masters and scholars of our university of the aforesaid town and to their successors the fines, forfeitures, amercements and other profits and liberties and

1405
Feb. 19

---

[1] See Cooper, *Annals*, i. 150.

aliis proficuis ac libertatibus et privilegiis quibuscumque eis
et predecessoribus suis per predictum nuper Regem seu dictos
progenitores suos ante hec tempora concessis: Salvis eciam
et exceptis huiusmodi finibus redempcionibus amerciamentis
exitibus forisfactis et catallis in casibus quando scolares dicte
universitatis vel servientes sui partes existunt sicut predictum
est. In cuius rei testimonium has litteras nostras fieri fecimus
patentes. Teste me ipso apud Westmonasterium decimo nono
die Februarii anno regni nostri sexto

SHELFORD.

pro octo marcis solutis in hanaperio.

Examinata per Iohannem Roderham et Henricum Shelford
clericos.

[1] Irrotulate in memorandis scaccarii de anno septimo Regis
Henrici quarti inter recorda de termino Sancti Hillarii ex parte
Rememoratoris Thesaurarii.

XVI. LITTERE PATENTES REGIS HENRICI QUINTI.

1419
Nov. 15

[2][H]enricus dei gracia Rex Anglie et Francie et Dominus
Hibernie omnibus ad quos presentes littere pervenerint
salutem. Inspeximus litteras patentes domini Henrici nuper
Regis Anglie patris nostri factas in hec verba: [H]enricus dei
gracia &c.

Here follows a copy of the Letters Patent of Henry IV. dated
in the 6th year of his reign and on the 19th of February 1405
hereinbefore printed and numbered XV. The present instrument
then proceeds as follows:—

Nos autem donaciones, concessiones et voluntates predictas
ratas habentes et gratas, eas pro nobis et heredibus nostris,
quantum in nobis est, acceptamus, approbamus, et dilectis
nobis nunc burgensibus ville predicte ac heredibus et
successoribus suis de gracia nostra speciali concedimus et
confirmamus, prout carta et littere predicte racionabiliter

[1] An endorsement.
[2] Original in Borough Archives with a fine impression of the great seal
in green wax appendant.

privileges whatsoever granted in time past to them and to their predecessors by the aforesaid late King or his said progenitors : Save also and except such fines, ransoms, amercements, forfeited issues and chattels in causes in which scholars of the said university or their servants are parties as is aforesaid. In witness whereof we have caused these our letters to be made patent. Witness myself at Westminster on the nineteenth day of February in the sixth year of our reign.

SHELFORD.

> for eight marks paid to the hanaper.
>
> Examined by John Roderham and Henry Shelford, clerks.
>
> Enrolled in the Memoranda of the Exchequer for the seventh year of King Henry the Fourth amongst the records of Hilary term on the part of the Treasurer's Remembrancer.

XVI.   LETTERS PATENT OF KING HENRY THE FIFTH.

[1] Henry by the grace of God King of England and France and Lord of Ireland to all to whom the present letters shall come greeting. We have inspected the letters patent of the lord Henry late King of England, our father, made in these words : Henry by the grace of God &c.

1419
Nov. 15

> Here follows a copy of the Letters Patent of Henry IV. dated in the 6th year of his reign and on the 19th of February 1405 hereinbefore translated and numbered XV. The present instrument then proceeds as follows :—

Now we, ratifying and according the said gifts, grants and injunctions, do, for ourselves and our heirs so far as in us lies, accept and approve and of our special grace do grant and confirm the same to our beloved the now burgesses of the town aforesaid and their heirs and successors, in such wise as the charter and letters aforesaid reasonably testify,

---

[1] See Cooper, *Annals*, i. 163.

4

testantur et prout iidem burgenses et successores sui huiusmodi fines, redempciones, amerciamenta et exitus forisfactos,
ac eciam catalla felonum, fugitivorum et utlagatorum, necnon
certificacionem et allocacionem in forma predicta, a tempore
confeccionis carte et litterarum predictarum habuerunt, ac
libertatibus predictis seu earum aliqua a tempore predicto
semper hactenus uti et gaudere consueverunt: Salvis semper
cancellario, magistris et scolaribus universitatis nostre ville
predicte et successoribus suis finibus, forisfacturis, amerciamentis et aliis proficuis ac libertatibus et privilegiis
quibuscumque, eis et predecessoribus suis, per predictum
nuper Regem seu dictos progenitores suos, ante hec tempora
concessis: Salvis eciam et exceptis huiusmodi finibus, redempcionibus, amerciamentis, exitibus forisfactis et catallis in
casibus quando scolares dicte universitatis vel servientes sui
partes existunt sicut predictum est.   In cuius rei testimonium
has litteras nostras fieri fecimus patentes.   Teste: Iohanne
Duce Bedfordie Custode Anglie, apud Westmonasterium
quinto decimo die Novembris anno regni nostri septimo.

pro duodecim marcis solutis in hanaperio

HASELEY.

Examinata per Henricum Kays et Thomam Haseley, clericos.

XVII.   LITTERE PATENTES REGIS HENRICI SEXTI.

1424
Feb. 3

[1][H]enricus dei gracia Rex Anglie et Francie et Dominus
Hibernie omnibus ad quos presentes littere pervenerint salutem.
[I]nspeximus litteras patentes carissimi domini et patris nostri
Regis defuncti factas in hec verba: [H]enricus dei gracia &c.

Here follows a copy of the Letters Patent of Henry V. dated
in the 7th year of his reign and on the 15th November 1419
hereinbefore printed and numbered XVI.   The present Charter
then proceeds as follows:—

Nos autem litteras predictas de eisdem donacionibus,

[1] Original in the Borough Archives with a nearly perfect great seal in green
wax appendant.

and in such wise as the said burgesses and their predecessors have had such fines, ransoms, amercements and forfeited issues, and also chattels of felons, fugitives and outlaws, also certificate and allowance in form aforesaid, from the time of the making of the charter and letters aforesaid, and have always hitherto been wont to use and enjoy the liberties aforesaid or any of them from the time aforesaid: Save always to the chancellor, masters and scholars of our university of the town aforesaid and to their successors the fines, forfeitures, amercements and other profits and liberties and privileges whatsoever, granted before now, to them and to their predecessors, by the aforesaid late King or his said progenitors: Save also and except such fines, ransoms, amercements, forfeited issues and chattels in cases in which scholars of the said university or their servants are parties, as is aforesaid. In witness whereof we have caused these our letters to be made patent. As witness: John Duke of Bedford Guardian of England at Westminster on the fifteenth day of November in the seventh year of our reign.

for twelve marks paid to the hanaper

HASELEY.

Examined by Henry Kays and Thomas Haseley, clerks.

XVII. LETTERS PATENT OF KING HENRY THE SIXTH.

[1]Henry by the grace of God King of England and France and Lord of Ireland to all to whom these present letters shall come greeting. We have inspected the letters patent of the dearest lord, our father the deceased King, made in these words: Henry by the grace of God &c.

1424 Feb. 3

> Here follows a copy of the Letters Patent of Henry V. dated in the 7th year of his reign and on the 15th November 1419 hereinbefore translated and numbered XVI. The present Charter then proceeds as follows : —

Now we approve, ratify and confirm the letters aforesaid

---

[1] See Cooper, *Annals,* i. 172, where a wrong date seems to be given.

4—2

concessionibus et voluntatibus, minime revocatis, de assensu
dominorum spiritualium et temporalium in parliamento nostro
apud Westmonasterium anno regni nostri primo tento existencium, approbamus, ratificamus et confirmamus, prout littere
predicte racionabiliter testantur, et prout iidem burgenses et
predecessores sui donacionibus, concessionibus et voluntatibus
predictis, a tempore confeccionis litterarum et confirmacionis
predictarum hucusque, racionabiliter uti et gaudere consueverunt. In cuius rei testimonium has litteras nostras fieri
fecimus patentes. Teste me ipso apud Westmonasterium
tercio die Februarii anno regni nostri secundo

per breve de privato sigillo

Haseley.

Examinata per Iohannem Spryngthorpe et Thomam Haseley,
clericos.

Trinitatis recorda anno XVII° regis Ricardi secundi nuper
Regis Anglie rotulo VII° ibidem prima carta irrotulata.

XVIII. Littere Patentes Regis Henrici Sexti.

1437
March 25

[1][H]enricus dei gracia Rex Anglie et Francie et Dominus
Hibernie omnibus ad quos presentes littere pervenerint
salutem. Inspeximus litteras domini Ricardi nuper Regis
Anglie secundi post conquestum factas in hec verba : Ricardus
dei gracia &c.

Here follows a copy of the Charter granted by Richard II.
in the 1st year of his reign and on the 8th of December 1377
hereinbefore printed and numbered XI. The present instrument
then proceeds as follows :—

Inspeximus eciam litteras patentes domini Henrici nuper

[1] Two originals (duplicate) in the Borough Archives, both with fragments of
the great seal in green wax appendant. That not used as the foundation of our
text was examined by John Bate and Richard Wetton in the place of Selby and
Sturgeon, and bears the note *Dupplicate per rotulum*.

concerning the said gifts, grants and injunctions (which have in no wise been revoked) by the assent of the lords spiritual and temporal present in our parliament at Westminster held in the first year of our reign, in such wise as the aforesaid letters reasonably testify, and in such wise as the said burgesses and their predecessors were wont reasonably to use and enjoy the said gifts, grants and injunctions, from the time of the making of the said letters and confirmation until now. In witness whereof we have caused these our letters to be made patent. Witness myself at Westminster on the third day of February in the second year of our reign

by writ of private seal

HASELEY.

Examined by John Spryngthorpe and Thomas Haseley, clerks.

The first Charter was enrolled on Roll No. 7 in the records of Trinity Term in the 17th year of King Richard II. sometime King of England.

XVIII. LETTERS PATENT OF KING HENRY THE SIXTH.

[1]Henry by the grace of God King of England and France and Lord of Ireland, to all to whom the present letters shall come greeting. We have inspected the letters of the lord Richard lately King of England the second after the conquest made in these words : Richard by the grace of God &c.

1437
March 25

Here follows a copy of the Charter granted by Richard II. in the 1st year of his reign and on the 8th of December 1377 hereinbefore translated and numbered XI. The present instrument then proceeds as follows :—

We have also inspected the letters patent of confirmation of the lord Henry, lately King of England, our grandfather,

[1] See Cooper, *Annals*, i. 186.

Regis Anglie avi nostri prefatis burgensibus de confirmacione
factas in hec verba : Henricus dei gracia &c.

Here follows a copy of the Letters Patent of Henry IV.
dated in the 6th year of his reign and on the 19th of February
1405, hereinbefore printed and numbered XV. The present
instrument then proceeds as follows :—

Nos autem cartas et litteras predictas de huiusmodi
libertatibus, franchesiis et quietanciis, minime revocatis, de
avisamento et assensu dominorum spiritualium et temporalium
ac comunitatis regni nostri Anglie in parliamento nostro apud
Westmonasterium anno regni nostri primo tento existencium
acceptamus approbamus et dilectis nobis nunc burgensibus
ville predicte ac heredibus et successoribus suis confirmamus,
prout carte et littere predicte racionabiliter testantur, et prout
iidem burgenses et antecessores sui libertatibus, franchesiis et
quietanciis illis, a tempore confeccionis cartarum et litterarum
predictarum semper hactenus, racionabiliter uti et gaudere
consueverunt. In cuius rei testimonium has litteras nostras
fieri fecimus patentes. Teste me ipso apud Westmonasterium
vicesimo quinto die Marcii anno regni nostri quintodecimo

per ipsum regem et consilium suum in parliamento

STURGEON.

Examinate per Ricardum Selby et Ricardum Sturgeon
clericos.

XIX. LITTERE PATENTES REGIS EDWARDI QUARTI.

1465
July 6

[1]Edwardus dei gracia Rex Anglie et Francie et Dominus
Hibernie omnibus ad quos presentes littere pervenerint
salutem. Inspeximus quandam peticionem nobis in parliamento nostro apud Westmonasterium vicesimo nono die
Aprilis anno regni nostri tercio summonito et per diversas
prorogaciones et adiornaciones usque vicesimum primum diem

---

[1] Original in the Borough Archives. Great seal in yellow wax appendant by
parchment tag.

to the aforesaid burgesses, made in these words : Henry by the grace of God &c.

> Here follows a copy of the Letters Patent of Henry IV. dated in the 6th year of his reign and on the 19th of February 1405, hereinbefore translated and numbered XV. The present instrument then proceeds as follows :—

Now, the said charters and letters aforesaid of such liberties, franchises and quittances (which have in no wise been revoked) we, with the advice and consent of the lords spiritual and temporal and of the commonalty of our realm of England present in our parliament held at Westminster in the first year[1] of our reign, do accept and approve and to our beloved the now burgesses of the town aforesaid and their heirs and successors do confirm the same, in such wise as the charters and letters aforesaid reasonably testify, and in such wise as the same burgesses and their predecessors have always hitherto reasonably been wont to use and enjoy these liberties, franchises and quittances from the time of the making of the charters and letters aforesaid. In witness whereof we have caused these our letters to be made patent. Witness myself at Westminster on the twenty-fifth day of March in the fifteenth year of our reign

By the King himself and his council in parliament
STURGEON.
Examined by Richard Selby and Richard Sturgeon, clerks.

XIX. LETTERS PATENT OF KING EDWARD THE FOURTH.

[2]Edward by the grace of God King of England and France and Lord of Ireland, to all to whom the present letters shall come greeting. We have inspected a certain petition exhibited (among others) to us in our Parliament summoned at Westminster on the twenty-ninth day of April in the third year of our reign and continued by divers prorogations and adjournments until the twenty-first day of January in the

1465
July 6

---

[1] A general confirmation of charters having been ordered by parliament in that year.

[2] See Cooper, *Annals*, i. 214.

Ianuarii anno regni nostri quarto continuato per comunitatem
regni nostri Anglie in dicto parliamento eodem vicesimo primo
die Ianuarii existentem ex parte maioris, ballivi et comunitatis ville nostre Cantebrigie inter alia exhibitam et in
filaciis cancellarie nostre residentem in hec verba *And also*
that Where the Maier, baillif and Cominalte of your Towne
of Cambrigge been yerely chargeable for the ferme thereof
be lxx. li. to your highnes and viii. li. and x. s. to the Priour
of Caldewell and xx. s. to the hous of Kyllyngworthe, and
the same Towne and also the inhabitauntez therin taxed at
every dysme and quinzisme graunted by parlement to xlvj.
li. xii. s. ii. d. ob., toward which charges the Maire, Baillifs
and Cominalte and all fermes, rentes and other casueltees of
the seid Towne and therto belongyng in certein not past
xl. li. yerely: And also dyvers and many places late mansions
there been appropred to the College of oure lady and seint
Nicholas there: And divers and many places beying somtyme
mancions there and inhabited with people and chargeable with
charges there beene utterly wasted and forletted; and divers
and many other places late inhabited with Craftes mene of
the seid Towne and in like wise than chargeable nowe been
inhabited with scolers and soo not chargeable; For which
causes grete parte of the inhabitauntes Craftes men late
dwellyng in the Towne been thens departed and daily departen and moo entenden soo to doo to the utterest empoverisshyng of the same Towne and be likely hode to the
utterest destruccion therof withoute youre gracious socour
and reliefe in that partie shewed; be consideracione of which
premisses Henry the sixt late kyng of this Reame, in dede
and not be right, by his lettres patentes beryng date at
Westminster the xviii. day of Iulii the xxiiii. yere of his
usurped reigne graunted for hym his heires and successours
that the Maier, Baillifs and Cominalte and the seid Towne to
xx. li. oonly and not over to hym of or for a dysme and
quynzisme and every other charge and parcell of the same
disme and quinzisme to hym by the Cominalte of the Reame
of Englond in his last parlemente giffen graunted and to be

fourth year of our reign, by the commonalty of our realm
of England present in the said parliament on the said
twenty-first day of January, on the part of the mayor,
bailiff and community of our town of Cambridge which
petition remains on the files of our Chancery in these words:
"*And also* that Where the Maier, baillif and Cominalte of
your Towne of Cambrigge been yerely chargeable for the
ferme therof be lxx. li. to your highnes and viii. li. and x. s.
to the Priour of Caldewell and xx. s. to the hous of Kyllyngworthe, and the same Towne and also the inhabitauntez
therin taxed at every dysme and quinzisme graunted by
parlement to xlvj. li. xii. s. ii. d. ob., toward which charges
the Maire, Baillifs and Cominalte and all fermes, rentes and
other casueltees of the seid Towne and therto belongyng in
certein not past xl. li. yerely: And also dyvers and many
places late mansions there been appropred to the College of
oure lady and seint Nicholas there: And divers and many
places beying somtyme mancions there and inhabited with
people and chargeable with charges there beene utterly
wasted and forletted; and divers and many other places late
inhabited with Craftes mene of the seid Towne and in like
wise than chargeable nowe been inhabited with scolers and
soo not chargeable; For which causes grete parte of the
inhabitauntes Craftes men late dwellyng in the Towne
been thens departed and daily departen and moo entenden
soo to doo to the utterest empoverisshyng of the same
Towne and be likely hode to the utterest destruccion therof
withoute youre gracious socour and reliefe in that partie
shewed; be consideracione of which premisses Henry the
sixt late kyng of this Reame, in dede and not be right, by
his lettres patentes beryng date at Westminster the xviii. day
of Iulii the xxiiii. yere of his usurped reigne graunted for
hym his heires and successours that the Maier, Baillifs and
Cominalte and the seid Towne to xx. li. oonly and not over
to hym of or for a dysme and quynzisme and every other
charge and parcell of the same disme and quinzisme to hym
by the Cominalte of the Reame of Englond in his last

paied shulden be assessed, taxed and tailed, and the same
xx. li. oonly and not over by that cause to hym shuld be
boundon to pay, and graunted over to the seid Maire,
Baillifs and Cominalte and their successours for hym his
heires and successours that, whensoever eny hoole disme
or quinzisme, or ·eny other charge or parcell of disme or
quinzisme, to hym his heires or successours by the Cominalte
of the Reame of Englond shuld happene to giffe or graunted,
that then the seid Maier, Baillifs and Cominalte and their
successours or the seid Towne to xx. li. oonly and not over
to every such disme and quinzisme soo to be giffen or
graunted shuld be assessed, taxed and tailed, and the same
xx. li. oonly and not over to hym his heires and successours
by that cause shuld be bounden and soo fro thensforth
for the quantite, rate and afferaunce of every disme and
quinzisme and every part or parcell of the same disme and
quinzisme to hym, his heires and successours to be giffen and
graunted to his use, his heires or successours, of the same
Maier, Baillifs and Cominalte and their successours to be
rered : And that the same Maire, Baillifs and Cominalte and
their successours and the seid Towneshipe of every somme
over the forseid xx. li. of theym by force of such disme or
quinzisme to him, his heires or successours, graunted and to
be graunted to his use, his heires or successours, by eny
mean to be rered, shuld be utterly quyte and discharged for
ever ; Although the same Maier, baillifs and Cominalte or
eny of theym to thiese maner grauntes be or shuld be parties,
doers, consenters or graunters or eny of theym be or shalbe
partie, doer, consenter or graunter ; And although these
maner graunte or grauntes be or shuld be, been or shuld
been, made under thiese wordes and termes of places exempt
not except by eny manner mean and forme, or other wordes
or termes of like force and effect, such manner graunt or
grauntes shuld be made, or alsmoche as the forseid Maier,
Baillifs and Cominalte and their predecessours xlvi. li. at every
hole disme and quinzisme to hym and his progenitours
graunted to theym afore tyme paiden notwithstondyng, as

parlemente giffen graunted and to be paied shulden be
assessed, taxed and tailed, and the same xx. li. oonly and
not over by that cause' to hym shuld be boundon to pay,
and graunted over to the seid Maire, Baillifs and Cominalte
and their successours for hym his heires and successours that,
whensoever eny hoole disme or quinzisme, or eny other
charge or parcell of disme or quinzisme, to hym his heires
or successours by the Cominalte of the Reame of Englond
shuld happene to giffe or graunted, that then the seid Maier,
Baillifs and Cominalte and their successours or the seid
Towne to xx. li. oonly and not over to every such disme
and quinzisme soo to be giffen or graunted shuld be assessed,
taxed and tailed, and the same xx. li. oonly and not over
to hym his heires and successours by that cause shuld be
bounden and soo fro thensforth for the quantite, rate and
afferaunce of every disme and quinzisme and every part or
parcell of the same disme and quinzisme to hym, his heires and
successours to be giffen and graunted to his use, his heires
or successours, of the same Maier, Baillifs and Cominalte
and their successours to be rered: And that the same Maire,
Baillifs and Cominalte and their successours and the seid
Towneshipe of every somme over the forseid xx. li. of theym
by force of such disme or quinzisme to him, his heires or
successours, graunted and to be graunted to his use, his
heires or successours, by eny mean to be rered, shuld be
utterly quyte and discharged for ever ; Although the same
Maier, baillifs and Cominalte or eny of theym to thiese
maner grauntes be or shuld be parties, doers, consenters, or
graunters or eny of theym be or shalbe partie, doer, consenter
or graunter ; And although these maner graunte or grauntes
be or shuld be, been or shuld been, made under thiese wordes
and termes of places exempt not except by eny manner
mean and forme, or other wordes or termes of like force and
effect, such manner graunt or grauntes' shuld be made, or
alsmoche as the forseid Maier, Baillifs and Cominalte and
their predecessours xlvi. li. at every hole disme and quinzisme
to hym and his progenitours graunted to theym afore tyme

the seid graunt therof pleinly appereth; And it is soo that by your gracious takyng uppon your highnes after your right and title the Croune of this Reame the seid graunte was voide; And for that cause your Tresorer and Barons of your Eschequer will not alowe the seid letres patentes: And doute is whether the provision made in your last parlement be sufficiant to helpe the seid Maier, Baillifs and Cominalte and your seid Towne, which not holpen, then they been but as undone: Wherfore that it please your highnes to ordeyn, stablissh and enacte in this your present parlement that the seid letres patentes be good and effectuell in your lawe accordyng to thentent of theym: And that the forseid Maier, Baillifs and Cominalte and their successours, their poverte considered, may have due allowaunce and discharge of the matiers conteyned in the same lettres patentes in all Courtes and places of the Reame withoute eny ambiguite or difficulte, by writtes oute of your Chauncery uppon the same letres patentes to be had, the same writtes to be had at all tymes necessarie and requisite withoute eny denyer. Inspeximus eciam quandam responsionem eidem peticioni per nos de avisamento et assensu dominorum spiritualium et temporalium in eodem parliamento similiter existentium ac comunitatis predicte necnon auctoritate eiusdem parliamenti factam, et in dorso eiusdem peticionis insertam, in hec verba Soit fait come il est desire. Nos autem tenores peticionis et responsionis predictarum ad requisicionem maioris, ballivi et comunitatis ville nostre predicte duximus exemplificandos per presentes. In cuius rei testimonium has litteras nostras fieri fecimus patentes. Teste me ipso apud Westmonasterium sexto die Iulii anno regni nostri quinto.

F AUKES.

Examinate per Iohannem Faukes et Thomam Ive, clericos.

[1] Irrotulate in memorandis scaccarii de anno VIII^{vo} Regis Edwardi quarti: videlicet inter recorda de Termino Pasche Rotulo xviii ex parte Rememoratoris Thesaurarii.

[1] An endorsement.

paiden notwithstondyng, as the seid graunt therof pleinly appereth ; And it is soo that by your gracious takyng uppon your highnes after your right and title the Croune of this Reame the seid graunte was voide ; And for that cause your Tresorer and Barons of your Eschequer will not alowe the seid letres patentes : And doute is whether the provision made in your last parlement be sufficiant to helpe the seid Maier, Baillifs and Cominalte and your seid Towne, which not holpen, then they been but as undone : Wherfore that it please your highnes to ordeyn, stablissh and enacte in this your present `parlement that the seid letres patentes be good and effectuell in your lawe accordyng to thentent of theym : And that the forseid Maier, Baillifs and Cominalte and their successours, their poverte considered, may have due allowaunce and discharge of the matiers conteyned in the same lettres patentes in all Courtes and places of the Reame withoute eny ambiguite or difficulte, by writtes oute of your Chauncery uppon the same letres patentes to be had, the same writtes to be had at all tymes necessarie and requisite withoute eny denyer." We have inspected likewise a certain answer to the said petition by us on the advice and consent of the lords spiritual and temporal, present in like manner in the said parliament, and of the aforesaid commonalty [of the realm], and by the authority of the said parliament made and inserted on the back of the said petition in these words " Let it be done as it is desired." Now we, at the request of the mayor, bailiff and commonalty of our town aforesaid have thought good that the tenours of the said petition and answer should be exemplified by these presents. In witness whereof we have caused these our letters to be made patent. Witness myself at Westminster on the sixth day of July in the fifth year of our reign.

FAUKES.

Examined by John Faukes and Thomas Ive, clerks.

Enrolled in the Memoranda of the Exchequer of the eighth year of King Edward the fourth : to wit, amongst the records of the Easter Term in Roll 18 on behalf of the Treasurer's Remembrancer.

XX. LITTERE PATENTES REGIS EDWARDI QUARTI.

1466
July 6

[1]Edwardus dei gracia Rex Anglie et Francie et Dominus Hibernie omnibus ad quos presentes littere pervenerint salutem. Inspeximus litteras patentes Henrici sexti nuper Regis Anglie in hec verba : Henricus dei gracia &c.

> Here follows a copy of the Letters Patent of Henry VI. dated in the 15th year of his reign and on the 25th of March 1437, hereinbefore printed and numbered XVIII. The present instrument then proceeds as follows :—

Nos autem cartas et litteras patentes ac omnia et singula contenta in eisdem rata habentes et grata, ea pro nobis et heredibus nostris, quantum in nobis est, acceptamus et approbamus, ac dilectis nobis nunc burgensibus ville predicte ac heredibus et successoribus suis ratificamus et confirmamus. In cuius rei testimonium has litteras nostras fieri fecimus patentes. Teste me ipso apud Westmonasterium sexto die Iulii anno regni nostri sexto.

XXI. LITTERE PATENTES REGIS HENRICI OCTAVI.

1510
April 29

[2][H]enricus dei gracia [R]ex [A]nglie et [F]rancie et [D]ominus [H]ibernie [O]mnibus ad quos presentes littere pervenerint salutem. [I]nspeximus litteras patentes domini Edwardi nuper regis Anglie quarti progenitoris nostri de confirmacione factas in hec verba : Edwardus dei gracia &c. :—

> Here follows a copy of the Letters Patent of Edward IV. dated in the 6th year of his reign and on the 6th of July 1466, hereinbefore printed and numbered XX. The present instrument then proceeds as follows :—

Nos autem cartas et litteras predictas ac omnia et singula

---

[1] From the Inspeximus of 2 Henry VIII. Original not forthcoming.

[2] Original in the Borough Archives, with a portion of the great seal appended by strings of green and white silk, in which gold thread is twisted.

XX. LETTERS PATENT OF KING EDWARD THE FOURTH.

[1]Edward by the grace of God King of England and France and Lord of Ireland, to all to whom the present letters shall come greeting. We have inspected the letters patent of Henry the Sixth late king of England in these words : Henry by the grace of God etc.

> Here follows a copy of the Letters Patent of Henry VI. dated in the 15th year of his reign and on the 25th of March 1437, hereinbefore translated and numbered XVIII. The present instrument then proceeds as follows ·—

Now we, ratifying and according the said charters and letters patent and all and singular the matters therein contained, do for ourselves and our heirs, so far as in us lies, accept and approve the same, and do ratify and confirm the same to our beloved the now burgesses of the said town, their heirs and successors. In witness whereof we have caused these our letters to be made patent. Witness myself at Westminster, the sixth day of July in the sixth year of our reign.

XXI. LETTERS PATENT OF KING HENRY THE EIGHTH.

[2]Henry by the grace of God King of England and France and Lord of Ireland, to all to whom the present letters shall come greeting. We have inspected the letters patent of confirmation of the lord Edward the fourth, lately King of England, our ancestor, made in these words: Edward by the grace of God &c. :—

> Here follows a copy of the Letters Patent of Edward IV. dated in the 6th year of his reign and on the 6th of July 1466, hereinbefore translated and numbered XX. The present instrument then proceeds as follows :—

Now we, ratifying and according the said charters and

---

[1] See Cooper, *Annals*, i. 215.
[2] See Cooper, *Annals*, i. 292.

in eisdem contenta rata habentes et grata, ea pro nobis et heredibus nostris, quantum in nobis est, acceptamus et approbamus ac dilectis nobis nunc burgensibus ville predicte ac heredibus et successoribus suis ratificamus et confirmamus, prout carte et littere predicte racionabiliter testantur. In cuius rei testimonium has litteras nostras fieri fecimus patentes. Teste me ipso apud Westmonasterium vicesimo nono die Aprilis anno regni nostri secundo.

YONG.

pro quadraginta solidis solutis in hanaperio.

Examinate per Wilelmum Malhom et Thomam Coweley, clericos.

Irrotulate.

XXII. LITTERE EXEMPLIFICATORIE REGIS HENRICI OCTAVI.

1530
May 15

[1][H]enricus octavus dei gracia Anglie et Francie [R]ex fidei defensor et Dominus Hibernie [O]mnibus Ballivis et Fidelibus suis salutem. [I]nspeximus quoddam recordum coram nobis habitum in hec verba: Placita coram domino Rege apud Westmonasterium in Termino Pasche anno regni Regis Henrici octavi vicesimo primo Rotulo xiij° inter placita Regis. ¶ Cantebriggia. ¶ Alias, scilicet quarto die Iulii anno regni domini Regis nunc decimo nono, apud Cantebriggiam in comitatu predicto coram Edwardo Slegge et Henrico Gylson, coronatoribus dicti domini Regis ville sue Cantebriggie predicte et libertates[2] eiusdem, super visum corporis Roberti Asshewelle, nuper de Cantebriggia predicta, laborer, ibidem mortui et interfecti, per sacramentum xij iuratorum extat presentatum, quod tercio die Iulii anno regni dicti domini Regis decimo nono supradicto, circa horam decimam post meridiem, in nocte eiusdem diei, predictus Robertus

---

[1] Original in the Borough Archives, with a seal in black wax (probably that of the King's Bench) appended by parchment tag.
[2] *Sic*: corr. *libertatis*.

letters and all and singular the matters therein contained, do for ourselves and our heirs, so far as in us lies, accept and approve the same, and do ratify and confirm the same to our beloved the now Burgesses of the said town, their heirs and successors, in such wise as the charters and letters aforesaid reasonably testify. In witness whereof we have caused these our letters to be made patent. As witness, Myself at Westminster on the twenty-ninth day of April in the second year of our reign.

YONG.

> For 40 shillings paid to the hanaper.
> Examined by William Malhom and Thomas Coweley, clerks.
> Enrolled.

[1]XXII. LETTERS EXEMPLIFICATORY OF KING HENRY THE EIGHTH.

Henry the Eighth by the grace of God King of England and France Defender of the Faith and Lord of Ireland, to all his Bailiffs and faithful People, greeting. We have inspected a certain record had before us in these words : Pleas before our lord the King at Westminster, in the Easter Term in the twenty-first year of the reign of King Henry the Eighth, in the 13th Roll amongst the pleas of the King. ¶ Cambridgeshire. ¶ Heretofore, to wit, on the 4th day of July in the nineteenth year of the reign of our lord the now King, at Cambridge in the county aforesaid before Edward Slegge, and Henry Gylson, the coroners of the said lord King of his said town of Cambridge and the liberty of the same, upon the view of the body of Robert Asshewell late of Cambridge aforesaid, labourer, there dead and slain, it is presented by the oath of twelve jurors that on the 3rd day of July in the aforesaid nineteenth year of the reign of the said lord King, about the tenth hour after noon, in the night of the same day, the aforesaid Robert Asshewell was in the peace of God

1530 May 15

---

[1] Not mentioned in Cooper's *Annals.*

Asshewelle fuit in pace Dei et dicti domini Regis, in quodam vico ibidem vocato Trumppyngtone Strete in villa Cantebriggie predicta, ibidem venit, eodem tercio die Iulii anno supradicto, quidam Iacobus Newland nuper de villa Cantebriggie predicta, in comitatu predicto, ffyssher, sive peddeler, circa horam predictam, vi et armis, videlicet baculo vocato a ffagott logge, ut felo dicti domini Regis, contra pacem ipsius Regis, coronam et dignitatem suas, ex malicia precogitata et insultu premeditato, per ipsum in Robertum Asshewelle, adtunc et ibidem inventum, insultum fecit, et ipsum Robertum Asshewelle cum predicto baculo precii unius obuli, quem idem Iacobus manibus suis tunc tenuit, prefatum Robertum Asshewelle super capud suum felonice percussit, unde cerebrum capitis sui exivit, dans ei tunc et ibidem plagam mortalem, de qua quidem plaga mortali idem Robertus Asshewelle incontinenter obiit, et sic idem Iacobus prefatum Robertum Asshewelle tunc et ibidem felonice et voluntarie interfecit et murderavit, contra pacem dicti domini Regis, et quam cito idem felo feloniam et murdrum predictas in forma predicta fecisset, fugam fecit, et habuit bona et catalla infra libertatem ville Cantebriggie predicte, in comitatu predicto, ad valenciam viginti marcarum tempore murdri predicti facti, que seisita fuerunt per maiorem et ballivos ville Cantebriggie predicte ut ius suum &c.: Quod quidem indictamentum dictus Rex nunc coram eo postea certis de causis venire fecit terminandum &c.: Per quod preceptum fuit vicecomiti quod non omittet &c. quin venire faceret prefatos maiorem et ballivos ville Cantebriggie ad respondendum domino Regi de bonis et catallis predictis &c.: Et modo, scilicet die lune proximo post mensem Pasche isto eodem Termino, coram domino Rege apud Westmonasterium, veniunt predicti maior ville Cantebriggie predicte necnon ballivi eiusdem ville per Thomam Skrymsher attornatum suum, et, habito auditu inquisicionis predicte, dicunt quod ipsi non intendunt quod dominus Rex nunc ipsos racione inquisicionis predicte, seu aliquorum bonorum et catallorum que fuerunt predicti Iacobi Newlande per maiorem et ballivos

and of the said lord King, in a certain street there called Trumppyngton Strete in the town of Cambridge aforesaid, and there came, on the said third day of July in the said year, a certain James Newland, late of the said town of Cambridge in the said county, fisher or pedlar, about the said hour, with force and arms, namely a stick called a "ffagott logge," as a felon of the said lord King, against the peace of the said King, his crown and dignity, of malice aforethought and premeditated assault, made therewith, on the said Robert Asshewell, then and there found, an assault, and with the aforesaid stick, of the price of one halfpenny, which the said James then held in his hands, did strike the aforesaid Robert Asshewell on his head feloniously, whereby the brain of his head issued, giving to him then and there a mortal wound, of which mortal wound the said Robert Asshewell incontinently died, and so the same James aforesaid did then and there feloniously and wilfully kill and murder the said Robert Asshewell against the peace of the said lord King, and, as soon as the said felon had committed the felony and murder aforesaid in manner aforesaid, he took to flight, and he had goods and chattels within the liberty of the town of Cambridge aforesaid, in the county aforesaid, to the value of twenty marks at the time when the murder aforesaid was committed, which were seized by the mayor and bailiffs of the town of Cambridge aforesaid as their right &c.: which indictment the said King has now, for certain causes, caused to come before him that it may be terminated &c.: Wherefore it was commanded to the sheriff that he should not omit &c., but should cause the said mayor and bailiffs of the town of Cambridge to come to answer to the lord King concerning the goods and chattels aforesaid &c.: And now, to wit, on the Monday next after the month of Easter in the said Term, before the lord King at Westminster, come the aforesaid mayor of the town of Cambridge aforesaid and the bailiffs of the said town, by Thomas Skrymsher their attorney, and, upon hearing had of the said inquest, they say that they do not understand that the now

predicte ville Cantebriggie seisitorum[1] et penes se retentorum,
impetere seu occasionare velit aut debet, aut quod iidem
maior et ballivi pro bonis et catallis illis aliquo modo domino
Regi de aliquo debito respondere aut onerari debent: quia,
protestando quod inquisicio predicta necnon materia in
eadem contenta minus sufficiens in lege existat ad ponendum
ipsos eidem inquisicioni respondere, pro placito tamen dicit[2],
quod predicta villa Cantebriggie est antiquus[3] burgus et unus
de antiquissimis burgis huius regni Anglie, [et][4] eedem burgus
et villa Cantebriggie sunt, et ante tempus et a tempore cuius
contrarii memoria hominum non existit, fuerunt unum corpus
et una comunitas in se incorporata, tam de burgensibus
eorumdem burgi et ville, quam de uno maiore et quatuor
ballivis per dictos burgenses eorumdem burgi et ville singulis
annis in festo sancti Michaelis Archangeli electis et eligendis;
et tam iidem burgenses quam predicti maior et ballivi ante
et per totum predictum tempus cuius contrarii memoria
hominum non existit, per nomen burgensium ville Cantebriggie quam per nomen maioris et ballivorum ville Cantebriggie placitaverunt et placitati fuerunt et adhuc existunt,
et persone[5] habiles ad perquirendum et habendum terras,
tenementa, libertates et franchesias et alia quecumque hereditamenta, per alterum et utrumque nomen predictorum
nominum, videlicet tam burgensium ville Cantebriggie quam
maioris et ballivorum ville Cantebriggie: et dicunt quod
dominus Ricardus nuper Rex Anglie et Francie secundus
per litteras suas patentes quas predicti maior et ballivi hic in
curia proferunt, et quarum data est apud Westmonasterium
nono die Decembris anno regni sui nono, inter alia ex sua
gracia speciali concessit pro se et heredibus suis et per
litteras predictas confirmavit burgensibus ville predicte heredibus et executoribus[6] suis burgensibus ville predicte im-

---

[1] *seitorum* MS.
[2] *Sic*: corr. *dicunt.*
[3] *antiqus* MS.
[4] *et* omitted in MS.
[5] *persones* MS.
[6] *Sic*: corr. *successoribus.*

lord King desires or ought to impeach or take occasion against them by reason of the inquest aforesaid, or of any the goods and chattels which belonged to the aforesaid James Newland, and were seized by the mayor and bailiffs of the aforesaid town of Cambridge and retained in their hands, or that the said mayor and bailiffs for the same goods and chattels ought in any wise to answer or be charged to the lord King as for a debt : for (protesting that the inquest aforesaid and the matter therein contained are insufficient in law to put them to reply to the said inquest) they, by way of plea, say that the aforesaid town of Cambridge is an ancient borough and one of the most ancient boroughs of this realm of England, and that the said borough and town of Cambridge are, and before time and from time of which the memory of man does not exist to the contrary, have been one body and one commonalty incorporate in itself, as well of the burgesses of the said borough and town as of one mayor and four bailiffs by the said burgesses of the said borough and town in each year on the feast of Saint Michael the Archangel elected and to be elected; and that as well the said burgesses as the aforesaid mayor and bailiffs before and throughout the whole aforesaid time of which the memory of man does not exist to the contrary, as well by the name of the burgesses of the town of Cambridge, as by the name of the mayor and bailiffs of the town of Cambridge, have pleaded and have been, and still are, impleaded, and have been and still are persons capable of purchasing and holding lands, tenements, liberties and franchises and other hereditaments whatsoever, as well by both or either of the names aforesaid, to wit, as well by the name of the burgesses of the town of Cambridge, as by that of the mayor and bailiffs of the town of Cambridge : and they say that the lord Richard the Second, sometime King of England and France, by his letters patent, which the aforesaid mayor and bailiffs here produce in court and of which the date is at Westminster on the ninth day of December in the ninth year of his reign, amongst other things of his special grace granted for himself and his

perpetuum omnimoda catalla felonum, fugitivorum et utlagatorum, de omnibus tenentibus et residentibus infra villam
et libertatem predictas, tam de extraneis quam de aliis quibuscumque, que infra villam et libertatem inveniri contigerint,
ita quod liceat eisdem burgensibus eadem catalla felonum et
fugitivorum in seisinam se ponere et ea ad usum eorundem
burgensium in auxilium firme ville predicte retinere possint,
absque impedimento eiusdem nuper Regis vel heredum
suorum iusticiariorum, vicecomitum aut aliorum ballivorum
seu ministrorum suorum vel heredum suorum quorumcumque,
et absque compoto vel alio raciocinio inde eidem nuper Regi
seu heredibus suis seu ministris dicti nuper Regis quibuscumque reddendo imperpetuum, prout in eisdem litteris
patentibus plenius[1] continetur: Quas quidem litteras patentes
predicti nuper Regis Ricardi secundi ac omnia singula in
eisdem litteris contenta dominus Rex nunc Henricus octavus
per litteras suas patentes, quas nunc iidem maior et ballivi
similiter hic in curia proferunt, quarum data est apud Westmonasterium xxix die Aprilis anno regni ipsius domini Regis
secundo, ratum habens et gratum, pro ipso domino Rege
nunc approbavit, ac burgensibus ville predicte et heredibus et
successoribus suis ratificavit et confirmavit, prout in eisdem
litteris patentibus predicti domini Regis nunc plenius continetur: Et iidem maior et ballivi dicunt quod predictus
Iacobus Newlande, tempore murdri predicti perpetrati, ac
tempore inquisicionis predicte capte, fuit et adhuc est liber
burgensis ville Cantebriggie predicte, et non scolaris universitatis Cantebriggie predicte, nec serviens alicuius scolaris
universitatis predicte; Virtute quarum quidem litterarum patencium prefatis burgensibus confectarum, predicti maior et
ballivi predicta bona et catalla unde in dicta inquisicione fit
mencio, ex quo tempore murdri predicti fuerunt predicti
Iacobi, post inquisicionem predictam captam, apud et infra
predictam villam Cantebriggie et tempore murdri predicti
per predictum Iacobum perpretati et postea inventa seisive-

---

[1] *plenis* MS.

heirs and by the letters aforesaid confirmed to the burgesses of the town aforesaid, to their heirs and executors [*corr.* successors], burgesses of the town aforesaid, for ever, all manner of chattels of felons, fugitives and outlaws, from all tenants and residents within the town and liberty aforesaid, as well from strangers as from all others which [chattels] might happen to be found within the town and liberty, in such wise that it should be lawful for the said burgesses to put themselves in seisin of the said chattels of felons and fugitives and retain the same for the use of the said burgesses in aid of the farm of the town aforesaid, without any hindrance by the said late King or his heirs by the justices, sheriffs or other bailiffs or ministers of him or of his heirs, and without rendering account or other reckoning for the same to the said late King or his heirs or to any the ministers of the said late King, for ever, as in the said letters patent is more fully contained : Which letters patent of the aforesaid late King Richard the Second and all and singular in the same letters contained, the now lord King Henry the Eighth by his letters patent, which now the same mayor and bailiffs likewise produce here in court, whereof the date is at Westminster on the 29th day of April in the second year of the reign of the said lord King, ratifying and according, did, for himself the now lord King approve the same and to the burgesses of the town aforesaid and their heirs and successors did ratify and confirm the same, in such wise as in the said letters patent of the aforesaid lord the now King is more fully contained: And the said mayor and bailiffs say that the aforesaid James Newland, at the time when the murder aforesaid was perpetrated, and at the time when the inquest aforesaid was taken, was and still is a free burgess of the town of Cambridge aforesaid, and not a scholar of the university of Cambridge aforesaid, nor a servant of any scholar of the university aforesaid : By virtue of which letters patent made to the aforesaid burgesses, the aforesaid mayor and bailiffs did seize the aforesaid goods and chattels whereof mention is made in the said inquest, which,

runt, et penes se in auxilium predicte firme eiusdem ville
Cantebriggie retinent et habent, prout eis bene licuit. Et
hoc predicti nunc maior et ballivi parati sunt verificare. Et
petunt iudicium si dominus Rex nunc pro predictis bonis et
catallis que fuerunt predicti Iacobi Newlande ulterius impetere aut ipsos de aliquo debito pro bonis et catallis illis
onerari. Et predictus Ricardus Lyster, generalis attornatus
domini Regis nunc, qui pro ipso Rege sequitur, pro ipso
Rege dicit quod titulum dictorum maioris et ballivorum per
ipsos superius placitatum et factum ad manutenendum[1] ipsos
habere et retinere bona et catalla predicta non est sufficiens
in lege, ad que ipse pro eodem domino Rege necesse non
habet nec per legem tenetur respondere. Et pro insuffici-
encia eorumdem placiti et tituli pro dicto domino Rege petit
judicium, et quod ipsi bona et catalla per ipsos ut predicitur
seisita dicto domino Regi respondere et quod ipsi ad finem
cum dicto domino Rege occasione seisionis et retencionis
eorumdem adiudicari debeant. Et predicti maior et ballivi,
ex quo ipsi sufficiens placitum et titulum ad manutenendum
ipsos maiorem et ballivos retinere et habere bona et catalla
predicta placitaverunt et demonstraverunt que ipsi parati
sunt verificare prout curia &c., et que predictus Ricardus
Lyster, qui sequitur &c., non dedicit nec ad ea aliqualiter
respondit set verificacionem illam superinde admittere omnino
recusat, ut prius petunt judicium, et quod breve patens
predictum eis [et][2] successoribus suis allocerentur &c.: Super
quo, visis et per curiam hic intellectis omnibus et singulis
premissis, servientibus domini Regis ad legem ac eiusdem
Regis attornato ad hoc convocatis et presentibus, pro eo
quod videtur curie hic quod placitum et titulum[3] dictorum
maioris et ballivi sufficientes in lege existunt ad manutenendum ipsos maiorem et ballivos retinere et habere bona et
catalla predicta, consideratum est quod littere patentes predicte dictis maiori et ballivis ville Cantebriggie predicte et

---

[1] *manutend'* MS.
[2] *et* omitted in MS.
[3] Corr. *titulus.*

at the time of the said murder did belong to the aforesaid
James, and which after the taking of the inquest aforesaid
were found at and within the said town of Cambridge, at the
time of the said murder perpetrated by the said James and
afterwards, and in their hands they do retain and hold the
same in aid of the aforesaid farm of the said town of Cambridge, as well they may.   And this the said now mayor and
bailiffs are ready to verify.   And they pray judgement
whether the now lord King, for the aforesaid goods and
chattels which belonged to the aforesaid James Newland, will
any further impeach them or will charge them with debt for
the same goods and chattels.   And the aforesaid Richard
Lyster, the Attorney-General of the now lord King, who sues
on the King's behalf, says for the King that the title of the
said mayor and bailiffs by themselves above pleaded and
made for maintaining them to have and retain the goods and
chattels aforesaid, is not sufficient in law, and that thereto he
on behalf of the said lord King has no need nor is bound by
law to answer.   And because of the insufficiency of the said
plea and title, he prays judgement for the said lord King,
and that they, for the goods and chattels, so seized by them
as aforesaid, ought to answer to the said lord King, and that
they ought to be adjudged to make fine with the said lord
King on account of the seizing and retaining of the same.
And the said mayor and bailiffs, for that they have pleaded
and shewn a sufficient plea and title to maintain them the
mayor and bailiffs in retaining and having the goods and
chattels aforesaid, which they are prepared to verify as the
court &c., and which the aforesaid Richard Lyster, who sues
&c., has not denied (nor has he in any wise replied to the
same but altogether refuses to admit the verification aforesaid), once more pray judgement, and that the said letter
patent to them and their successors, be allowed &c.   Whereupon, all and singular the said premises being seen and
understood by the court here, and the Sergeants-at-Law
to the lord King and the Attorney of the said King being
for this purpose convoked and assembled, for that it appears

successoribus suis in hac parte allocentur: Et quod predicti nunc maior et ballivi bona et catalla predicta virtute litterarum patencium predictarum habeant et gaudeant: et quod ipsi eant inde sine die salvo semper iure Regis si quod &c.: Quod quidem recordum coram nobis sic habitum duximus exemplificandum per presentes. In cuius rei testimonium has litteras nostras fieri fecimus patentes. Teste: Johanne Fitz Iamys apud Westmonasterium quinto decimo die Maii anno regni nostri vicesimo secundo.

XXIII. Littere Patentes Regis Edwardi Sexti.

1549
May 13 Edwardus[1] sextus dei gracia Anglie Francie et Hibernie Rex fidei defensor et in terra ecclesie Anglicane et Hibernice supremum caput omnibus ad quos presentes littere pervenerint. salutem.   Inspeximus litteras patentes celebris memorie domini Henrici nuper Regis Anglie-octavi, patris nostri precharissimi, de confirmacione factas in hec verba: Henricus dei gracia &c.:—

> Here follows a copy of the letters patent of Henry VIII. dated in the 2nd year of his reign and on the 29th of April 1510, hereinbefore printed and numbered XXI.   The present instrument then proceeds as follows:—

Inspeximus cartam domini Henrici quondam Regis Anglie factam in hec verba: Henricus dei gracia &c.:—

> Here follows a copy of the writ of Henry II. hereinbefore printed and numbered II.   The present instrument then proceeds as follows:—

---

[1] Original in the Borough Archives.   Three large skins.   Initial elaborately adorned with portrait of the King &c.   Great seal nearly perfect.

to the court here that the plea and title of the said mayor and bailiffs are sufficient in law to maintain them the mayor and bailiffs in retaining and having the goods and chattels aforesaid, it is considered that the letters patent aforesaid to the said mayor and bailiffs of the town of Cambridge aforesaid and their successors in this behalf be allowed: and that the aforesaid now mayor and bailiffs do have and enjoy the goods and chattels aforesaid by virtue of the letters patent aforesaid: and that they go hence without day, saving always the right of the King if any &c.: which record so had before us we have thought good to be exemplified by these presents. In witness whereof we have caused these our letters to be made patent. As witness: John Fitzjames at Westminster on the fifteenth day of May in the twenty-second year of our reign.

XXIII. LETTERS PATENT OF KING EDWARD THE SIXTH.

[1]Edward the Sixth by the grace of God of England, France and Ireland King, Defender of the Faith, and of the Church of England and Ireland upon earth the Supreme Head, to all to whom the present letters shall come, greeting. We have inspected the letters patent of confirmation of the lord Henry the Eighth, of famous memory, late King of England, our dearest father, made in these words: Henry by the grace of God &c.:—

1549
May 13

> Here follows a copy of the letters patent of Henry VIII. dated in the 2nd year of his reign and on the 29th of April 1510, hereinbefore translated and numbered XXI. The present instrument then proceeds as follows :—

We have inspected a charter of the lord Henry sometime King of England made in these words: Henry by the grace of God &c.:—

> Here follows a copy of the writ of Henry II. hereinbefore translated and numbered II. The present instrument then proceeds as follows:—

---

[1] See Cooper, *Annals,* ii. 17.

Inspeximus eciam quoddam breve domini Henrici quondam Regis Anglie de prohibicione in hec verba: Henricus Rex Anglie &c.:—

> Here follows a copy of the writ of Henry I. hereinbefore printed and numbered I. The present instrument then proceeds as follows:—

Inspeximus eciam quandam aliam cartam quam dominus Henricus tercius quondam Rex Anglie fecit burgensibus de Cantebrige in hec verba: Henricus dei gracia &c.:—

> Here follows a copy of the charter granted by Henry III. in the 40th year of his reign and on the 11th of April 1256, hereinbefore printed and numbered VII. The present instrument then proceeds as follows:—

Inspeximus eciam quandam aliam cartam domini Ricardi quondam Regis Anglie factam in hec verba: Ricardus dei gracia &c.:—

> Here follows a copy of the charter granted by Richard II. in the 5th year of his reign and on the 1st of May 1382, hereinbefore printed and numbered XII. The present instrument then proceeds as follows:—

Nos autem cartas et litteras predictas ac omnia et singula in eisdem contenta rata habentes et grata, ea pro nobis et heredibus nostris, quantum in nobis est, acceptamus et approbamus, ac dilectis nobis nunc burgensibus ville predicte ac eorum heredibus et successoribus ratificamus et confirmamus, prout carte et littere predicte racionabiliter testantur. In cuius rei testimonium has litteras nostras fieri fecimus patentes. Teste me ipso apud Westmonasterium terciodecimo die Maii anno regni nostri secundo.

MILSENT.

Examinate per {Georgium Throkmarton / Petrum Ayssheton} Clericos.

We have inspected also a certain writ of prohibition of the lord Henry sometime King of England in these words : Henry King of England &c. :—

> Here follows a copy of the writ of Henry I. hereinbefore translated and numbered I. The present instrument then proceeds as follows :—

We have inspected also a certain other charter which the lord Henry the Third sometime King of England made to the burgesses of Cambridge in these words : Henry by the grace of God &c. :—

> Here follows a copy of the charter granted by Henry III. in the 40th year of his reign and on the 11th of April 1256, hereinbefore translated and numbered VII. The present instrument then proceeds as follows :—

We have inspected also a certain other charter of the lord Richard late King of England made in these words : Richard by the grace of God &c. :—

> Here follows a copy of the charter granted by Richard II. in the 5th year of his reign and on the 1st of May 1382, hereinbefore translated and numbered XII. The present instrument then proceeds as follows :—

Now we, ratifying and according the said charters and letters and all and singular in the same contained, do, for us and our heirs, so far as in us lies, accept and approve the same, and to our beloved the now burgesses of the town aforesaid, and their heirs and successors, do ratify and confirm the same, in such wise as the charters and letters aforesaid reasonably testify. In witness whereof we have caused these our letters to be made patent. As witness : Myself at Westminster the thirteenth day of May in the second year of our reign.

MILSENT.

Examined by {George Throckmarton / Peter Ayssheton} Clerks.

XXIV. Littere Exemplificatorie Regis Edwardi Sexti[1].

1548
May 13

Edwardus sextus dei gracia Anglie, Francie et Hibernie Rex, fidei defensor, et in terra ecclesie Anglicane et Hibernice supremum caput omnibus ad quos presentes littere pervenerint salutem. Inspeximus tenorem recordi et processus loquele que fuit coram nobis, sine brevi nostro, inter Iohannem Longe et Willelmum Burton, de quadam transgressione eidem Iohanni per prefatum Willelmum apud Cantebriggiam[2] illata, ut dicebatur, quem coram nobis in Cancellariam nostram venire fecimus, in hec verba:—Tenor recordi et processus, de quibus in billa huic sedule attachiata fit mentio, et coram domino Rege Termino Sancte Trinitatis anno regni Regis Ricardi secundi post conquestum sexto irrotulato sequitur in hec verba ro. lxxv:—Cantabrigia ¶ Willelmus Burton attachiatus fuit ad respondendum Iohanni Longe de placito trangressionis per billam, et sunt plegii de prosequendo scilicet Iohannes Whichobbe et Robertus Beylam, et unde idem Iohannes Longe in propria persona sua queritur quod predictus Willelmus die lune proximo post festum Omnium Sanctorum anno regni domini Edwardi nuper Regis Anglie, avi domini Regis nunc, quadragesimo nono, vi et armis, scilicet gladiis baculis &c. ipsum Iohannem Longe apud Cantebriggiam cepit et imprisonavit, videlicet per unum diem, quousque idem Iohannes Longe finem per quadraginta solidos cum predicto Willelmo pro deliberacione sua habenda fecisset, detinuit, et alia enormia ei intulit, contra pacem dicti avi &c., unde dicit quod deterioratus est et dampnum habet ad valenciam decem librarum, et inde producit sectam &c.: Et predictus Willelmus in propria persona sua venit. Et super hoc venit Robertus de Soham attornatus maioris et ballivorum ville Cantebriggie ad libertates suas petendas, et calump-

---

[1] Original in the Borough Archives. Fragments of the great seal in brown wax appended by parchment tag.

[2] MS. Cantebregg'.

¹XXIV. LETTERS EXEMPLIFICATORY OF KING EDWARD
THE SIXTH.

Edward the Sixth by the grace of God King of England,   1548
France and Ireland, Defender of the Faith and of the Church   May 13
of England and Ireland on earth the Supreme Head, to all to
whom the present letters shall come, greeting. We have
inspected the tenour of the record and process of the suit
which was before us, without our writ, between John Longe
and William Burton, touching a certain trespass committed
at Cambridge by the aforesaid William against the said John,
as was alleged, which [record and process] we have caused to
come before us in our chancery, [and which ran] in these
words:—The tenour of the record and process, whereof
mention is made in the bill attached to this schedule, and
which was enrolled on Roll No. 75 before the lord King
in Trinity Term in the sixth year of the reign of King
Richard the Second since the Conquest, in these words:—
Cambridgeshire. ¶ William Burton was attached by bill
to answer John Longe concerning a plea of trespass, and
there are pledges for the prosecution, namely John Whichobbe
and Robert Beylam, and therein the said John Longe in his
own person complains that the said William, on Monday next
after the feast of All Saints in the forty-ninth year of the
reign of the lord Edward sometime King of England, the
grandfather of the lord now King, by force and arms, to wit,
with swords and staves &c., took and imprisoned the said
John Longe at Cambridge, to wit, for one day, and detained
the said John Long until he had made fine by forty shillings
with the said William for his deliverance, and other enormous
things to him did, against the peace of the said grandfather
&c., whereby he [John] says that he has loss and damage
to the value of ten pounds, and thereof he produces suit &c.:
And the aforesaid William comes in his own person. And
thereupon comes Robert of Soham, the attorney of the mayor

¹ See Cooper, *Annals,* ii. 17.

niat inde libertatem suam, videlicet habendi cognicionem
placiti predicti coram prefatis maiore et ballivis in gilda aula
sua apud Cantebriggiam ; quia dicunt quod villa Cantebriggie
est antiquus[1] burgus et a toto tempore extitit[2] et nuper fuit in
possessione domini Henrici filii Willelmi Conquestoris nuper
Regis Anglie progenitoris domini Regis nunc, qui quidem
Henricus nuper Rex habuit in eodem burgo ballivos suos,
qui quidem ballivi tempore quo burgus ille fuit in manibus
predicti Regis Henrici habuerunt cognicionem placitorum,
tam de terris et tenementis in eodem burgo et suburbio
eiusdem existentibus, quam de transgressionibus, convencionibus et aliis contractibus quibuscumque in eodem burgo
et suburbio emergentibus, et tenuerunt inde placita coram
eisdem ballivis apud Cantebriggiam, qui quidem Henricus
nuper Rex per cartam suam quam proferunt in curia, que est
sine data, tradidit et ad firmam dimisit tunc burgensibus de
Cantebriggia villam suam de Cantebriggia, tenendam de ipso
tunc Rege et heredibus suis, per eandem firmam quam vicecomes Cantebriggie sibi reddere solebat, qui quidem Henricus
quondam Rex &c. per aliam cartam suam, quam proferunt
in curia, que similiter est sine data, concessit quod si quis
ibidem forisfecerit ibidem faciat rectum. Et dicunt quod
virtute concessionum predictarum ballivi ville predicte, qui
tunc fuerant[3], tenuerunt omnia placita tam de terris et tenementis in eodem burgo et suburbio existentibus, quam de
transgressionibus [convencionibus] et aliis contractibus quibuscumque in eisdem burgo et suburbio emergentibus. Et dicunt
quod postmodum Henricus filius imperatricis quondam Rex
&c. per cartam suam, quam proferunt &c., precepit quod
burgenses sui de Cantebriggia haberent et tenerent ita bene et
in pace et iuste omnes libertates et liberas consuetudines suas
in rivagiis et in omnibus aliis rebus sicut carta Regis Henrici
avi sui eis testatur. Et dicunt quod, tam tempore predicti
Regis Henrici filii imperatricis &c., quam predicti Regis Henrici

---

[1] *antiqus* MS.
[2] *extiterit* MS.
[3] Corr. *fuerunt.*

and bailiffs of the town of Cambridge for claiming their liberties, and challenges thereof their liberty, to wit, of having cognizance of the aforesaid plea before the aforesaid mayor and bailiffs in their gildhall at Cambridge; for they say that the town of Cambridge is an ancient borough, and existed from all time, and was of late in the possession of the lord Henry the son of William the Conqueror sometime King of England, the ancestor of the lord now King, and that the said Henry sometime King had in the same borough his bailiffs, which bailiffs at the time when that borough was in the hands of the aforesaid King Henry had cognizance of pleas, as well touching lands and tenements being in the same borough and the suburb of the same, as also touching trespasses, covenants and other contracts whatsoever arising in the same borough and suburb, and held pleas thereof before the said bailiffs at Cambridge, and that the said Henry sometime King, by his charter, which they produce in court, which is without date, delivered and to farm let, to the then burgesses of Cambridge, his town of Cambridge, to hold of himself the then King and his heirs by the same farm which the sheriff of Cambridge was wont to render to him; and that the said Henry sometime King &c., by another charter of his which they produce in court, which likewise is without date, granted that if any one should forfeit there, he should there do right. And they say that by virtue of the aforesaid grants the bailiffs of the aforesaid town, who then were, held all pleas, as well touching lands and tenements being in the said borough and suburb, as concerning trespasses, [covenants,] and other contracts whatsoever arising in the said borough and suburb. And they say that afterwards Henry son of the Empress, sometime King &c., by his charter which they produce &c., ordered that his burgesses of Cambridge should have and hold as well and peaceably and rightly all their liberties and free customs in the river-banks and in all other things as the charter of King Henry his grandfather witnessed to them. And they say that, as well in the time of the aforesaid King Henry son of the Empress &c., as of the

avi &c., ballivi burgi predicti, qui pro tempore fuerant, similiter
tenuerunt coram eis omnia placita infra dictum burgum et
suburbium emergencia in forma predicta; et ipsi et omnes
successores sui similiter postea tenuerunt coram eis omnia
placita predicta in forma predicta. Et dicunt quod dominus
Iohannes quondam Rex &c. per cartam suam anno regni sui
sexto concessit burgensibus suis de Cantebriggia gildam
mercatoriam, et quod nullus eorum placitaret extra muros
burgi de Cantebriggia de ullo placito preter placita de tenuris
exterioribus exceptis monetariis et ministris suis, et quod
haberent terras suas et tenuras et vadimonia et debita omnia
quecumque¹ ea debeant, et de terris suis et tenuris que infra
burgum sunt, rectum eis teneatur secundum consuetudinem
burgi, et de omnibus aliis debitis suis que accomodata fuerunt
apud Cantebriggiam et de vadimoniis ibidem factis placita
apud Cantebriggiam teneantur.   Et ulterius dicunt quod
idem Iohannes quondam² Rex &c., per aliam cartam suam
anno regni sui octavo, concessit et per eandem cartam suam
confirmavit burgensibus suis de Cantebriggia villam de
Cantebriggia cum omnibus pertinenciis suis habendam et
tenendam imperpetuum de ipso tunc Rege et heredibus suis
sibi et heredibus suis, reddendo inde annuatim ad scaccarium
suum antiquam firmam, scilicet quadraginta libras albas et
viginti libras numero de incremento pro omni servicio, per
manus eorum ad duo scaccaria anni; et quod ipsi et heredes
sui haberent et tenerent predictam villam cum omnibus
pertinenciis suis bene et in pace, libere et quiete, integre,
plenarie et honorifice, in pratis et pascuis, molendinis, aquis
et stagnis, cum omnibus libertatibus et liberis consuetudinibus
suis; et quod facerent de se ipsis prepositum quem voluerint
et quando voluerint.   Et dicunt quod, post concessionem
predictam, burgenses ville predicte quolibet anno eligerent³
prepositum suum et ballivos ville predicte in crastino nativi-
tatis beate Marie; quiquidem prepositus et ballivi semper

---

¹ Sic MS.
² *quandam* MS.
³ Sic MS.

aforesaid King Henry the grandfather &c., the bailiffs of the aforesaid borough, for the time being, likewise held before them all pleas arising within the said borough and suburb in form aforesaid ; And they and all their successors likewise, afterwards have held before them all the aforesaid pleas in form aforesaid. And they say that the lord John sometime King &c. by his charter in the sixth year of his reign, granted to his burgesses of Cambridge a gild merchant, and that none of them should plead beyond the walls of the borough of Cambridge concerning any plea, save pleas of external tenures, except his moneyers and servants, and that they should have their lands and tenures and pledges and all debts, no matter who should owe the same, and that touching their lands and tenures which are within the borough, right should be holden to them according to the custom of the borough, and concerning all other their debts, which were lent at Cambridge, and concerning pledges there made, pleas should be holden at Cambridge. And further they say that the said John sometime King &c., by another charter of his, in the eighth year of his reign, granted and by his said charter confirmed to his burgesses of Cambridge the town of Cambridge with all its appurtenances, to have and to hold for ever, of him the then King and his heirs, to them and their heirs, rendering therefor yearly to his exchequer the ancient farm, namely forty pounds blanch and twenty pounds by tale by way of increase, for all service by their hands at the two exchequers of the year ; and that they and their heirs should have and hold the aforesaid town with all its appurtenances, well and peaceably, freely and quietly, wholly and fully and honourably, in meadows and pastures, mills, water and pools, with all their liberties and free customs ; and that they should make from among themselves a reeve whom they would and when they would. And they say that, after the aforesaid grant, the burgesses of the aforesaid town in every year chose their reeve and bailiffs of the aforesaid town on the morrow of the Nativity of the Blessed Mary ; and the said reeve and bailiffs always held before them at Cambridge all the aforesaid pleas,

tenuerunt coram eis apud Cantebriggiam omnia placita predicta, videlicet de terris et tenementis tenuerunt curias suas
et dederunt inde quinque dies per annum, videlicet die lune
proximo post festum Sancti Mathei appostoli et evangeliste,
et die lune proximo post festum sancte Lucie virginis, et die
lune proximo post diem dominicam in medio quadragesime,
et die lune proximo post festum Sancte Trinitatis, et die lune
proximo post festum sancti Iacobi appostoli ; et eciam tenuerunt placita de transgressionibus et aliis contractibus et
convencionibus per intrinsecos factis qualibet die martis per
annum ; et de quibuscumque transgressionibus, contractibus
et convencionibus et aliis rebus inter forinsecos et intrinsecos
et forinsecos et forinsecos de die in diem ; et similiter tenuerunt curiam suam de gilda mercatoria inter mercatores et
mercatores de mercandisis suis de die in diem et de hora in
horam secundum exigenciam querele ; et similiter predicti
prepositi et ballivi tenuerunt ibidem quolibet anno duas letas,
videlicet unam post festum Sancti Michaelis et aliam post
festum Pasche, et ceperunt presentaciones de omnibus articulis
que ad letam et visum franci plegii pertinent et ceperunt inde
puniciones delinquencium ; et similiter omnes successores sui,
officia predicta in burgo predicto gerentes, omnia placita
predicta coram eis tenuerunt in forma predicta ; quas quidem
libertates et consuetudines predictas dominus Henricus filius
Regis Iohannis quondam Rex Anglie per cartas suas quas
proferunt in curia tunc burgensibus suis ville predicte postea
concessit et confirmavit, quarum cartarum una data est apud
Westmonasterium vicesimo primo die Aprilis anno regni sui
undecimo, et altera carta[1] data est apud Westmonasterium
duodecimo die Aprilis anno regni sui quadragesimo ; et
ulterius concessit idem Henricus quod de cetero placitare
possint infra villam predictam omnia placita libertatem tangencia, tam de vetito namio, quam de aliis placitis que sine
iusticiariis suis placitare possint, ita quod nullus vicecomes
aut alius ballivus ipsius Regis intromitteret se de aliquibus
ad libertates suas spectantibus, nisi per defectum predictorum

---

[1] MS. *alterius carte.*

to wit, concerning lands and tenements they held their courts and gave for this five days yearly, namely, on the Monday next after the feast of Saint Matthew [Sept. 21] the apostle and evangelist, and on the Monday next after the feast of Saint Lucy the Virgin [Dec. 13], and on the Monday next after the Sunday in Mid Lent, and on the Monday next after the feast of the Holy Trinity, and on the Monday next after the feast of Saint James the apostle [July 25]; and also they held pleas touching trespasses and other contracts and covenants made by those within the town on every Tuesday throughout the year; and concerning all manner of trespasses, contracts and covenants and other matters between strangers and those within the town, and between strangers and strangers [they held plea] from day to day; and likewise they held their court of the gild merchant, between merchants and merchants, concerning their merchandises, from day to day and from hour to hour, according to the exigence of the complaint; and likewise the aforesaid reeves and bailiffs held there in every year two leets, namely, one after the feast of Saint Michael and the other after the feast of Easter, and received presentments concerning all articles which pertain to the leet and the view of frank-pledge and took thence the penalties of delinquents; and likewise all their successors, bearing the aforesaid offices in the aforesaid borough, held all the aforesaid pleas before them in form aforesaid; and the aforesaid liberties and customs the lord Henry son of King John, sometime King of England, by his charters which they produce in court, afterwards granted and confirmed to his then burgesses of the aforesaid town; of which charters one is dated at Westminster on the twenty-first day of April in the eleventh year of his reign, and the other charter is dated at Westminster on the twelfth day of April in the fortieth year of his reign; and moreover the same Henry granted that henceforth they should be able to plead within the aforesaid town all pleas touching their liberty, as well concerning vee de nam [replevin], as concerning other pleas which they could plead without his Justices, so that no sheriff or other

burgensium vel ballivorum suorum eiusdem ville ; et quod
iidem burgenses de seipsis eligere possint et creare coronatores
in villa predicta, ad attachiamenta placitorum corone sue
infra predictam villam Cantebriggie emergencia facienda,
usque ad eventum Iusticiariorum suorum, sicut alibi ad
coronatores suos pertinuit ; et prohibuit idem Rex super
forisfacturam decem librarum ne quis eos contra libertates
et concessiones huiusmodi vexare, molestare vel inquietare
presumat. Et proferunt hic in curia cartam predictam
premissa testificantem, cuius data apud Westmonasterium
undecimo die Aprilis anno regni sui quadragesimo. Ac
postmodum dominus Edwardus quondam Rex Anglie, pro-
avus domini Regis nunc, predictas cartas et confirmaciones
progenitorum suorum inspiciendo, easdem donaciones, concessiones et confirmaciones predictas ratas habens et gratas,
eas pro se et heredibus suis quantum in ipso fuit predictis
burgensibus et eorum heredibus ac successoribus concessit et
confirmavit, sicut carte predicte racionabiliter testantur ; et
preterea, volens idem Rex iisdem burgensibus graciam facere
ampliorem, concessit eis predictis pro se et heredibus suis quod
licet ipsi aliqua vel aliquibus libertatum et quietanciarum
predictarum hactenus plene usi non fuerant, ipsi nichilominus,
heredes ac successores sui predicti, libertatibus et quietanciis
predictis et earum qualibet de cetero, absque inquietacione
vel impedimento ipsius Regis vel heredum suorum aut
ministrorum suorum quorumcumque, racionabiliter gaudeant
et utantur ; et quod de transgressionibus seu contractibus in
eisdem burgo et suburbio factis non placitent nec implacitentur
extra burgum illum, nisi res ipsa tangat ipsum Regem vel
heredes suos ; et quod super transgressionibus et contractibus
illis aut aliis factis intrincesis per forinsicos[1] minime convincantur, set solomodo per comburgenses suos, nisi factum illud
tangat ipsum Regem vel heredes suos aut comunitatem burgi
predicti. Ac postmodum dominus Rex nunc, dictas cartas
progenitorum suorum inspiciendas[2], donaciones, concessiones,

[1] Sic MS.
[2] MS. *inspiciendo.*

bailiff of the King himself should meddle with any matters relating to their liberties, except upon default of the aforesaid burgesses or of their bailiffs of the same town ; and that the said burgesses might be able to choose from among themselves and create coroners in the aforesaid town, to make attachment of the pleas of his crown arising within the aforesaid town of Cambridge, until the coming of his Justices, as pertained to his coroners elsewhere ; and the same King forbad under a penalty of ten pounds that any one should presume to vex, molest or disturb them against such liberties and grants. And they [the burgesses] produce here in court the aforesaid charter testifying the premisses, and dated at Westminster on the eleventh day of April in the fortieth year of his reign. And [they say that] afterwards the lord Edward sometime King of England, the great-grandfather of the now lord King, inspecting the aforesaid charters and confirmations of his ancestors, and ratifying and according the said gifts, grants and confirmations, did for himself and his heirs, as far as in him lay, grant and confirm the same to the aforesaid burgesses, their heirs and successors, as the aforesaid charters reasonably testify ; and moreover, the said King, wishing to confer an ampler favour on the said burgesses, granted to them aforesaid for himself and his heirs, that, although they theretofore had not fully used all or some of the liberties and quittances aforesaid, nevertheless they, their heirs and successors aforesaid might reasonably enjoy and use the liberties and quittances aforesaid and any of these henceforth, without let or hindrance by the King or his heirs or any his ministers, and that concerning trespasses or contracts made in the said borough and its suburbs, they should not plead nor be impleaded outside that borough unless the matter should concern the King or his heirs ; and that concerning such trespasses and contracts or other internal affairs they should in no wise be convicted by foreigners, but only by their fellow-burgesses, unless the matter should concern the King or his heirs or the commonalty of the borough aforesaid. And [they say that] afterwards the lord now King, inspecting the said charters of

confirmaciones, libertates ac quietancias in cartis predictis contentas ratas habens et gratas, eas pro se et heredibus suis, quantum in ipso est, acceptavit, approbavit, ratificavit, et per cartam suam eisdem burgensibus et eorum heredibus ac successoribus concessit et confirmavit, prout carta predicta predicti Edwardi proavi sui racionabiliter testatur, et prout iidem burgenses libertatibus et quietanciis predictis semper a tempore concessionis et confeccionis carte predicte racionabiliter uti et gaudere consueverunt. Et proferunt hic in curia cartam domini Regis nunc premissa testificantem, cuius data est apud Westmonasterium octavo die Decembris anno regni sui primo. Et dicunt quod maior et ballivi burgi predicti, qui pro tempore fuerunt, semper a tempore confeccionis predicte carte predicti Edwardi proavi &c., habuerunt cognicionem omnium placitorum in burgo predicto emergencium, tenendorum in burgo predicto in forma predicta. Et dicunt quod huiusmodi libertas maiori et ballivis ville predicte coram domino Rege nunc extitit allocata videlicet termino Sancti Hillarii anno regni domini Regis nunc secundo, Rotulo lviij., inter Iohannem Scothowe querentem et Adam Savage de Cantebriggia de placito transgressionis; et similiter termino Sancti Hillarii anno regni domini Regis nunc tercio Rotulo xlix., inter Thomam Redere de Cantebriggia querentem et Willelmum Baylif et Rogerum Harleston de capcione et detencione catallorum &c.; et similiter termino Sancti Michaelis anno regni domini Edwardi nuper Regis Anglie, avi domini Regis nunc, tricesimo septimo, Rotulo lxxxxvij., inter Willelmum Shyrwynke querentem et Iohannem filium Stephani Morice de placito transgressionis; et eciam termino Sancti Hillarii anno eiusdem avi &c. xxxiij°., Rotulo Ciij., inter Iohannem With querentem et Iohannem Freng de placito transgressionis &c. Et super hoc dominus Rex mandavit Iusticiariis suis hoc breve suum clausum in hec verba:—Ricardus dei gracia Rex Anglie et Francie et Dominus Hibernie, dilectis et fidelibus suis Roberto Tresilian et sociis suis Iusticiariis ad placita coram nobis tenenda assignatis salutem. Quia maior, ballivi et burgenses ville nostre Cante-

his ancestors, and ratifying and according the gifts, grants, confirmations, liberties and quittances contained in the aforesaid charters, did for himself and his heirs, so far as in him lay, accept, approve and ratify the same, and by his charter did grant and confirm the same to the said burgesses, their heirs and successors, in such wise as the charter aforesaid of the aforesaid Edward his great-grandfather reasonably testifies, and in such wise as the said burgesses always, from the time of the granting and making of the aforesaid charter, have been wont reasonably to use and enjoy the liberties and quittances aforesaid. And they produce here in court the charter of the lord now King, testifying the premisses, of which the date is at Westminster on the eighth day of December in the first year of his reign. And they say that the mayor and bailiffs of the borough aforesaid, for the time being, have always from the time of the making of the aforesaid charter of the aforesaid Edward the great-grandfather &c., had cognizance of all pleas arising in the borough aforesaid, to be held in the borough aforesaid in form aforesaid. And they say that such liberty is allowed to the mayor and bailiffs of the town aforesaid before the lord now King, to wit, in the Hilary term in the second year of the reign of the lord now King on Roll No. 58 [in a suit] between John Scothowe plaintiff and Adam Savage of Cambridge in a plea of trespass; and likewise in the Hilary term of the third year of the reign of the lord now King on Roll No. 49 [in a suit] between Thomas Redere of Cambridge plaintiff and William Bayliff and Roger Harleston touching a taking and detention of chattels &c.; and likewise in the Michaelmas term in the thirty-seventh year of the reign of the lord Edward, sometime King of England, the grandfather of the lord now King, on Roll No. 97 [in a suit] between William Shyrwynke plaintiff and John the son of Stephen Morice in a plea of trespass; and also in the Hilary term in the 33rd year of the same grandfather &c., on Roll No. 103 [in a suit] between John With plaintiff and John Freng concerning a plea of trespass &c. And hereupon the lord King sent

briggie, tam per cartas progenitorum nostrorum quondam
Regum Anglie, quas confirmavimus, quam per cartam nostram,
clamant habere diversa privilegia, quietancias, immunitates,
liberas consuetudines, donaciones, concessiones, ferias ac alias
libertates, quibus ipsi et antecessores sui, maiores, ballivi et
burgenses ville predicte, a tempore confeccionis cartarum et
confirmacionis predictarum, semper hactenus usi sunt et gavisi,
sicut dicunt: Vobis mandamus quod, visis cartis predictis,
ipsos maiorem, ballivos et burgenses omnibus et singulis
privilegiis, quietanciis, immunitatibus, liberis consuetudinibus,
donacionibus, concessionibus, feriis et libertatibus in eisdem
contentis coram vobis uti et gaudere permittatis, iuxta
tenorem cartarum et confirmacionis predictarum, prout eis uti
debent ipsique et omnes antecessores sui, maiores, ballivi et
burgenses eiusdem ville, privilegiis, quietanciis, immunitatibus,
liberis consuetudinibus, donacionibus, concessionibus, feriis et
libertatibus illis a tempore predicto semper hactenus racionabiliter uti et gaudere consueverunt: Salvis dumtaxat et
exceptis libertatibus et privilegiis cancellario et scolaribus
universitatis Cantebriggie et successoribus suis per cartas
progenitorum nostrorum seu nostras aut per litteras patentes
eorumdem progenitorum nostrorum seu nostras concessis:
Teste me ipso apud Westmonasterium vicesimo quinto die
Iulii anno regni nostri septimo. Per quod iidem maior et
ballivi ut prius petunt cognicionem istius placiti in forma
predicta &c. Et visis cartis dictis, necnon allocacionibus
predictis coram domino Rege residentibus, quia manifeste
constat curia quod huiusmodi libertas alias eis extitit allocata
in casu consimili. Ideo habeant inde libertatem suam &c.
Et super hoc predictus attornatus prefixit diem partibus
predictis coram prefatis maiore et ballivis in gilda aula apud
Cantebriggiam die martis in festo Translacionis sancti Thome
martyris et dictum est prefato attornato quod partibus predictis plena et celeris iusticia exhibeat: alioquin redeant &c.
Inspeximus eciam tenorem recordi et processus loquele que
fuit coram Senescallo et Marescallo Hospicii nostri apud
Cantebriggiam die martis proxima post festum translacionis

to his Justices this his writ close in these words :—Richard by the grace of God King of England and France and Lord of Ireland, to his beloved and faithful Robert Tresilian and his fellows, Justices assigned to hold pleas before ourselves, greeting. Whereas the mayor, bailiffs and burgesses of our town of Cambridge, as well by the charters of our ancestors sometime Kings of England, which we have confirmed, as by our charter, claim to have divers privileges, quittances, immunities, free customs, gifts, grants, fairs and other liberties, which they and their predecessors, mayors, bailiffs and burgesses of the town aforesaid from the time of the making of the charters and of the confirmation aforesaid always hitherto have used and enjoyed, so they say : We command you that, having seen the aforesaid charters, you do allow them, the said mayor, bailiffs and burgesses to use and enjoy before you all and singular the privileges, quittances, immunities, free customs, gifts, grants, fairs and liberties contained in them, according to the tenour of the charters and of the confirmation aforesaid, in such wise as they ought to use the same and as they and all their predecessors, mayors, bailiffs and burgesses of the same town, have always heretofore been wont reasonably to use and enjoy those privileges, quittances, immunities, free customs, gifts, grants, fairs and liberties from the time aforesaid : Save always and except the liberties and privileges granted to the chancellor and scholars of the university of Cambridge and their successors by the charters of our ancestors or by our own, or by the letters patent of the same our ancestors, or by our own : Witness myself at Westminster on the twenty-fifth day of July in the seventh year of our reign. Wherefore the said mayor and bailiffs once more seek cognizance of this plea in form aforesaid &c. And the said charters having been seen, and also the allowances aforesaid remaining with our lord the King, because it manifestly appears to the court that such liberty was heretofore allowed in a similar case : Therefore they shall have their liberty therein &c. And thereupon the aforesaid attorney [of the borough] fixed a day for the parties

sancti Thome Martiris proxime preterito inter Thomam
Lodeworth et Galfridum Castur de Cantebriggia de triginta
[et octo[1]] solidis, quos idem Thomas a prefato Galfrido
exigit, necnon allocaciones libertatum maiori et ballivis
ville predicte iuxta libertates et consuetudines eis per cartas
progenitorum nostrorum quondam Regum Anglie quas confirmavimus concessas in hec verba: [Inspeximus tenorem
recordi et processus loquele que fuit] coram nobis [in hec
verba]: Placita [aule Hospicii domini Regis existentis apud
Cantebriggiam die mercurii proxima[2]] post festum translacionis
sancti Thome Martiris coram Senescallo et Marescallo Hospicii [predicti et anno regni[2]] Regis Ricardi secundi post
conquestum septimo.   Galfridus Castur de Cantebriggia attachiatus fuit per billam ad respondendum Thome Lodeworth
de placito debiti; et unde idem Thomas in propria persona
sua queritur de predicto Galfrido et dicit[3] quod ei debet et
iniuste detinet triginta et octo solidos, eo quod idem Galfridus
ibidem emit in xv Michaelis anno regni Regis secundi Ricardi
sexto coreum de predicto Thome pro summa predicta solvenda quandocumcque &c.; qui quidem Thomas petiit[4]
summam pecunie supradicte sibi solvi et licet idem Galfridus
de solucione dictorum triginta et octo solidorum sepius per
predictum Thomam requisitus eandem summam solucione
omnino recusat et sic iniuste detinet, unde deterioratus est
et dampnum habet ad valenciam quadraginta solidorum, et
inde producit sectam: Et predictus Galfridus presens in curia
&c.: Super quo venit Robertus Iugler attornatus maioris et
ballivorum ville Cantebriggie ad libertates suas petendas et
calumpniandas, et calumpniat inde libertatem suam, videlicet
habendum cognicionem placiti predicti coram prefatis maiore
et ballivis in gilda aula sua apud Cantebrigiam.

---

[1] Defaced and illegible.
[2] Defaced and illegible where the document has been folded. Words defaced
in the original supplied from P. R. O. County Placita, Chancery, Cambridge,
No. 13.
[3] MS. *dicet.*
[4] A word defaced, supplied from P. R. O. County Placita, Chancery, Cambridge, No. 13.

aforesaid before the aforesaid mayor and bailiffs in the gildhall at Cambridge on the Tuesday the feast of the Translation of Saint Thomas the Martyr, and the aforesaid attorney is ordered to shew full and speedy justice to the parties aforesaid : otherwise let them return &c. We have inspected also the tenour of the record and process of the suit which was held before the Steward and Marshal of our Household at Cambridge on the Tuesday next after the feast of the Translation of Saint Thomas the Martyr last past, [in a plea] between Thomas Lodeworth and Geoffrey Castur of Cambridge concerning thirty-eight shillings, which the said Thomas exacts from the aforesaid Geoffrey, and also the allowances of liberties to the mayor and bailiffs of the town aforesaid according to the liberties and customs granted to them by the charters of our ancestors sometime Kings of England, which we have confirmed in these words : We have inspected the tenour of the record and process of the suit which was held before us in these words :—Pleas of the Hall of the lord King's household being at Cambridge on Wednesday next after the feast of the Translation of Saint Thomas the Martyr before the Steward and Marshal of the said Household and in the seventh year of the reign of King Richard the Second after the conquest. Geoffrey Castur of Cambridge was attached by bill to answer Thomas Lodeworth concerning a plea of debt ; and hereupon the said Thomas in his own person complains of the aforesaid Geoffrey and says that he owes to him and unjustly detains thirty-eight shillings, because the said Geoffrey there bought in the quindene of St Michael, in the sixth year of the reign of King Richard the Second, a hide from the aforesaid Thomas for the sum aforesaid to be paid whensoever &c. : and the said Thomas sought the aforesaid sum of money to be paid to him, and although the said Geoffrey was frequently called upon for payment of the said thirty-eight shillings by the aforesaid Thomas, he altogether refuses the said sum in payment and so unjustly detains it, whereby he is injured and has damage to the value of forty shillings, and thereof he produces suit :

Here follows a copy of the recital of the history of the borough, hereinbefore printed p. 80 (quia dicunt quod villa Cantabriggie est antiquus burgus, &c.) to p. 88 (Johannem Freng de placito transgressionis).

Per quod iidem maior et ballivi ut prius petunt cognicionem istius placiti in forma predicta &c.: Et visis cartis predictis, ante tempus memorie quam post, et diligenter examinatis, necnon allocacionibus predictis coram domino Rege residentibus, quia manifeste constat curie quod huiusmodi libertas eis alias extit[1] allocata in casu consimili, licet tamen expresse non exprimantur, coram Senescallo et Marescallo, per verba specialia in cartis ante tempus memorie, habito tamen respectu ad cartas predictas et ad alias cartas ex post facto factas, necnon ad allocaciones placitorum coram eis adjudicatas et cartas et confirmaciones Regis nunc et ad alias causas, letas, curias, motas: Ideo habeant inde libertatem suam &c.: Et super hoc predictus attornatus prefixit diem partibus predictis coram maiore et ballivis in gilda aula apud Cantebrigiam die veneris proxima post festum translacionis Sancti Thome martiris, et dictum est prefato attornato quod partibus predictis plena et celeris justicia exhibeatur: alioquin reddeant &c.: Nos autem tenores recordorum et processuum ac allocacionis predictorum ad requisicionem maioris et burgensium ville Cantebrigie duximus exemplificandas per presentes: In cuius rei testimonium has litteras nostras fieri fecimus paterntes. Teste me ipso apud Westmonasterium terciodecimo die Maii anno regni nostri secundo.

Examinate per Georgium Throkmorton et Petrum Ayssheton, Clericos.

---

[1] Corr. *extitit.*

And the aforesaid Geoffrey being present in court &c.: On which comes Robert Jugler the attorney of the mayor and bailiffs of the town of Cambridge to seek and claim their liberties, and he challenges their liberty therein, namely to have cognizance of the aforesaid plea before the aforesaid mayor and bailiffs in their gildhall at Cambridge.

> Here follows a copy of the recital of the history of the borough, hereinbefore translated p. 81 (for they say that the town of Cambridge is an ancient borough, &c.) to the foot of p. 89 (John Freng concerning a plea of trespass).

Wherefore the said mayor and bailiffs once more seek cognizance of that plea in form aforesaid &c.: And the charters aforesaid, before the time of memory and after, being seen and diligently examined, and also the allowances aforesaid remaining with the lord King, because it manifestly appears to the court that such liberty was heretofore allowed to them in a similar case, (although nevertheless [such liberties] are not expressly stated,) before the Steward and Marshal, by special words in charters before the time of memory, respect nevertheless being had to the charters aforesaid and to other charters made subsequently, as also to the allowances of pleas adjudged before them and the charters and confirmations of the now King, and to other causes, leets, moots, courts: Therefore let them have their liberty herein &c.: and thereupon the aforesaid attorney [of the borough] fixed a day for the parties aforesaid before the mayor and bailiffs in the gildhall at Cambridge on the Friday next after the Translation of Saint Thomas the martyr, and the aforesaid attorney is ordered to shew full and speedy justice to the parties aforesaid: otherwise let them return &c.: Now we have thought good that the tenour of the records and processes and allowance aforesaid at the request of the mayor and burgesses of the town of Cambridge be exemplified by these presents: In witness whereof we have caused these our letters to be made patent. Witness myself at Westminster on the thirteenth day of May in the second year of our reign.

> Examined by George Throckmorton and Peter Ayssheton, Clerks.

XXV. Littere Patentes Regine Elizabethe.

1589
Aug. 15
[1]Elizabeth dei gracia Anglie, Francie et Hibernie Regina, fidei defensor &c. omnibus ad quos he litere nostre patentes pervenerint salutem. Cum maior ballivi et burgenses ville nostre Cantebrigie in comitatu Cantebrigie ante tricesimum annum inclyti ac precharissimi patris nostri domini Henrici dei gracia nuper Regis Anglie octavi, de tempore in tempus existentes a tempore cuius contrarii memoria hominum non existit, habuerunt ac usi fuerunt habere et tenere quotannis quandam feriam sive nundinas apud Barnewell et Sturbridge in predicto comitatu Cantebrigie ac infra libertatem ville nostre Cantebrigie tentam sive tentas, ac per nomen nundinarum de Sturbridge cognitam seu cognitas incipientem sive incipientes quolibet anno in festo sancti Bartholomei Apostoli et ab eodem festo continue usque decimum quartum diem proxime post festum exaltacionis sancte crucis singulis annis durantem sive durantes, unacum omnibus et omnimodis iurisdictionibus, authoritatibus, curiis, proficuis curiarum, liberis consuetudinibus, tolnetis, doccagiis, picagiis, stallagiis, opellis, groundagiis, advantagiis, commoditatibus, proficuis, easiamentis, et aliis libertatibus quibuscumque, ad huiusmodi feriam sive nundinas pertinentibus vel quoquo modo spectantibus. Exceptis nonnullis libertatibus, potestatibus, iurisdiccionibus, immunitatibus, prescripcionibus, consuetudinibus, easiamentis, preheminenciis, proficuis, et commoditatibus universitati nostre Cantebrigie infra easdem nundinas habitis, usitatis et perceptis : Quequidem nundine per laudabilem industriam maioris, ballivorum, et burgensium ville Cantebrigie predicte de tempore in tempus existentium loci ipsius commoditate, academie vicinitate, et temporis opportunitate opitulantibus in longe maximas ac celeberrimas tocius Anglie

---

[1] Original in the Borough Archives. The initials are elaborately ornamented with a portrait of the Queen and the Tudor arms. A perfect great seal in a tin box appendant.

XXV. LETTERS PATENT OF QUEEN ELIZABETH.

[1]Elizabeth by the grace of God of England, France and
Ireland Queen, Defender of the Faith &c., to all to whom
these our letters patent shall come greeting. Whereas the
mayor, bailiffs and burgesses of our town of Cambridge in the
county of Cambridge before the thirtieth year of our illustrious
and dearest father the lord Henry the Eighth by the grace of
God sometime King of England, from time to time being,
from the time of which the memory of men does not run to
the contrary, have had and have been used to have and hold
yearly a certain feast or fair, held at Barnwell and Sturbridge
in the aforesaid county of Cambridge and within the liberty
of our town of Cambridge, and known by the name of
Sturbridge Fair, beginning in each year on the feast of
St Bartholomew the Apostle and lasting from the same feast
continuously until the fourteenth day next after the feast of
the exaltation of the Holy Cross in every year, together with
all and every the jurisdictions, authorities, courts, profits of
courts, free customs, tolls, dockages, pickages, stallages,
booths, groundages, advantages, commodities, profits, easements, and other liberties whatsoever pertaining to such feast
or fair or in any way concerning it : Saving certain liberties,
powers, jurisdictions, immunities, prescriptions, customs, easements, preeminences, profits, and commodities had, used and
taken by our university of Cambridge within the said fair :
Which fair by the laudable industry of the mayor, bailiffs and
burgesses of the aforesaid town of Cambridge, from time to
time being, by the convenience of the place itself, the neigh-
bourhood of the university and the favourableness of the
time helping, has become by far the largest and most famous
fair in all England, whence very much of use is derived as

1589
Aug. 15

[1] Cooper, *Annals*, i. 466.

nundinas evaserint, unde plurimum utilitatis tam mercatoribus
per universum regnum Anglie ubicque locorum dispersis ad
easdem nundinas concurrentibus, ac merces et mercandisas
satis ibidem brevi tempore vendentibus, quam eciam emptoribus ad nundinas illas de singulis tocius regni partibus ad
pisces salsos, butirum, caseum, mel, salem, linum, canabum,
picem et bitumen, aliasque merces et mercandizas quascunque emendum ac providendum venientibus effluxit: Ac
cum ex proficuis earundem nundinarum maior, ballivi et
burgenses dicte ville Cantebrigie de tempore in tempus per
tempus immemoratum existentes, non solum maximam partem
septuaginta librarum legalis monete Anglie pro feodi firma
ville Cantebrigie predicte ac aliarum libertatum ac franchesiarum suarum per chartas diversorum progenitorum nostrorum
Regum Anglie reservatarum levaverint, verum eciam earundem
nundinarum beneficio eandem villam in viis, stratis, fossis ac
aliis oneribus quam plurimis supportare et manutenere per
totum tempus predictum usque tricesimum annum regni
precharissimi patris nostri predicti satis habiles effecti sunt
et potentes: Ac cum universis commoditatibus antedictis
non obstantibus, postea videlicet die mercurii proxime post
crastinum purificacionis beate Marie anno regni illustrissimi
ac precharissimi patris nostri domini Henrici nuper Regis
Anglie octavi tricesimo, per Johannem Baker attornatum
dicti nuper patris nostri precharissimi in curia eiusdem nuper
patris nostri apud Westmonasterium coram Iusticiariis eiusdem nuper patris nostri ad placita coram ipso nuper domino
Rege ac patre nostro tenenda assignatis, datum fuit eidem
curie intelligi et informari quod maior, ballivi et burgenses
dicte ville Cantebrigie in comitatu Cantebrigie ad tunc pro
tempore existente, per quatuor annos tunc ultime elapsos et
amplius usi fuerunt et adtunc utebantur habere nundinas sive
feriam apud Barnewell et Sturbridge in comitatu Cantebrigie
in crastino sancti Bartholomei Appostoli et ab eodem crastino
continue usque decimum quartum diem proxime post festum
exaltacionis Sancte Crucis sequentem singulis annis, tenendas
cum omnibus libertatibus et liberis consuetudinibus ad huius-

well by the merchants dispersed throughout the whole realm
of England in every place coming together to the said fair,
and selling their wares and merchandise sufficiently there in
a short time, as also by the buyers coming to this fair from
all parts of the whole realm to buy and provide salt fish,
butter, cheese, honey, salt, flax, canvas, pitch and bitumen
and other wares and merchandise whatsoever : And whereas
from the profits of the said fair the mayor, bailiffs and
burgesses of the said town of Cambridge from time to time
being from time immemorial, not only have raised the greatest
part of the seventy pounds of lawful money of England for
the fee farm of the town of Cambridge aforesaid and of their
other liberties and franchises reserved by the charters of
divers of our ancestors the Kings of England, but also by the
benefit of the said fair have been rendered sufficiently fitted
and able to support and maintain the said town in ways,
streets, ditches, and other very numerous burdens during
the whole time aforesaid until the thirtieth year of the reign
of our dearest father aforesaid : And whereas all the conveniences aforesaid notwithstanding, afterwards, to wit on the
Wednesday next after the morrow of the purification of the
Blessed Mary in the thirtieth year of the reign of our most
illustrious and dearest father the lord Henry the Eighth
sometime King of England, by John Baker attorney of our
said late dearest father in the court of our said late father at
Westminster before the Justices of our said late father
assigned to hold pleas before himself sometime lord King
and our father, the said court was given to understand and
was informed that the mayor, bailiffs and burgesses of the
said town of Cambridge in the county of Cambridge then for
the time being, for four years then last past and longer had
used and still used to have a fair or feast at Barnwell
and Sturbridge in the county of Cambridge on the morrow
of Saint Bartholomew the Apostle and from the said
morrow continuously until the fourteenth day next following
after the feast of the exaltation of the Holy Cross in
each year, to be held with all liberties and free customs

modi feriam sive nundinas spectantibus, necnon habere et tenere ibidem per totum tempus predictum per senescallos et alios ministros suos curiam pedis pulverisati et colore eiusdem capere et attachiare nonnullos dicti nuper domini Regis ac patris nostri subditos ad nundinas et feriam predictas confluentes, et eos tam per corpora quam per bona et catalla sua multocies inquietare et aggravare, ac diversas fines, redempciones et amerciamenta de huiusmodi dicti nuper patris nostri subditis capere, et ad solum commodum dicti maioris, ballivorum et burgensium detinere et convertere, ac eciam habere omnimodas alias forisfacturas et regalitates quascunque infra precincta nundinarum seu ferie predictarum apud Barnewell et Sturbridge predictas annuatim tempore ferie seu nundinarum earundem contingentes: Et quod de omnibus et singulis libertatibus et franchesiis supradictis predicti maior, ballivi et burgenses per spacium dictorum quatuor annorum et amplius super dictum dominum Regem apud Barnewell et Sturbridge predictas in dicto comitatu Cantebrigie usurpaverunt in dicti domini Regis et sue regie prerogative grave damnum et preiudicium ac in magnum contemptum ipsius domini Regis, prout per informacionem predictam in dicta curia dicti nuper domini Regis ac patris nostri precharissimi remanentem, plenius liquet: Super qua quidem informacione dictis tunc maiore, ballivis et burgensibus ville Cantebrigie predicte premunitis existentibus ad respondendum quo warranto claimabant habere libertates, franchesias et privilegia predicta, si quid pro se et successoribus suis in extinctionem informacionis predicte dicere vellent aut scirent: Ac eisdem maiore, ballivis et burgensibus die lune proxima post crastinum Assencionis Domini anno regni predicti nuper patris nostri precharissimi tricesimo primo, coram ipso domino Rege et patre nostro precharissimo apud Westmonasterium per attornatum suum comparentibus, et diversis diebus interloquendi eis in eadem curia datis et concessis: Tandem die mercurii in crastino sancti Johannis Baptiste anno regni dicti nuper domini Regis et patris nostri precharissimi tricesimo primo: Quia dicti adtunc maior, ballivi et burgenses, nolentes

belonging to such feast or fair, also to have and to hold there through all the time aforesaid by their stewards and other ministers a court of pie-powder and under colour of the same to take and to attach divers subjects of the said late lord King and our father coming to the fair and feast aforesaid and oftentimes to disquiet and trouble them as well in body as in their goods and chattels and to take divers fines, re-demptions and amercements from such subjects of our said late father, and to detain and convert them to the sole use of the said mayor, bailiffs and burgesses, and also to have all other kinds of forfeitures and regalities whatsoever within the precincts of the fair or feast aforesaid at Barnwell and Sturbridge aforesaid annually happening at the time of the said feast or fair : And that in all and singular the liberties and franchises abovesaid the aforesaid mayor, bailiffs and burgesses for the space of the said four years and more have usurped upon the said lord King at Barnwell and Sturbridge aforesaid in the said county of Cambridge, to the grave loss and prejudice of the said lord King and of his royal prerogative and to the great contempt of the said lord King himself as more fully appears by the aforesaid information remaining in the said court of the said late lord King and our dearest father : On which information, the said then mayor, bailiffs and burgesses of the town of Cambridge aforesaid being summoned to answer by what warrant they claimed to have the liberties, franchises and privileges aforesaid, if they wished to or could say anything for themselves and their successors in answer to the information aforesaid : And the said mayor, bailiffs and burgesses on the Monday next after the morrow of the Ascension of the Lord in the thirty-first year of the reign of our aforesaid late dearest father, before the lord King himself and our dearest father at Westminster appearing by their attorney, and several days being given and granted to them for imparling in the said court : At length on the Wednesday on the morrow of Saint John the Baptist in the thirty-first year of the reign of the said late lord King and our dearest father : Because the said then mayor, bailiffs and burgesses not wishing to contend with our said dearest

cum dicto patre nostro precharissimo in hac parte contendere
aut libertates suas predictas defendere, sed semetipsos quoad
feriam seu nundinas de Sturbridge predictas ac alias libertates
in eadem informacione specificatas, voluntatem et bene-
placitum dicti nuper patris nostri precharissimi humillime sub-
mittentes, nihil dixerunt in extincione informacionis predicte:
Concessum et consideratum fuit per curiam dicti domini Regis
ac patris nostri quod omnes et singule libertates, franchesie et
privilegia in informacione predicta specificata in manus dicti
patris nostri precharissimi seisirentur et remanerent, prout per
recordum inde in dicta curia dicti nuper patris nostri remanentem[1] plenius poterit apparere: Cumque maior, ballivi et burgenses nostri dicte ville nostre Cantebrigie nunc pro tempore
existentes, per dilectum et fidelem nostrum Rogerum Northe
militem, dominum Northe de Kirtling, summum et capitalem
dicte ville senescallum, nobis humillime supplicaverint quatenus
nos reginea pietate moti feriam predictam vocatam Sturbridge
Fayre cum omnibus libertatibus et liberis consuetudinibus
antedictis eisdem maiori, ballivis et burgensibus concedere
dignaremur: Nos equis postulacionibus eorundem maioris,
ballivorum et burgensium favorabiliter annuentes, longum et
continuum usum earundem nundinarum vocatarum Sturbridge
fayer per eosdem maiorem, ballivos et burgenses eorumque
predecessores in forma predicta habitum considerantes, ac
proficua et utilitates tam mercatoribus quam emptoribus ad
easdem nundinas venientibus, ac eciam maiori, ballivis et
burgensibus ville predicte et universitati nostre predicte pro-
venientes, perpendentes firme insuper nostre continuacioni
(unde maxima pars ex proficuis earundem nundinarum levari
solebat), prospicere volentes: Ac ut dicta villa nostra Cantebrigie tam in oneribus suis supportetur quam sub prospero
et pacifico regimine nostro augeatur et condecoretur desiderantes: Ex gracia nostra speciali ac ex certa sciencia et mero
motu nostris dictam feriam sive nundinas de ˌ Sturbridge
quotannis apud Barnewell et Sturbridge infra libertatem
dicte ville Cantebrigie tenendas, ac in festo Sancti Bartholomei Appostoli annuatim incepturas, et ab eodem festo

---

[1] Sic MS.

father in this matter or to defend their aforesaid liberties, but
most humbly submitting themselves, as touching the feast or
fair of Sturbridge aforesaid and other liberties specified in the
same information, to the will and good pleasure of our said late
dearest father, said nothing in answer to the information aforesaid : It was granted and determined by the court of the said
lord King and our father that all and singular the liberties,
franchises and privileges specified in the information aforesaid should be seized and should remain in the hands of our
said dearest father, as by the record thereof remaining in the
said court of our said late father may more fully appear :
And whereas our mayor, bailiffs and burgesses of our said
town of Cambridge now for the time being, applying by our
beloved and faithful Roger North knight, Lord North of
Kirtling, the high and chief steward of the said town, have
most humbly entreated us that we, moved by our queenly
pity, would deign to grant the fair aforesaid called " Sturbridge
Fayre " with all the liberties and free customs aforesaid to
the said mayor, bailiffs and burgesses : We, favourably re-
garding the just petitions of the said mayor, bailiffs and
burgesses, considering the long and continuous use of the
said fair called " Sturbridge fayer " by the said mayor, bailiffs
and burgesses and their predecessors held in the form aforesaid, and desiring to increase the profits and advantages
accruing as well to merchants as to buyers coming to the
same fair, and also to the mayor, bailiffs and burgesses of the
town aforesaid and to our aforesaid university, considering
further the continuation of our farm (whereof the greatest
part was wont to be levied from the profits of the said fair) :
And desiring that our said town of Cambridge may both be
supported in its burdens and be increased and adorned
under our prosperous and peaceful rule : Of our special grace
and from our certain knowledge and mere motion We give
and grant, and for us, our heirs and successors (as far as in
us lies) we restore out of our hands, deliver, confirm, ratify
and approve by these presents that the said feast or fair of
Sturbridge be held yearly at Barnwell and Sturbridge within

continue usque decimum quartum diem proxime post festum
exaltacionis Sancte Crucis annuatim temporibus futuris duraturas, unacum omnibus et omnimodis antedictis proficuis,
commoditatibus, easiamentis, curie proficuis, curie authoritatibus, iurisdiccionibus, facultatibus edificandi, construendi,
erigendi, cooperiendi, removendi, locandi, necnon ordinandi
et disponendi opellas locis earundem nundinarum et opellarum consuetis, et aliis libertatibus, franchesiis et liberis
consuetudinibus universis quibus ipsi nunc maior, ballivi et
burgenses eorumve predecessores in nundinas predictas aliquibus temporibus retroactis usi aut gavisi fuerunt, prefatis
maiori, ballivis et burgensibus ville nostre Cantebrigie et
eorum successoribus imperpetuum : Damus et concedimus ac
pro nobis, heredibus et successoribus nostris (quantum in
nobis est) restituimus extra manus nostras, deliberamus, confirmamus, ratificamus et approbamus per presentes : Salvis
tamen et semper acceptis¹ et reservatis tam nobis, heredibus
et successoribus nostris quam cancellario, magistris et scholaribus dicte universitatis nostre Cantebrigie et successoribus
suis, omnibus et singulis privilegiis, libertatibus, franchesiis,
immunitatibus, preheminenciis, potestatibus, iurisdiccionibus,
prescripcionibus, consuetudinibus, easiamentis, proficuis, commoditatibus, et advantagiis quibuscunque [tentis] a dictis
cancellario, magistris et scholaribus universitatis nostre Cantebrigie aut eorum aliquo, aut ab eorum ministris, famulis,
servientibus, aut ab eorum aliquo aut ab aliqua vel aliquibus
dicte universitatis nostre Cantebrigie personis priviligiatis in
dictis nundinis, feria seu feriis predictis anglice vocatis Sturbridge fayre, vel infra precincta earumdem, vel in aliquibus
subditorum nostrorum cetibus, conventibus seu congregacionibus, infra suburbia ville nostre Cantebrigie vel infra villam de
Barnewell, aut eiusdem ville campos et limites, antehac vulgariter vocatis Sturbridge Fayre, vel in aliquibus locis ubi
ferie sive nundine vulgariter vocate Sturbridge fayre ante hec
tempora tenebantur, que racione, causa, vigore, vel virtute
alicuius donacionis, concessionis seu confirmacionis nostre vel

¹ Corr. *exceptis.*

the liberty of the said town of Cambridge, and begin on the feast of Saint Bartholomew the Apostle yearly, and from the same feast last continuously unto the fourteenth day next after the feast of the exaltation of the Holy Cross yearly in future times, together with all and every the aforesaid profits, advantages, easements, profits of court, authorities of court, jurisdictions, powers of building, constructing, erecting, covering, removing, placing, as also of ordering and disposing the booths in the accustomed places of the said fair and booths with all other liberties, franchises and free customs which they the now mayor, bailiffs and burgesses or their predecessors have used or enjoyed in the aforesaid fair at any time past, to the aforesaid mayor, bailiffs and burgesses of our town of Cambridge and their successors for ever : Save however and always excepting and reserving as well to us, our heirs and successors as to the chancellor, masters and scholars of our said university of Cambridge and their successors, all and singular the privileges, liberties, franchises, immunities, preeminences, powers, jurisdictions, prescriptions, customs, easements, profits, conveniences and advantages whatsoever [held] by the said chancellor, masters and scholars of our university of Cambridge or any of them, or by their ministers, attendants, servants or any of them, or by any person or persons of our said university of Cambridge privileged in the said fair, feast or feasts aforesaid, called in English "Sturbridge fayre," or within the precincts of the same, or in any assemblies, conventions or congregations of our subjects within the suburbs of our town of Cambridge, or within the town of Barnwell or the fields and boundaries of the same town, heretofore commonly called "Sturbridge Fayre" or in any places where the feast or fair commonly called "Sturbridge fayre" before these times was held, which by reason, cause, authority or power of any gift, grant or confirmation of us or of our ancestors had or done before these times, or of any act of parliament, or which were held by themselves or any of them in the fair, feast or feasts aforesaid or in the precincts of the same or in the said

progenitorum nostrorum ante hec tempora habite seu facte aut alicuius actus parliamenti aut que per ipsos aut ipsorum aliquem in nundinis, feria seu feriis predictis aut precinctis earumdem, vel in dictis cetibus, conventibus, seu congregacionibus, vel in dictis locis ubi ferie seu nundine vulgariter vocate Sturbridge faire antehac tenebantur, habite, gavise, usitate aut percepte fuerunt aliquo tempore per maiorem partem viginti annorum proxime preteritorum, his litteris nostris patentibus aut hac concessione, restitucione seu deliberacione nostra, aut aliqua lege, causa, re vel materia quacumque in contrarium inde aliquo modo non obstante: Habendam, tenendam, utendam et gaudendam eandem feriam sive nundinas unacum omnibus et omnimodis antedictis proficuis, commoditatibus, easiamentis, curie proficuis, curiarum authoritatibus, iurisdiccionibus, facultatibus edificandi, construendi, erigendi, cooperiendi, removendi, locandi, necnon ordinandi et disponendi opellas locis earumdem nundinarum et opellarum consuetis, et aliis libertatibus, franchesiis et liberis consuetudinibus universis quibus ipsi nunc maior, ballivi et burgenses eorumve predecessores temporibus retroactis (ut prefertur) usi vel gavisi fuerunt (exceptis preexceptis) prefatis maiori, ballivis et burgensibus eorumque successoribus imperpetuum, predicto iudicio in predicto brevi de quo warranto reddito aut aliquo actu, ordinacione, abusu, non usu, aut aliqua alia re, causa vel materia quacumque in aliquo non obstante: Volumus insuper et pro nobis, heredibus et successoribus nostris, ex certa sciencia et mero motu nostris prefatis maiori, ballivis et burgensibus et eorum successoribus (quantum in nobis est) damus et concedimus per presentes, quod ipsi et eorum successores de tempore in tempus futuro tempore existente ordinaciones, regulas et statuta (secundum formam et effectum harum litterarum patentum) quoad pacificam et quietam gubernacionem nundinarum predictarum, ac tam quoad edificacionem, erectionem, cooperturam, locacionem, dislocacionem, remocionem, limitacionem, preficcionem, et ordinacionem opellarum quarumcunque infra nundinas predictas de cetero erigendarum, quam eciam quoad dis-

assemblies, conventions, or congregations, or in the said places where the feast or fair commonly called "Sturbridge faire" hitherto was held, or enjoyed, used or taken at any time through the greater part of the twenty years last past, these our letters patent, or this our grant, restitution or delivery, or any law, cause, thing or matter whatsoever to the contrary thereof in any way notwithstanding: To have, hold, use and enjoy the same feast or fair together with all and every the aforesaid profits, conveniences, easements, profits of court, authorities of courts, jurisdictions, powers of building, constructing, erecting, covering, removing, placing and also of ordering and disposing booths in the accustomed places of the said fair and booths, with all other liberties, franchises and free customs which they the now mayor, bailiffs and burgesses or their predecessors in times past (as has been said before) have used or enjoyed (things before excepted being excepted) to the aforesaid mayor, bailiffs and burgesses and their successors for ever, the aforesaid judgement given in the aforesaid writ of "quo warranto" or any act, ordinance, abuse, nonuser or any other thing, cause or matter whatever in anything notwithstanding: We will moreover and for us, our heirs and successors, of our certain knowledge and mere motion, we give and grant by these presents, to the aforesaid mayor, bailiffs and burgesses and their successors (as far as in us lies) that they and their successors from time to time in future time being, may and can make, set up, issue and establish ordinances, rules and statutes (according to the form and effect of these letters patent) concerning the peaceful and quiet government of the fair aforesaid, both as touching the building, erection, covering, placing, displacing, removing, limiting, fixing and ordering of booths whatsoever within the fair aforesaid henceforth to be erected, and also as touching the dispositions and assurances of the same by last wills, donations, surrenders, or otherwise to be made: Also as touching each of the arts, faculties, occupations or mysteries, for gathering, ordering, directing, arranging and deputing the merchants, workmen and artificers (holding

posiciones et assurancias earundem per ultimas voluntates, donaciones, sursumreddiciones aut aliter fiendas: Necnon quoad singulam artium, facultatum, occupacionum seu misteriorum, mercatores, opifices atque artifices (opellas seu staciones aliquas in nundinis predictis tenentes sive occupantes) coniunctim (prout decet) locis, opellis et stacionibus unicuique earumdem artium, facultatum, occupacionum et misteriorum mercatoribus, opificibus et artificibus designatis et consuetis (specialiter vero in quodam loco earundem nundinarum vocato Cheapeside) collocandis, ordinandis, designandis, disponendis et deputandis, facere, constituere, edere et stabilire possint et valeant, imperpetuum vel ad tempus prout eis magis expedire videbitur, duraturas et inviolabiliter observandas, dummodo ordinaciones, regule et statuta huiusmodi iuri, titulo sive interesse alicuius burgensis dicte ville Cantebrigie, legittime et secundum consuetudines et ordinaciones dicte ville tenentis seu possidentis aliquam opellam in nundinis predictis non preiudicent, nec libertatibus aut privilegiis cancellarii, magistrorum et scholarium universitatis nostre Cantebrigie, nec consuetudinibus suis antehac per maiorem partem viginti annorum proxime preteritorum usitatis aliqualiter derogent, nec legibus aut statutis regni nostri Anglie fuerint repugnantes: Ac dummodo huiusmodi ordinaciones, regule aut statuta non prohibeant nec restringant aliquam personam per universitatem predictam privilegiatam a conduccione alicuius opelle seu opellarum in nundinis predictis: Ac que quidem ordinaciones, regulas aut statuta tam per prefatos maiorem, ballivos et burgenses aut eorum successores imposterum edenda et stabilienda quam per eos aut eorum predecessores antehac edita seu stabilita de tempore in tempus, mutandi, revocandi, reiiciendi, adnichillandi aut secundum eorum discreciones confirmandi, necnon alia quecumque de tempore in tempus edendi, ordinandi et stabiliendi prout temporis mutatio et rerum eventus exigebit[1] eisdem maiori ballivis et burgensibus eorumque successoribus pro nobis heredibus et successoribus nostris (quantum in nobis est)

[1] Sic MS.

or occupying any booths or stations in the aforesaid fair) jointly (as is becoming) in the places, booths and stations marked out and accustomed for each of the said arts, faculties, occupations and mysteries for the merchants, workmen and artificers (especially in a certain place of the said fair called Cheapeside), for ever, or for the time being, as to them shall seem more expedient, to continue and to be inviolably observed, provided that such ordinances, rules and statutes shall not prejudice the right, title or interest of any burgess of the said town of Cambridge, lawfully and according to the customs and ordinances of the said town, holding or possessing any booth in the fair aforesaid, nor shall in any way derogate from the liberties or privileges of the chancellor, masters and scholars of our university of Cambridge or their customs used heretofore for the greater part of twenty years last past, nor shall be repugnant to the laws or statutes of our realm of England : And provided that such ordinances, rules or statutes shall not prohibit nor restrain any person privileged by the university aforesaid from holding any booth or booths in the fair aforesaid : And these ordinances, rules or statutes as well those in future to be issued or established by the aforesaid mayor, bailiffs and burgesses or their successors as those issued or established by them or their predecessors beforetime from time to time, we for ourselves our heirs and successors (as far as in us lies) of our certain knowledge and mere motion give full present authority, and grant power of changing, revoking, rejecting, annulling or, according to their discretions, of confirming, and also of issuing, ordering and establishing any others from time to time as the change of time and the course of events shall require, to the said mayor, bailiffs and burgesses and their successors : Now we forbid and expressly prohibit by these presents any sellers of any goods, called in English mercery wares or grocery wares, to be placed elsewhere in the said fair or to occupy any stall or station for selling such goods in the said fair except in the aforesaid place called Cheapeside, nor any woollen clothes or any clothes made of woollen

ex certa sciencia et mero motu nostris plenam authoritatem
presentem damus et concedimus facultatem : Nolumus autem
sed expresse prohibemus per presentes aliquos venditores
aliquarum mercium anglice appellatarum mercery wares seu
grocery wares alibi in nundinis predictis locari vel aliquam
opellam seu stacionem ad huiusmodi merces vendendum in
nundinis illis occupare nisi in predicto loco vocato Cheapeside,
nec aliquos pannos laneos seu vestimenta aliqua facta ex
pannis laneis alibi in eisdem nundinis vendicioni exponi
preterquam in loco consueto ibidem vocato le Duddery, nec
aliquos aurifabros alibi in eisdem nundinis locari seu merces
suas in aliquibus opellis vendicioni exponere, nisi tantum in
loco earundem nundinarum antiquitus appellato Soper lane
alias Gouldsmiths Rowe, nec aliquos fabros stanarios anglice
pewterers vel brasyers alibi in nundinis illis merces suas
vendicioni exponere nisi solummodo in stacionibus et opellis
earundem nundinarum consuetis in Pewtry rowe et Brasyer
Rowe ibidem : Providemus tamen et expresse volumus per
presentes quod omnes et singuli burgenses nostri ville predicte
qui secundum ordinaciones antehec[1] in eadem villa factas et
consuetudines eiusdem ville hactenus usitatas aliquam seu
aliquas opellam seu opellas in nundinis predictis de prefatis
maiore, ballivis et burgensibus modo tenent sibi, heredibus et
assignatis suis burgensibus dicte ville vel pro termino vite vel
annorum sive huiusmodi opellam seu opellas perquirerint[1] sive
eam vel eas per dissessum hereditarium acceperint, earundem
opellarum quamlibet sibi, heredibus et assignatis suis burgensibus dicte ville, vel pro termino vite vel annorum secundum seperales eorum status, titulos, interesse et terminos quos
in eisdem, iuxta ordinaciones in eadem villa antehac factas et
stabilitas ac publica eorundem maioris, ballivorum et burgensium authoritate in eadem villa nuper confirmatas ac
secundum consuetudines eiusdem ville hactenus usitatas
habent, de cetero habeant et teneant ac habere et tenere
valeant harum presencium litterarum nostrarum patencium
beneficio ac vigore, et in tam amplis modo ac forma ac si hec

[1] Sic MS.

cloth to be exposed for sale elsewhere in the said fair except in the accustomed place there called the Duddery, or any goldsmiths to be placed elsewhere in the said fair or to expose their goods for sale in any stalls, except only in the place of the said fair of old called Soaper Lane or Goldsmiths' Row, or any tin-smiths, in English pewterers or brasiers, to expose their goods for sale elsewhere in the fair except only in the accustomed stations and stalls of the said fair in Pewtry Row and Brazier Row there: But we provide and expressly will by these presents that all and singular our burgesses of the town aforesaid who, according to the ordinances heretofore made in the said town and the customs of the said town hitherto used, now hold any stall or stalls in the aforesaid fair from the aforesaid mayor, bailiffs and burgesses for themselves their heirs and assigns, burgesses of the said town, or for a term of life or of years, whether they have acquired such stall or stalls or have received it or them by hereditary descent, henceforth may have and hold and can have and hold each of the same stalls to themselves, their heirs and assigns, burgesses of the said town, or for the term of life or of years according to their several estates, titles, interest and terms which they have in the same, according to the ordinances in the same town heretofore made and established, and by the public authority of the said mayor, bailiffs and burgesses in the said town lately confirmed, and according to the customs of the said town hitherto used, by benefit and virtue of these our present letters patent, and in as ample a manner and form as if this our present charter had been made and granted to each burgess aforesaid, as far as concerns their stalls which now they hold from the beforenamed mayor, bailiffs and burgesses in the aforesaid fair and in form aforesaid: Provided always that in order that unity and concord may be the better fostered and preserved between the chancellor, masters and scholars of our university of Cambridge aforesaid and the mayor, bailiffs and burgesses of our said town of Cambridge: We do not will nor do we intend that these our letters patent or anything contained

presens charta nostra cuilibet burgensi predicto quoad opellas
suas quas modo de prefatis maiore, ballivis et burgensibus in
nundinis predictis ac in forma predicta tenent, esset confecta
atque concessa : Proviso semper quod quo melius unitas et
concordia inter cancellarium, magistros et scholares universitatis nostre Cantebrigie predicte ac maiorem, ballivos
et burgenses dicte ville nostre Cantebrigie foveatur et con-
servetur : Nolumus neque intendimus has literas nostras
patentes aut quicquam contentum in eisdem intelligi, accipi
vel torqueri ad tollendum, coarctandum, diminuendum aut in
dubium vocandum ullam partem libertatum, franchesiarum,
immunitatum, potestatum, iurisdiccionum, prescripcionum, consuetudinum, easiamentorum, beneficiorum aut commoditatum
a dictis cancellario, magistris et scholaribus aut eorum aliquo
aut ab eorum ministris, famulis seu servientibus aut eorum
aliquo in nundinis, ferie[1] sive feriis predictis vocatis Sturbridge
fayre habitam, gavisam, usitatam vel perceptam, racione, causa,
vigore seu virtute alicuius concessionis, actus parliamenti, prescripcionis, aut consuetudinis cuiuscumque, aut ab ipsis vel
ipsorum aliquo in nundinis predictis vel in aliquibus subditorum
nostrorum cetibus, conventibus seu congregacionibus infra
suburbia ville nostre Cantebrigie vel infra villam de Barnewell
aut eiusdem ville campos et limites antehac vulgariter vocatis
Sturbridge Fayre, vel in aliquibus locis ubi ferie seu nundine
vulgariter vocate Sturbridge Fayre ante hec tempora tenebantur, habitam, gavisam, usitatam vel perceptam aliquo
tempore per maiorem partem viginti annorum proxime preteritorum : Set quod predictis cancellario, magistris et scholaribus ac successoribus suis eorumque singulis et ipsorum
ministris, famulis et servientibus quibuscumque bene liceat
et licebit in nundinis sive feriis predictis uti, frui, gaudere,
habere, tenere et percipere omnia et omnimoda libertates,
franchesias, immunitates, potestates, iurisdicciones, prescrip-
ciones, consuetudines, easiamenta, beneficia, et commoditates
per nos seu per aliquem progenitorum aut predecessorum
nostrorum seu per authoritatem parliamenti ipsis aut ipsorum

[1] Sic MS.

in them should be understood, taken or twisted to the taking away, restricting, diminishing or calling in question any part of the liberties, franchises, immunities, powers, jurisdictions, prescriptions, customs, easements, benefits or commodities had, enjoyed, used or received by the said chancellor, masters and scholars or any of them or by their ministers, officers or servants or any of them in the fair or feast aforesaid called Sturbridge fayre, by reason, cause, power or virtue of any concession, act of parliament, prescription or custom whatsoever had, enjoyed, used or received by them or any of them, in the fair aforesaid or in any assemblies, conventions or congregations of our subjects within the suburbs of our town of Cambridge or within the town of Barnwell or the fields and limits of the said town heretofore commonly called Sturbridge Fayre, or in any places where the feast or fair commonly called Sturbridge Fayre before these times was held, at any time through the greater part of twenty years last past: But that it may and shall be fully lawful to the aforesaid chancellor, masters and scholars and their successors and to each of them and to their ministers, officers and servants whomsoever in the fair or feast aforesaid to use, take, enjoy, have, hold and receive all and every the liberties, franchises, immunities, powers, jurisdictions, pre-scriptions, customs, easements, benefits, and advantages by us or by anyone of our ancestors or predecessors or by authority of parliament given, granted or confirmed to them or to any of them, or had, received, used or enjoyed by them or any of them in the said fair, assemblies, conventions or places aforesaid commonly called Sturbridge faire at any time through the greater part of twenty years last past, in as ample manner and form, to whatever effect, object or intent,

B. C.   8

alicui data, concessa aut confirmata vel ab ipsis aut ipsorum
aliquo in eisdem nundinis, cetibus, conventibus seu locis predictis vulgariter vocatis Sturbridge faire aliquo tempore per
maiorem partem viginti annorum proxime preteritorum
habita, percepta, usitata aut gavisa in tam amplis modo et
forma ad quemcumque effectum, propositum seu intencionem,
ac[1] si he litere nostre patentes maiori, ballivis et burgensibus
ville nostre Cantebrigie predicte omnino facte non fuissent
absque ullo scrupulo, dubitacione seu questione de, in, aut
super ea re movendis, his literis nostris patentibus aut materia
seu re aliqua in eisdem contenta in aliquo non obstante :
Proviso semper et nostra voluntas et intencio est quod he
litere nostre patentes aut aliqua res seu materia quacumque
in eisdem superius contenta nullo modo se extendat neque
quovismodo intelligatur, interpretetur seu accipiatur ad tollendum, evacuandum, restringendum, diminuendum seu coarctandum privilegia, libertates, immunitates, preheminencias
authoritates, iurisdicciones, proficua, commoditates, advantagia
seu eorum aliqua vel aliquos ante hec tempora per nos sive
progenitores nostros maiori, ballivis et burgensibus dicte ville
nostre Cantebrigie data, tradita seu concessa, queque nunc
virtute et pretextu aliquarum literarum nostrarum patencium
aut progenitorum nostrorum vel racione et vigore alicuius
actus parliamenti antehac editi seu provisi pleno et integro
robore iure existit seu existunt et debuit existere poterit seu
poterint : Sed quod he litere nostre patentes atque omnia et
singula in eisdem contenta omni modo habeantur, accipiantur
et interpretentur imperpetuum contra nos, heredes et successores nostros, atque omnes alias personas atque personam,
corpus politicum atque corpora politica nunc aut imposterum
aliquod ius, titulum aut interesse de, aut in, predictis nundinis,
feria seu feriis de Sturbridge habentes aut vendicantes aut
habencia seu vendicancia quam liberatissime ad omnem usum,
commodum et utilitatem ipsorum maioris, ballivorum et
burgensium et successorum suorum : Et quod dicti maior,
ballivi et burgenses et eorum successores his literis nostris

[1] Sic MS.

as if these our letters patent to the mayor, bailiffs and burgesses of our town of Cambridge aforesaid had in no wise been made, without any scruple, doubt or question being moved of, in, or on this matter, these our letters patent or any matter or thing in the same contained in any wise notwithstanding : Provided always and our will and intention is that these our letters patent or any thing or matter whatsoever in the same above contained in no way shall extend nor in any way shall be understood, interpreted or received to the taking away, avoiding, restricting, diminishing or contracting the privileges, liberties, immunities, preeminences, authorities, jurisdictions, profits, commodities, advantages or any of them given, granted or conceded before these times by us or our ancestors to the mayor, bailiffs and burgesses of our said town of Cambridge, which now by virtue and pretext of any letters patent of us or of our ancestors or by reason and virtue of any act of parliament heretofore issued or provided in full and entire force in law exists or exist and ought to exist and may exist : But that these our letters patent and all and singular the matters contained therein in every way may be had, received and interpreted for ever against us, our heirs and successors, and all other persons and person, body politic and bodies politic, now or hereafter having or claiming any right, title or interest of, or in, the aforesaid fair or feast of Sturbridge, as freely as possible, to all use, advantage and profit of the said mayor, bailiffs and burgesses and their successors : And that the said mayor, bailiffs and burgesses and their successors may and can use these our letters patent for ever in any form of law, to all effects and intents as shall seem to them most useful or to be more expedient, any thing or matter whatsoever in these presents or in any law, ordinance or matter whatsoever to the contrary thereof in

patentibus imperpetuum uti possint et valeant in quacumque
iuris forma ad omnes effectus et intenciones prout iis maxime
commodum meliusve expedire videbitur, aliqua re seu materia
quacumque in presentibus aut aliqua lege, ordinacione seu
materia quacumque in contrarium inde in aliquo non obstantibus. In cuius rei testimonium has literas nostras fieri
fecimus patentes. Teste me ipsa apud Drayton decimo
quinto die Augusti anno regni nostri tricesimo primo.

Powle.

per breve de privato sigillo et de dato predicto auctoritate
parliamenti.

examinate per Willelmum Brevit.

XXVI.   Littere Patentes Jacobi Primi.

1605
April 30 [1] Iacobus dei gratia Anglie Scotie Francie et Hibernie
Rex fidei defensor &c. omnibus ad quos presentes litere
pervenerint salutem. Cum burgus noster de Cantabrigia in
comitatu Cantabrigie sit burgus antiquus et populosus et
burgenses burgi illius quandoque per nomen maioris, ballivorum et burgensium eiusdem burgi quandoque per nomen
burgensium burgi illius et quandoque per alia nomina ville
predicte necnon diversas libertates, franchesias, immunitates,
consuetudines, preheminencias, et alia hereditamenta habuerunt, usi et gavisi fuerunt ac habent, utuntur et gaudent
tam per seperales et diversas cartas ǀet literas patentes
diversorum progenitorum et antecessorum nostrorum Regum
et Reginarum Anglie quam eciam racione diversarum
prescripcionum et consuetudinum in eodem burgo usitatarum
et habitarum cumque dilecti subditi nostri modo maior,
ballivi et burgenses burgi de Cantabrigia predicta nobis
humillime supplicaverunt quatenus nos eisdem maiori, ballivis
et burgensibus graciam et munificenciam nostram regiam in
hac parte exhibere et extendere velimus : Quodque nos pro
meliori gubernacione et regimine eiusdem burgi dictos ma-

---

[1] In the Borough Archives. On two large skins. A fragment of the great
seal in brown wax appendant. The initials are adorned with the royal arms.

any wise notwithstanding. In witness whereof we have caused these our letters to be made patent. Witness myself at Drayton on the fifteenth day of August in the thirty-first year of our reign.

POWLE.

by writ of Privy seal and of the aforesaid date by authority of parliament.

Examined by William Brevit.

XXVI. LETTERS PATENT OF JAMES THE FIRST.

[1]James by the grace of God of England Scotland France and Ireland King Defender of the Faith &c. to all to whom the present letters shall come greeting. Whereas our borough of Cambridge in the county of Cambridge is an ancient and populous borough, and our burgesses of that borough sometimes under the name of the mayor, bailiffs and burgesses of the same borough, sometimes under the name of the burgesses of that borough, and sometimes under other names of the town aforesaid have had, used and enjoyed and also have, use, and enjoy divers liberties, franchises, immunities, customs, preeminences, and other hereditaments as well by separate and divers charters and letters patent of divers of our ancestors and predecessors, Kings and Queens of England, as also by reason of divers prescriptions and customs used and had in the same borough, and whereas our beloved subjects the now mayor, bailiffs and burgesses of the borough of Cambridge aforesaid have supplicated us most humbly that we would be willing to shew and extend in this behalf our royal grace and munificence to the said mayor, bailiffs and burgesses : And that we for the better government and ruling

1605
April 30

---

[1] See Cooper, *Annals*, iii. 17.

iorem, ballivos et burgenses eiusdem burgi in unum corpus corporatum et politicum per nomen maioris, ballivorum et burgensium burgi de Cantabrigia per literas nostras patentes confirmare, facere, constituere et creare dignaremur cum augmentacionibus et addicionibus quorumdam libertatum, privilegiorum et franchesiarum prout nobis melius videbitur expedire: Nos igitur volentes quod decetero imperpetuum continuo habeatur unus certus et indubitatus modus in eodem burgo, de et in regimine et gubernacione eiusdem burgi et populi nostri in eodem burgo inhabitantis ac aliorum ibidem confluentium: Ac eciam ut pax nostra ceteraque facta iusticie et boni regiminis ibidem melius custodiri et fieri valeant et possint, sperantesque quod si maior, ballivi et burgenses dicti burgi et successores sui maiores et ampliores ex concessione nostra regali gaudere possint dignitates, privilegia, iurisdicciones, libertates et franchesias tunc ad servicia que poterint[1] nobis heredibus et successoribus nostris, impendenda et exhibenda, specialius fortiusque sentiant se obligatos: Necnon ad humilem peticionem et rogacionem predilectorum et fidelium conciliarii nostri Thome domini Ellesmere domini cancellarii Anglie nunc capitalis senescalli burgi predicti et Iohannis Fortescue militis ducatus nostri Lancastrie cancellarii ac moderni recordatoris burgi predicti de gracia nostra speciali ac ex certa sciencia et mero motu nostris voluimus, ordinavimus, constituimus, concessimus et declaravimus ac per has literas nostras patentes pro nobis, heredibus et successoribus nostris, volumus, ordinamus, constituimus, concedimus et declaramus quod dictus burgus de Cantabrigia de cetero imperpetuum sit et erit et permanebit liber burgus de se et quod homines eiusdem burgi liberi sint burgenses, et quod habeant omnes libertates et liberas consuetudines ad liberum burgum spectantes imperpetuum et quod maior, ballivi et burgenses eiusdem burgi quodque burgenses burgi illius, sive antehac legittime incorporati fuerunt sive non, de cetero imperpetuum sine ulla questione seu ambiguitate imposterum fiendi sint et

---

[1] Corr. *pertinent.*

of the same borough would deign to confirm, make, constitute
and create the said mayor, bailiffs and burgesses of the same
borough into one body corporate and politic by the name of
the mayor, bailiffs and burgesses of the borough of Cambridge
by our letters patent with augmentations and additions of
certain liberties, privileges and franchises as shall seem good
and expedient to us: We therefore willing that henceforth for
ever continually there should be one certain and undoubted
method in the same borough of and in the ruling and government of the same borough and of our people dwelling in
the same borough and of others coming together there : and
also that our peace and other deeds of justice and good ruling
there may be able to be and should be better kept and done,
and hoping that if the mayor, bailiffs and burgesses of the
said borough and their successors enjoy from our royal
concession greater and ampler dignities, privileges, jurisdictions, liberties and franchises then they will feel themselves more specially and strongly bound to discharge and
fulfil the services which pertain to us, our heirs and successors:
Moreover at the humble petition and request of our well-
beloved and faithful councillor Thomas Lord Ellesmere Lord
Chancellor of England now high steward of the borough
aforesaid and of John Fortescue, knight, Chancellor of our
Duchy of Lancaster and the now recorder of the borough
aforesaid, of our special grace and from our certain knowledge
and mere motion we have willed, ordained, constituted,
granted and declared and by these our letters patent for us,
our heirs and successors, we will, ordain, constitute, grant and
declare that the said borough of Cambridge henceforth for
ever may be and shall be and shall remain a free borough of
itself and that the men of the said borough may be free
burgesses and that they may have all liberties and free
customs belonging to a free borough for ever, and that the
mayor, bailiffs and burgesses of the said borough and also the
burgesses of that borough, whether beforetime they have
been lawfully incorporated or not, henceforth for ever without
any question or ambiguity hereafter shall be made and shall

erunt unum corpus corporatum et politicum in re, facto et
nomine, per nomen maioris, ballivorum et burgensium burgi
de Cantabrigia: ac omnes burgenses burgi predicti per nomen
maioris, ballivorum et burgensium burgi de Cantabrigia unum
corpus corporatum et politicum in re, facto et nomine realiter
et ad plenum pro nobis, heredibus et successoribus nostris,
erigimus, facimus, ordinamus, constituimus et declaramus per
presentes et quod per idem nomen habeant successionem
perpetuam, et quod ipsi per nomen maioris, ballivorum et
burgensium burgi de Cantabrigia sint et erunt perpetuis
futuris temporibus persone habiles et in lege capaces ac
corpus corporatum et politicum in lege capax ad habendum,
perquirendum, recipiendum, possidendum, gaudendum et retinendum terras, tenementa, libertates, privilegia, iurisdicciones,
franchesias et hereditamenta quecunque, cuiuscunque generis,
nature vel speciei fuerint sibi et successoribus suis, in feodo
et perpetuitate sive pro termino anni vel annorum aut aliter
quocunque modo, necnon bona et catalla quecunque, necnon
ad dandum, concedendum, dimittendum, alienandum, assignandum et disponendum terras, tenementa et hereditamenta
predicta ; Et quod imperpetuum per idem nomen maioris,
ballivorum et burgensium burgi de Cantabrigia placitare et
implacitari, respondere et responderi, defendere et defendi
valeant et possint in quibuscunque curiis et locis coram nobis,
heredibus et successoribus nostris ac coram quibuscunque
iudicibus et iusticiariis et aliis personis et officiariis nostri,
heredum vel successorum nostrorum, aut aliorum quorumcunque, in omnibus et singulis accionibus, placitis, sectis,
querelis, causis, materiis et demandis quibuscunque, cuiuscunque sunt aut erunt generis, nature seu speciei in tam
amplis modo et forma prout aliqui alii ligei nostri huius regni
nostri Anglie persone habiles et in lege capaces sive aliquod
aliud corpus corporatum et politicum infra regnum nostrum
Anglie habere, perquirere, recipere, possidere, gaudere, placitare et implacitari, respondere et responderi, defendere et
defendi, facere, permittere sive exequi possint et valeant : Et
quod predicti maior, ballivi et burgenses burgi predicti et

be one body corporate and politic in deed, fact and name
by the name of the mayor, bailiffs and burgesses of the
borough of Cambridge: and all the burgesses of the borough
aforesaid by the name of the mayor, bailiffs and burgesses of
the borough of Cambridge, we erect, make, ordain, constitute
and declare by these presents, for us our heirs and successors,
one body corporate and politic in deed, fact and name,
really and fully, and that by the said name they may have
perpetual succession, and that they themselves by the name
of the mayor, bailiffs and burgesses of the borough of Cambridge may be and shall be in all future times persons fit and
capable in law and a body corporate and politic capable in
law to have, obtain, receive, possess, enjoy and retain lands
tenements, liberties, privileges, jurisdictions, franchises and
hereditaments whatsoever, of whatever kind, nature or species
they may be, for themselves and their successors, in fee and
perpetuity, whether for a term of a year or of years or
otherwise, in whatsoever manner, and goods and chattels
whatsoever, also to give, grant, demise, alienate, assign and
dispose of the lands, tenements and hereditaments aforesaid ;
and that for ever by the said name of the mayor, bailiffs and
burgesses of the borough of Cambridge they may be qualified
and be able to plead and to be impleaded, to answer and to
be answered, to defend and to be defended, in whatsoever
courts and pleas before us, our heirs and successors and
before whatsoever judges and justices and other persons and
officers of us, our heirs or successors, or of others whomsoever,
in all and singular actions, pleas, suits, complaints, causes,
matters and demands whatsoever, of whatsoever kind, nature
or species they are or shall be, in as ample a manner and form
as any other our lieges of this our realm of England, persons
qualified and capable in law, or any other body corporate and
politic within our realm of England are able to and can have,
acquire, receive, possess, enjoy, plead and be impleaded,
answer and be answered, defend and be defended, make,
permit or execute: And that the aforesaid mayor, bailiffs
and burgesses of the borough aforesaid and their successors

successores sui habeant imperpetuum comune sigillum pro
causis et negociis suis quibuscunque ac successorum suorum
agendis serviturum : Et quod bene licebit eisdem maiori,
ballivis, burgensibus et successoribus suis sigillum illud ad
libitum suum de tempore in tempus frangere, mutare et de
novo facere, prout eis melius fieri videbitur : Et ulterius de
uberiori gracia nostra volumus et per presentes pro nobis,
heredibus et successoribus nostris concedimus predictis maiori,
ballivis et burgensibus burgi predicti et eorum successoribus
quod maior, ballivi et burgenses burgi predicti pro tempore
existente vel maior pars eorundem, quorum maiorem burgi
predicti pro tempore existente unum esse volumus, habeant
et habebunt plenam authoritatem, potestatem et facultatem
condendi, constituendi, ordinandi, faciendi et stabiliendi de
tempore in tempus talia et huiusmodi leges, statuta, iura,
ordinaciones et constituciones qualia eis sive maiori parti
eorundem, quorum maiorem burgi predicti pro tempore
existente unum esse volumus, bona, utilia, salubria, honesta et
necessaria iuxta eorum sanas discreciones fore videbuntur
pro bono regimine et gubernacione maioris, ballivorum et
burgensium burgi predicti et omnium et singulorum aliorum
burgensium, officiariorum, ministrorum, artificum, inhabitan-
cium et residencium quorumcunque infra burgum predictum et
libertates eiusdem pro uberiori bono publico, comuni utilitate
ac bono regimine burgi predicti : Ac eciam pro meliori
gubernacione, disposicione, locacione et dimissione terrarum,
possessionum, revencionum et hereditamentorum prefatorum
maioris, ballivorum et burgensium burgi predicti ac res
et causas alias quascunque burgi predicti statum, iura et
interesse eiusdem burgi tangentes seu quoquo modo concernentes : Quodque maior, ballivi et burgenses burgi predicti pro tempore existente vel eorum maior pars, quorum
maiorem burgi predicti pro tempore existente unum esse
volumus, quociescunque huiusmodi leges, iura, constituciones
et ordinaciones condiderint, fecerint vel stabiliverint in forma
predicta huiusmodi et talia penas, puniciones, et penalitates, per
imprisonamentum corporis seu corporum vel per fines et

may have for ever a common seal to be kept for transacting all the causes and businesses whatsoever of them and their successors: And that it shall be fully lawful to the said mayor, bailiffs and burgesses and their successors from time to time at their pleasure to break, change and re-make that seal as it shall seem to them best to be done: And further of our more abundant grace we will and by these presents for us, our heirs and successors, we grant to the aforesaid mayor, bailiffs and burgesses of the borough aforesaid and their successors that the mayor, bailiffs and burgesses of the borough aforesaid for the time being or the greater part of them, of whom we will that the mayor of the borough aforesaid for the time being shall be one, may have and shall have full authority, power and capacity of framing, constituting, ordaining, making and establishing from time to time such and suchlike laws, statutes, rules, ordinances and constitutions as to them or to the greater part of them, of whom we will that the mayor of the borough aforesaid for the time being shall be one, shall appear to be good, useful, salutary, lawful and necessary according to their sound discretions for the good ruling and governing of the mayor, bailiffs and burgesses of the borough aforesaid and of all and singular the other burgesses, officers, servants, artificers, inhabitants and residents whomsoever within the borough aforesaid and the liberties thereof, for the greater public good, the common weal and the good ruling of the borough aforesaid: And also for the better governing, disposition, letting and demising of lands, possessions, revenues and hereditaments aforesaid of the mayor, bailiffs and burgesses of the borough aforesaid and other things and causes whatsoever of the aforesaid borough, touching or in any way concerning the estate, rights and interests of the said borough: And that the mayor, bailiffs and burgesses of the borough aforesaid for the time being or the greater part of them, of whom we will that the mayor of the borough aforesaid for the time being shall be one, as often as they shall have framed, made or established such laws, rules, constitutions and ordinances in form aforesaid, may make,

amerciamenta vel per eorum utrumque erga et super omnes
delinquentes contra huiusmodi leges, instituta, iura, ordinaciones et constituciones sive eorum aliquod sive aliqua,
qualia et que eisdem maiori, ballivis et burgensibus pro tempore
existente sive eorum maiori parti, quorumque maiorem burgi
predicti pro tempore existente unum esse volumus, necessaria,
opportuna et requisita pro observacione earundem [1] legum,
ordinacionum et constitucionum melius fieri videbuntur, facere
ordinare, limitare et providere, ac eadem fines et amerciamenta
levare et habere possint et valeant ad opus et usum maioris,
ballivorum et burgensium burgi predicti et successorum
suorum absque impedimento nostri aut heredum vel successorum nostrorum aut alicuius sive aliquorum officiariorum
vel ministrorum nostrorum vel heredum aut successorum
nostrorum et absque aliquo compoto nobis, heredibus seu
successoribus nostris, inde reddendo : Que omnia et singula
leges, ordinaciones, iura, ordinaciones et constituciones sic ut
prefertur facienda observari volumus sub penis in eisdem
continendis : Ita tamen quod leges, ordinaciones, constituciones, imprisonamenta, fines et amerciamenta huiusmodi
sint racionabilia et non sint repugnancia vel contraria legibus,
statutis, consuetudinibus sive iuribus regni nostri Anglie seu
racionabilibus et laudabilibus prescripcionibus et consuetudinibus in eodem burgo antique usitatis et consuetis : Et ut
maior, ballivi et burgenses burgi predicti et eorum successores
de tempore in tempus onera et expensas burgi predicti melius
sustinere et supportare possint et valeant de gracia nostra
speciali, certa sciencia et mero motu nostris concessimus ac
per presentes pro nobis, heredibus et successoribus nostris
concedimus et licenciam specialem, legittimam et licitam
facultatem, potestatem et authoritatem damus prefatis maiori,
ballivis et burgensibus burgi predicti et successoribus suis ad
habendum, perquirendum, recipiendum et retinendum eis et
successoribus suis imperpetuum tam de nobis, heredibus et
successoribus nostris, quam de quibuscunque subditis et ligeis
nostris aut de aliis quibuscunque sive aliqua alia persona sive

---

[1] MS. *eorundem.*

ordain, limit and provide such and suchlike pains, punishments and penalties, by imprisonment of the body or the bodies, or by fines and amercements, or by either of them, towards and upon all delinquents against such laws, institutions, rules, ordinances and constitutions or any one or more of them, as to the said mayor, bailiffs and burgesses for the time being or to the greater part of them, of whom we will that the mayor of the borough aforesaid for the time being shall be one, shall appear necessary, fit and requisite for the observance of the said laws, ordinances and constitutions, and the said fines and amercements they may and can levy and have, to the use and advantage of the mayor, bailiffs and burgesses of the borough aforesaid and of their successors, without any hindrance from us, or our heirs and successors, or from any one or more officers or servants of us or of our heirs and successors, and without any account thereof to be rendered to us or our heirs or successors: Which all and singular the laws, ordinances, rules, ordinances and constitutions as is before said we will to be caused to be observed under the penalties contained in the same: But so that such laws, ordinances, constitutions, imprisonments, fines and amercements be reasonable and be not repugnant or contrary to the laws, statutes, customs or rights of our realm of England or the reasonable and laudable prescriptions and customs, in the said borough of old used and accustomed: And that the mayor, bailiffs and burgesses of the borough aforesaid and their successors from time to time can and may be better able to sustain and support the burdens and expenses of the borough aforesaid, of our special grace, certain knowledge and mere motion, we have granted and by these presents, for us, our heirs and successors, we grant and give special, legitimate and lawful licence, faculty, power and authority to the aforesaid mayor, bailiffs and burgesses of the borough aforesaid and their successors, to have, acquire, receive and retain to them and to their successors for ever, as well from us, our heirs and successors, as from any our subjects and lieges and from others whomsoever, whether from any other person or any

aliquibus aliis personis quibuscunque, mesuagia, terras, tenementa, rectorias, decimas, redditus, revenciones, servicia et
alia possessiones et hereditamenta quecunque infra villam
Cantabrigie predicte seu infra suburbia, libertates, limites aut
precincta eiusdem ville existencia que de nobis, heredibus vel
successoribus nostris non tenentur imediate in capite nec per
servicium militare, dummodo eadem mesuagia, terre, tenementa, rectorie, decime, redditus, revenciones, servicia et alia
possessiones seu hereditamenta per eosdem maiorem, ballivos
et burgenses burgi predicti et successores suos sic ut prefertur
habenda, perquirenda, recipienda et retinenda in toto non
excedant valorem sexaginta librarum per annum, statuto de
terris et tenementis ad manum mortuam non ponendis aut
aliquo alio statuto, actu, ordinacione, provisione seu restriccione
in contrarium inde antehac habito, facto, edito, ordinato seu
proviso, aut aliqua causa vel materia quacunque in aliquo
non obstante: Damus eciam ac per presentes pro nobis,
heredibus et successoribus nostris, concedimus cuicunque
subdito nostro et quibuscunque subditis nostris, heredum et
successorum nostrorum, potestatem, licenciam et authoritatem
quod mesuagia, terras, tenementa, rectorias, decimas, redditus,
revenciones, servicia et alia possessiones et hereditamenta
quecunque infra villam predictam aut infra suburbia, libertates, limites seu precincta eiusdem ville existencia, que de
nobis, heredibus vel successoribus nostris non tenentur
imediate in capite nec per servicium militare prefatis maiori,
ballivis et burgensibus burgi predicti et successoribus suis
dare, legare, concedere, alienare sive conveiare possint et
valeant, dummodo eadem messuagia, terre, tenementa, rectorie,
decime, redditus, revenciones, servicia et alia possessiones et
hereditamenta non excedant clarum annuum valorem sexaginta librarum per annum, statuto de terris et tenementis ad
manum mortuam non ponendis aut aliquo alio statuto, actu,
ordinacione, provisione seu restriccione inde in contrarium
antehac habito, facto, edito, ordinato seu proviso non obstante:
Et ulterius de ampliori gratia nostra speciali ac ex certa sciencia
et mero motu nostris concessimus, approbavimus, ratificavi-

other persons whomsoever, messuages, lands, tenements,
rectories, tithes, rents, revenues, services and other possessions
and hereditaments whatsoever being within the town of
Cambridge aforesaid or within the suburbs, liberties, limits
and precincts of the said town, which are not held immediately
from us, our heirs or successors, in chief, nor by military
service, provided that the said messuages, lands, tenements,
rectories, tithes, rents, revenues, services and other possessions
or hereditaments by the said mayor, bailiffs and burgesses of
the borough aforesaid and their successors so as is aforesaid,
to be held, acquired, received and kept, do not in the whole
exceed the value of sixty pounds a year, the statute against
putting lands and tenements in mortmain and any other
statute, act, ordinance, provision or restriction heretofore had,
made, issued, ordained or provided to the contrary or any
cause or matter whatever in any wise notwithstanding : We
give also and by these presents we grant for us, our heirs and
successors, to every the subject or subjects of us, our heirs
and successors, power, licence and authority that he or they
can and may be able to give, bequeath, grant, alienate or
convey to the mayor, bailiffs and burgesses aforesaid of the
borough aforesaid and their successors, messuages, lands,
tenements, rectories, tithes, rents, revenues, services and other
possessions and hereditaments whatsoever, being within the
town aforesaid or within the suburbs, liberties, limits or
precincts of the said town, which are not held immediately
of us, our heirs or successors, in chief, nor by military service,
provided that the said messuages, lands, tenements, rectories,
tithes, rents, revenues, services and other possessions and
hereditaments do not exceed the clear yearly value of
sixty pounds a year, the statute against putting lands
and tenements in mortmain, or any other statute, act,
ordinance, provision or restriction heretofore had, made,
issued, ordained or provided to the contrary notwithstanding : And furthermore of our ampler special grace and
from our certain knowledge and mere motion we have
granted, approved, ratified and by these presents we grant

mus et confirmavimus ac per presentes pro nobis, heredibus
et successoribus nostris concedimus, approbamus, ratificamus
et confirmamus prefatis maiori, ballivis et burgensibus burgi
de Cantabrigia predicta et successoribus suis omnia et
omnimoda, tot, tanta, talia, eadem, huiusmodi et consimilia
concessiones, liberas consuetudines, libertates, privilegia,
franchesias, imunitates, quietancias, exempciones, ferias,
nundinas, mercata, theolonea, tolneta, iurisdicciones, commoditates, emolumenta, terras, tenementa et hereditamenta,
quot, quanta, qualia, et que maior, ballivi et burgenses burgi
de Cantabrigia predicta aut eorum aliqui, modo legittimo
habent, tenent, gaudent et utuntur, aut habere, tenere,
uti aut gaudere debent per nomen maioris, ballivorum
et burgensium burgi de Cantabrigia aut per nomen ballivorum et burgensium burgi de Cantabrigia aut per nomen
burgensium burgi de Cantabrigia sive per quecunque alia
nomina sive per quodcunque aliud nomen vel per quamcunque incorporacionem vel corpus politicum seu pretextu
cuiuscunque incorporacionis vel corporis politici premissa
aut eorum aliqua data seu concessa fuere predictis maiori,
ballivis et burgensibus aut aliquibus seu alicui predecessorum
suorum racione vel pretextu aliquarum cartarum aut literarum patencium per aliquem progenitorum sive antecessorum
nostrorum quoquo modo antehac factarum, confirmatarum
vel concessarum aut racione vel pretextu alicuius legittime
prescripcionis, usus seu consuetudinis antehac habite seu
usitate seu quocunque alio legali modo, iure seu titulo, licet
eadem seu eorum aliquod vel aliqua antehac usi non fuerunt
vel fuit, aut abusi vel male usi vel discontinuati fuerunt vel
fuit, aut licet eadem aut eorum aliquod vel aliqua deperdita
aut forisfacta sint aut fuerint : Habendum tenendum et gaudendum eadem terras et tenementa, libertates, privilegia,
franchesias, iurisdicciones et cetera premissa eisdem maiori,
ballivis et burgensibus burgi predicti et successoribus suis
imperpetuum : Reddendo inde nobis, heredibus et successoribus nostris talia huiusmodi et consimilia redditus, servicia,
denariorum summas et tenurias que proinde nobis antehac

approve, ratify and confirm for us, our heirs and successors,
to the aforesaid mayor, bailiffs and burgesses of the borough
of Cambridge aforesaid and to their successors, all and every,
so many, so great, such, the same, of this kind and like
concessions, free customs, liberties, privileges, franchises,
immunities, quittances, exemptions, feasts, fairs, markets,
takings, tolls, jurisdictions, conveniences, emoluments, lands,
tenements and hereditaments of such sort, quantity and
nature, and which the mayor, bailiffs and burgesses of the
borough of Cambridge aforesaid, or any of them, in a lawful
manner have, hold, enjoy and use, or ought to have, hold, use
or enjoy by the name of the mayor, bailiffs and burgesses of
the borough of Cambridge, or by the name of the bailiffs and
burgesses of the borough of Cambridge, or by the name of
the burgesses of the borough of Cambridge, or by whatever
other names, or by whatever other name, or by whatever
incorporation or body politic, or on pretext of whatever incorporation or body politic, the premises or any of them have
been given or granted to the aforesaid mayor, bailiffs and
burgesses or to any one or more of their predecessors, by
reason or pretext of any charters or letters patent made,
confirmed or granted by any of our ancestors or predecessors
in any way heretofore, or by reason or pretext of any lawful
prescription, use or custom heretofore had or used, or by any
other legal manner, right or title, although the same or any
one or more of them heretofore have or has not been used or
have or has been abused or badly used, or have or has been
discontinued, or although the same or any one or more of them
have or has been lost or forfeited : To have, hold and enjoy
the said lands and tenements, liberties, privileges, franchises,
jurisdictions and other premises to the said mayor, bailiffs and
burgesses of the borough aforesaid and to their successors for
ever : Rendering thence to us, our heirs and successors, such,
such like, and similar rents, services, sums of money and
tenures which to us heretofore have been thence due, payable

debita, solubilia et de iure consueta fuerunt: Quare volumus
et per presentes pro nobis, heredibus et successoribus nostris,
concedimus prefatis maiori, ballivis et burgensibus burgi
de Cantabrigia predicta et successoribus suis quod habeant,
teneant, utantur et gaudeant ac plene habere, tenere, uti et
gaudere possint et valeant imperpetuum omnia et omnimoda
predicta terras, tenementa, redditus, revenciones, libertates,
liberas consuetudines, privilegia, authoritates, quietancias et
hereditamenta quecunque predicta secundum tenorem et
effectum harum literarum nostrarum patencium, sine occasione vel impedimento nostri heredum vel successorum nostrorum quorumcunque: Nolentes quod iidem maior, ballivi
et burgenses burgi predicti vel eorum aliqui vel aliquis nec
aliquis burgensis burgi predicti racione premissorum sive
eorum alicuius per nos vel per heredes nostros, iusticiarios,
vicecomites, escaetores aut alios ballivos seu ministros nostros
heredum seu successorum nostrorum quorumcunque inde occasionentur, molestentur, vexentur seu graventur, molestetur,
vexetur, gravetur seu in aliquo perturbetur: Volentes et per
presentes firmiter pro nobis heredibus et successoribus nostris
mandantes et precipientes tam Thesaurario, Cancellario et
Baronibus Scaccarii nostri, heredum et successorum nostrorum,
ac omnibus et singulis aliis iudicibus et iusticiariis nostris
heredum et successorum nostrorum, quam Attornato et
Solicitore nostro generali pro tempore existente et eorum
cuilibet et omnibus aliis officiariis et ministris nostris quibuscunque, quod nec ipsi nec eorum aliquis sive aliqui aliquod
breve seu summonicionem de quo warranto seu aliquod aliud
breve seu brevia vel processus nostros quecunque versus
predictos maiorem, ballivos et burgenses burgi predicti seu
eorum aliquos seu homines vel inhabitantes burgi predicti
vel eorum aliquem vel aliquos, pro aliquibus causis, rebus,
materiis, offensis, clamatibus, usurpacionibus aut eorum aliquo
per ipsos sive eorum aliquos, debitis, clamatis, attemptis,
usitatis, habitis sive usurpatis ante diem confeccionis presencium prosequantur aut continuant aut prosequi aut
continuari faciant aut causabunt seu eorum aliquis faciet

and of right accustomed : Wherefore we will and by these presents for us, our heirs and successors, we grant to the beforenamed mayor, bailiffs and burgesses of the borough of Cambridge aforesaid and to their successors that they may have, hold, use and enjoy, and may be able to and can fully have, hold, use and enjoy for ever all and every the aforesaid lands, tenements, rents, reversions, liberties, free customs, privileges, authorities, quittances and hereditaments whatsoever aforesaid, according to the tenour and effect of these our letters patent, without hindrance or impediment of us, our heirs or successors, whatsoever: Being unwilling that the said mayor, bailiffs and burgesses of the borough aforesaid or any one or more of them or any burgess of the borough aforesaid by reason of the premises or any of them, by us or by our heirs, justices, sheriffs, escheators or other bailiffs or ministers of us our heirs or successors whomsoever should herein be hindered, molested, vexed or impeded or in any wise disturbed: Willing and by these presents firmly, for us our heirs and successors, ordering and enjoining, as well the Treasurer, Chancellor and Barons of the Exchequer of us, our heirs and successors, and all and singular the other judges and justices of us, our heirs and successors, as our Attorney and Solicitor General for the time being and either of them, and all other our officers and ministers whomsoever, that neither they nor any one or more of them may prosecute or continue or cause to be prosecuted or continued any writ or summons of quo warranto or any other our writ or writs or processes whatever against the aforesaid mayor, bailiffs and burgesses of the borough aforesaid or any of them or the men or inhabitants of the borough aforesaid or any one or more of them, for any causes, things, matters, offences, claims, usurpations or any of them by any one or more of them due, claimed, attempted, used, held, or usurped before the day of

aut causabit: Volentes eciam quod maior, ballivi et burgenses burgi illius vel eorum aliqui per aliquem vel aliquos
iusticiarios, iudices, officiarios vel ministros predictos in aut
pro debito, usu, clameo vel abusu, libertate, franchesia aut
iurisdiccione infra burgum de Cantabrigia predicta suburbia
aut precincta eiusdem ante diem confeccionis harum literarum
nostrarum patencium minime molestentur aut impedientur
aut ad ea aut eorum aliquod respondere compellantur : Et
ulterius de ampliori gracia nostra speciali ac ex certa sciencia
et mero motu nostris volumus et per presentes pro nobis
heredibus et successoribus nostris concedimus prefatis maiori,
ballivis et burgensibus burgi predicti et successoribus suis
quod he litere nostre patentes vel irrotulamenta earumdem erunt in omnibus et per omnià firme, valide, bone,
sufficientes et effectuales in lege erga et contra nos, heredes
et successores nostros, tam in omnibus curiis nostris quam
alibi infra regnum nostrum Anglie absque aliquibus confirmacionibus, licenciis vel tolleracionibus de nobis, heredibus
vel successoribus nostris, imposterum per predictos maiorem,
ballivos et burgenses burgi predicti et successores suos
procurandis impetrandis aut obtinendis : Non obstante male
nominando vel male recitando aut non recitando aliquorum
premissorum aut alicuius partis vel parcelle premissorum
in hiis literis nostris patentibus mencionatorum vel reci-
tatorum: Et non obstante non inveniendo officium vel
inquisicionem premissorum aut alicuius inde parcelle per
que titulus noster invenire debuit ante confeccionem harum
literarum nostrarum patencium : Et non obstante statuto
in parliamento domini Henrici nuper Regis Anglie sexti
antecessoris nostri anno regni sui decimo octavo facto et
edito: Et non obstante statuto de terris et tenementis ad
manum mortuam non ponendis et non obstante aliquibus
aliis defectionibus in non recte nominando naturas, genera,
species, quantitates aut qualitates premissorum aut alicuius
inde parcellam: Proviso semper et firmiter per presentes
pro nobis heredibus et successoribus nostris prefatis maiori,
ballivis et burgensibus burgi predicti et successoribus suis

the making of these presents : Willing also that the mayor, bailiffs and burgesses of that borough or any of them by any one or more justices, judges, officers or ministers aforesaid in or for any debt, usage, claim or abuse, liberty, franchise or jurisdiction within the borough of Cambridge aforesaid, the suburbs or precincts of the same, before the day of the making of these our letters patent should in no way be molested or hindered or be compelled to answer these or any of them : And further of our ampler special grace and from our certain knowledge and mere motion, for us, our heirs and successors, we will and by these presents we grant to the before-named mayor, bailiffs and burgesses of the borough aforesaid and their successors, that these our letters patent or enrolments of the same shall be in all things and by all means, firm, strong, good, sufficient and effectual in law towards and against us, our heirs and successors, as well in all our courts as elsewhere within our realm of England, without any confirmations, licences or tolerations from us our heirs or successors hereafter to be procured, sought or obtained by the aforesaid mayor, bailiffs and burgesses of the borough aforesaid and their successors : Notwithstanding the badly naming or badly reciting or not reciting of any of the premises or of any part or parcel of the premises mentioned or recited in these our letters patent : And notwithstanding the not finding of an office or inquisition of the premises or of any parcel thereof by which our title ought to have been found before the making of these our letters patent : And notwithstanding the statute made and promulgated in the parliament of the lord Henry the Sixth sometime King of England our ancestor in the eighteenth year of his reign : And notwithstanding the statute against putting lands and tenements in mortmain, and notwithstanding any other defects in not rightly naming the natures, kinds, species, quantities or qualities of the premises or of any parcel thereof: Provided always and firmly by these presents for us, our heirs and successors, we enjoin and command the aforesaid mayor, bailiffs and burgesses of the borough afore-

precipimus et mandamus quod he litere nostre patentes aut
aliquod in eisdem contentum non aliqualiter extendat ad
preiudicium, enervacionem seu impedimentum iurisdiccionum,
privilegiorum, libertatum, finium, forisfacturarum, amerciamentorum, proficuum seu hereditamentorum quorumcunque
cancellario, magistris et scholaribus universitatis nostre
Cantabrigie aut alicui seu aliquibus predecessorum suorum
per quodcunque nomen incorporacionis seu per quecunque
nomina incorporacionis per nos aut aliquos aut aliquem
progenitorum aut antecessorum nostrorum nuper regum
seu reginarum Anglie concessos seu mencionatos fore concessos, sed quod iidem cancellarius, magistri et scholares
et successores sui omnibus talibus iurisdiccionibus, privilegiis,
libertatibus, finibus, forisfacturis, amerciamentis, proficuis et
hereditamentis habeant, teneant et gaudeant ac habere, tenere
et gaudere valeant et possint libere, pacifice et quiete, hiis
presentibus aut aliquo in eisdem contento non obstante:
Volumus eciam et per presentes concedimus prefatis maiori,
ballivis et burgensibus burgi de Cantabrigia quod habeant
et habebunt has literas nostras patentes sub magno sigillo
nostro Anglie debito modo factas et sigillatas absque fine
seu feodo magno vel parvo nobis in hanaperio Cancellarie
nostre seu alibi ad usum nostrum quoquomodo reddendo
seu solvendo: Eo quod expressa mencio de vero valore
annuo aut de aliquo[1] alio valore vel certitudine premissorum
sive eorum alicuius aut de aliis donis sive concessionibus
per nos seu per aliquem progenitorum sive predecessorum
nostrorum prefatis maiori, ballivis et burgensibus burgi de
Cantabrigia predicta ante hec tempora factis in presentibus
minime facta existit aut aliquo statuto, actu, ordinacione,
provisione, proclamacione sive restriccione in contrarium
inde antehac habito, facto, edito, ordinato sive proviso aut
aliqua alia re, causa vel materia quacunque in aliquo non
obstante. In cuius rei testimonium has literas nostras fieri
fecimus patentes. Teste me ipso apud Westmonasterium

---

[1] MS. *aliquo aliquo.*

said and their successors, that these our letters patent or
anything contained in them shall not in any way extend to
the prejudice, weakening or hindering of the jurisdictions,
privileges, liberties, fines, forfeitures, amercements, profits or
hereditaments whatsoever granted, or mentioned to be granted,
to the chancellor, masters and scholars of our university of
Cambridge or to any one or more of their predecessors, by
whatever name of incorporation or by whatever names of
incorporation, by us or any one or more of our ancestors or
predecessors sometime kings or queens of England, but that
the said chancellor, masters and scholars and their successors
may have, hold and enjoy and may be able to and can have,
hold and enjoy all such jurisdictions, privileges, liberties, fines,
forfeitures, amercements, profits and hereditaments freely,
peacefully and quietly, these presents or anything contained
in them notwithstanding: We will also and by these presents
we grant to the beforenamed mayor, bailiffs and burgesses
of the borough of Cambridge that they may have and shall
have these our letters patent under our great seal of England
in the proper manner made and sealed without fine or fee
great or small in any way to be rendered or paid to us into
the hanaper of our Chancery or elsewhere to our use : Any
omission in these presents of an express mention of the
true annual value or of any other value or certitude of the
premises or any of them, or of other gifts or grants, made
by us or by any of our ancestors or predecessors before these
times to the beforenamed mayor, bailiffs and burgesses of the
borough of Cambridge aforesaid, or any statute, act, ordinance,
provision, proclamation or restriction heretofore had, made,
issued, ordained or provided or any other thing, cause or
matter whatsoever in any wise to the contrary hereof notwithstanding. In witness whereof we have caused these our
letters to be made patent. Witness myself at Westminster

tricesimo die Aprilis anno regni nostri Anglie, Francie et Hibernie tercio et Scocie tricesimo octavo.

T. RAVENSCROFTE.

per breve de privato sigillo &c.

Taxatur finis pro confirmacione priorum libertatum iiij li.

T. ELLESMERE, *Cancellarius.*

XXVII.   LITTERE PATENTES CAROLI PRIMI.

1632
Feb. 6

[1] Carolus dei gracia Anglie, Scotie, Francie et Hibernie Rex, fidei defensor, &c. omnibus ad quos presentes pervenerint salutem. Cum burgus noster Cantabrigie in comitatu nostro Cantabrigie sit burgus antiquus et populosus, cumque maior, ballivi et burgenses eiusdem burgi diversas libertates, franchesias, consuetudines, immunitates et preheminencias habuerunt ac usi et gavisi fuerunt, tam racione et pretextu diversarum cartarum et literarum patencium per diversos progenitores et antecessores nostros nuper Reges vel Reginas Anglie antehac factarum, concessarum seu confirmatarum quam racione et pretextu diversarum prescripcionum, usuum et consuetudinum in eodem burgo ab antiquo usitatarum et consuetarum: Cumque dilecti subditi nostri modo maior, ballivi et burgenses eiusdem burgi nobis humiliter supplicaverunt quatenus nos, pro meliori regimine, gubernacione et melioracione eiusdem burgi, graciam et munificenciam nostram regiam in hac parte graciose extendere et exhibere velimus, quodque nos predictos maiorem, ballivos et burgenses eiusdem burgi per quodcunque nomen sive per quecunque nomina modo in-

---

[1] Rot. Pat. 7 Car. I., p. 12.   Copy in Cross Book, p. 192.   Original not in Borough Archives.

on the thirtieth day of April in the third year of our reign of England, France and Ireland and the thirty-eighth of Scotland.

T. RAVENSCROFT.

by writ of Privy Seal, &c.

The fine for confirmation of former liberties is taxed £4.

T. ELLESMERE, *Chancellor.*

XXVII.   LETTERS PATENT OF CHARLES THE FIRST.

[1]Charles by the grace of God of England, Scotland, France and Ireland King, Defender of the Faith, &c. to all to whom these presents shall come, greeting.   Whereas our borough of Cambridge in our county of Cambridge is an ancient and populous borough, and whereas the mayor, bailiffs and burgesses of the said borough have had and have used and enjoyed divers liberties, franchises, customs, immunities and preeminences, as well by reason and pretext of divers charters and letters patent heretofore made, granted or confirmed by divers our ancestors and predecessors sometime Kings or Queens of England as by reason and pretext of divers prescriptions, uses and customs in the said borough from old time used and accustomed: And whereas our beloved subjects the now mayor, bailiffs and burgesses of the said borough have most humbly supplicated us that we, for the better ruling, government and amelioration of the said borough, would be willing graciously to extend and shew our royal grace and munificence in this respect, and that we would be willing to make, ordain, constitute, erect and create the aforesaid mayor, bailiffs and burgesses of the said borough by whatever name or by whatever names they may now be

1632
Feb. 6

---

[1] See Cooper, *Annals*, iii. 245—6.

corporati sint vel antehac incorporati fuerunt, et utrum
antehac incorporati fuerint sive non, in unum corpus corporatum et politicum per nomen maioris, ballivorum et
burgensium burgi Cantabrigie facere, ordinare, constituere,
redigere et creare velimus cum augmentacionibus et addicionibus quorumdam libertatum, privilegiorum et franchesiarum
prout nobis melius fieri et fore videbitur : Nos igitur publicum
bonum et utilitatem eiusdem burgi graciose desiderantes,
volentesque quod de cetero imperpetuum continuo habeatur
unus certus et indubitatus modus de et pro regimine et
gubernacione eiusdem burgi et populi nostri ibidem inhabitantis et aliorum illuc influentium, et quod burgus predictus
de cetero imperpetuum sit, erit et permaneat burgus pacis et
quietis ad formidinem et terrorem malorum delinquentium et
in premium bonorum : Sperantesque eciam quod si amplior
ex concessione nostra gaudere poterint libertates et privilegia tunc ad servicia que poterint nobis, heredibus et
successoribus nostris impendenda et exhibenda specialius
fortiusque sentiant se obligatos : De gracia nostra speciali ac
ex certa sciencia et mero motu nostris voluimus, ordinavimus,
constituimus, declaravimus et concessimus ac per presentes
pro nobis heredibus et successoribus nostris volumus et
ordinamus, constitu[i]mus, declaramus et concedimus quod
dictus burgus Cantabrigie sit, erit et permaneat de cetero
imperpetuum liber burgus de se, et quod maior, ballivi et
burgenses burgi predicti[1] et successores sui de cetero imperpetuum sint et erunt vigore presencium unum corpus corporatum et politicum in re, facto et nomine per nomen maioris, ballivorum et burgensium burgi Cantabrigie ac eos per
nomen maioris, ballivorum et burgensium burgi Cantabrigie
unum corpus corporatum et politicum in re, facto et nomine,
realiter et ad plenum, pro [nobis] heredibus et successoribus
nostris incorporamus, erigimus, facimus, ordinamus, constitu[i]mus, creamus, confirmamus, ratificamus et declaramus per
presentes et quod per idem nomen habeant successionem

---

[1] For "maior...predicti" the Letters Patent of Charles II. read "burgenses et
inhabitantes burgi de Cantabrigia predicta."

incorporated, or heretofore have been incorporated, and whether they have heretofore been incorporated or not, into one body corporate and politic by the name of the mayor, bailiffs and burgesses of the borough of Cambridge, with augmentations and additions of certain liberties, privileges and franchises as to us shall seem best : We therefore graciously desiring the public good and advantage of the said borough, and willing that henceforth for ever continually there shall be held one certain and undoubted mode of and for the ruling and government of the said borough and of our people there dwelling and of others resorting thither, and that the borough aforesaid henceforth for ever may be, shall be and remain a borough of peace and quietness to the fear and terror of evil-doers and to the reward of the good : And hoping also that if, from our grant, they shall be able to enjoy liberties and privileges more amply, then they may feel themselves more specially and more strongly bound to pay and render the services which they may be able to do to us, our heirs and successors : Of our special grace and from our certain knowledge and mere motion we have willed, ordained, constituted, declared and granted and by these presents for us, our heirs and successors, we will and ordain, constitute, declare and grant that the said borough of Cambridge may be, shall be and remain henceforth for ever a free borough of itself, and that the mayor, bailiffs and burgesses of the borough aforesaid[1] and their successors henceforth for ever may be and shall be, by virtue of these presents, one body corporate and politic, in deed, fact and name, by the name of the mayor, bailiffs and burgesses of the borough of Cambridge, and by the name of the mayor, bailiffs and burgesses of the borough of Cambridge we incorporate, erect, make, ordain, constitute, create, confirm, ratify and declare them by these presents one body corporate and politic in deed, fact and name, really and fully, for [us] our heirs and successors : And that by the same name they shall have perpetual succession :

[1] For "mayor...aforesaid" the Letters Patent of Charles II. read "burgesses and inhabitants of the borough of Cambridge aforesaid."

perpetuam: Et quod ipsi per nomen maioris, ballivorum et burgensium burgi Cantabrigie sint et erunt perpetuis futuris temporibus persone habiles et in lege capaces ac corpus corporatum et politicum et in lege capax ad habendum, perquirendum, recipiendum, possidendum, gaudendum et retinendum[1] mesuagia, terras, tenementa, libertates, privilegia, iurisdicciones, franchesias et alia hereditamenta quecunque, cuiuscunque sint generis, nature vel speciei, sibi et successoribus suis, in feodo et perpetuitate seu ad terminum vite, vitarum, anni vel annorum vel aliter quocunque modo, necnon bona et catalla quecunque, necnon ad dandum, concedendum, dimittendum, alienandum, locandum, assignandum et disponendum eadem[1] mesuagia, terras, tenementa et hereditamenta necnon bona et catalla quecunque ac ad omnia et singula alia facta et res facienda et exequenda per nomen predictum: Et quod per idem nomen maioris, ballivorum et burgensium burgi Cantabrigie placitare et implacitari, respondere et responderi, defendere et defendi valeant et possint in quibuscunque curiis, placeis et locis coram nobis heredibus et successoribus nostris ac coram quibuscunque iudicibus et iusticiariis et aliis officiariis, personis et ministris nostris, heredum et successorum nostrorum, aut aliorum quorumcunque in omnibus et singulis accionibus, querelis, sectis, placitis, causis, materiis et demandis quibuscunque, cuiuscunque sunt aut erunt generis, nature vel speciei eisdem et in tam amplis modo et forma prout alii ligei nostri huius regni nostri Anglie, persone habiles et in lege capaces sive aliquod aliud corpus corporatum et politicum infra hoc regnum nostrum Anglie habere, perquirere, recipere, possidere, gaudere, retinere, dare, concedere, dimittere, alienare, assignare et disponere, placitare et implacitari, respondere et responderi, defendere et defendi, facere, permittere, sive exequi possint et valeant, prout antehac de antiquo consueverunt: Et quod maior, ballivi et burgenses burgi predicti et successores sui de cetero imperpetuum habeant comune sigillum pro causis et negociis

---

[1] The Letters Patent of Charles II. insert "maneria."

And that they themselves by the name of the mayor, bailiffs
and burgesses of the borough of Cambridge may be and
shall be in all future times persons fit and in law capable and
a body corporate and politic and in law capable to have,
acquire, receive, possess, enjoy and retain[1] messuages, lands,
tenements, liberties, privileges, jurisdictions, franchises and
other hereditaments whatsoever, of whatsoever kind, nature or
species they may be, for themselves and their successors in
fee and perpetuity or for a term of life or lives, of a year
or years, or otherwise, in whatever manner; also goods and
chattels whatsoever; and to give, grant, demise, alienate, let,
assign and dispose of the said[1] messuages, lands, tenements
and hereditaments, and goods and chattels whatsoever, and
to do and carry out under the name aforesaid all and singular
other acts and deeds: And that under the said name of the
mayor, bailiffs and burgesses of the borough of Cambridge
they may be able to and can plead and be impleaded, answer
and be answered, defend and be defended in whatsoever courts,
places and localities before us our heirs and successors and
before whatsoever judges and justices and other officers, persons
and ministers of us, our heirs and successors, or of others
whomsoever in all and singular actions, complaints, suits, pleas,
causes, matters and demands whatsoever, of whatsoever kind,
nature or species they are or shall be, by the same and in as
ample manner and form as our other lieges of this our realm
of England, persons fit and in law capable, or any other body
corporate and politic within this our kingdom of England
can and are able to have, acquire, receive, possess, enjoy,
retain, give, grant, demise, alienate, assign and dispose,
plead and be impleaded, answer and be answered, defend and
be defended, do, permit or execute, as heretofore from old
time they have been accustomed: And that the mayor, bailiffs
and burgesses of the borough aforesaid and their successors
henceforth for ever may have a common seal to be kept for
carrying out the causes and businesses of themselves and of

[1] The Letters Patent of Charles II. insert "manors."

suis et successorum suorum quibuscunque agendis serviturum:
Et quod bene liceat et licebit eisdem maiori, ballivis et
burgensibus burgi predicti et successoribus suis sigillum illud
ad libitum suum de tempore in tempus frangere, mutare et de
novo facere prout eis melius fieri et fore videbitur expediens,
prout antehac de antiquo habuerunt et consueverunt: Et
ulterius de uberiori gracia nostra volumus ac per presentes pro
nobis heredibus et successoribus nostris concedimus prefatis
maiori, ballivis et burgensibus burgi predicti et successoribus
suis quod de cetero imperpetuum sit et erit infra burgum predictum unus de burgensibus burgi predicti qui erit et vocabitur maior burgi predicti, quodque sint et erunt duodecim de
capitalibus burgensibus burgi predicti in forma inferius in hiis
presentibus expressa eligendi, preter maiorem burgi predicti,
qui erunt et nominabuntur aldermanni ac de privato consilio
burgi predicti prout de antiquo ut prefertur consueverunt,
quodque similiter sint et erunt infra burgum predictum
viginti quatuor de aliis discretioribus burgensibus eiusdem
burgi qui erunt et nominabuntur de comuni concilio burgi
predicti: Et volumus ac per presentes pro nobis, heredibus et
successoribus nostris concedimus quod predicti viginti quatuor
de comuni consilio burgi predicti pro tempore existente erunt
de tempore in tempus assistentes et auxiliantes maiori et
aldermannis dicti burgi pro tempore existente in omnibus
causis, rebus, negociis et materiis quibuscunque dictum
burgum tangentibus seu quoquomodo concernentibus tocies
quocies et quandocunque per maiorem burgi predicti pro
tempore existente requisiti fuerint prout usitatum et consuetum hactenus fuit et de antiquo gavisi fuerunt: Volumus
eciam ac per presentes pro nobis heredibus et successoribus
nostris statuimus et ordinamus quod de cetero imperpetuum
sint et erunt duo thesaurarii in idem corpus corporatum et
politicum maiori, ballivis et burgensibus burgi predicti et
successoribus suis incorporati et uniti infra burgum Cantabrigie predicte et eos thesaurarios burgi predicti plene et
realiter incorporamus, unimus et consolidamus imperpetuum
per presentes eligendos per maiorem, ballivos et burgenses

their successors whatsoever : And that it may be and shall be
lawful for the said mayor, bailiffs and burgesses of the
borough aforesaid and their successors to break, change and
make anew from time to time that seal at their pleasure,
as to them shall seem most expedient, as heretofore from
old time they have had and were wont to have : And further
of our fuller grace we will, and by these presents for us, our
heirs and successors we grant, to the beforenamed mayor,
bailiffs and burgesses of the borough aforesaid and to their
successors, that henceforth for ever there may be and shall
be within the borough aforesaid one of the burgesses of the
borough aforesaid who shall be, and shall be called, mayor
of the borough aforesaid, and that there may be and shall
be twelve of the chief burgesses of the borough aforesaid
to be chosen in the form expressed below in these presents,
besides the mayor of the borough aforesaid, who shall be
and shall be called aldermen and of the private council
of the borough aforesaid, as from old time, as it is said,
they were accustomed, and that likewise there may be and
shall be within the borough aforesaid twenty-four of the
other more discreet burgesses of the said borough who shall
be and shall be called of the common council of the borough
aforesaid : And we will and by these presents for us, our heirs
and successors we grant, that the aforesaid twenty-four of
the common council of the borough aforesaid for the time
being shall be from time to time assisters and helpers to the
mayor and aldermen of the said borough for the time being
in all causes, things, businesses and matters whatsoever
touching or in any way concerning the said borough as often
as and whensoever they have been called on by the mayor of
the borough aforesaid for the time being as has been used
and accustomed hitherto and as they have enjoyed from old
time : We will also and by these presents for us our heirs and
successors we enact and ordain that henceforth for ever there
may be and shall be two treasurers in the said body corporate and politic, to be incorporated and united to the mayor,
bailiffs and burgesses of the borough aforesaid, and their

burgi predicti vel maiorem partem eorumdem pro tempore existente ad omnia et singula quecunque ad predictum officium thesaurarii spectantia exequenda et performanda sacramentis suis, non solum pro fideli et debita execucione officii[1] sui coram maiore burgi nostri predicti vel deputato suo pro tempore existente, verum eciam pro fideli et plena conservacione libertatum et privilegiorum universitatis nostre Cantabrigie coram cancellario vel procancellario universitatis nostre predicte vel deputato suo in universitate nostra predicta existente iisdem die, loco, modo et forma ac verbis quibus maior et ballivi burgi nostri predicti singulis annis sacramenta sua respective prestare tenentur, super sancta Dei evangelia prius prestanda: Quibus quidem cancellario vel procancellario aut deputato suo pro tempore existente ac maiori burgi nostri predicti vel deputato suo pro tempore existente plenam potestatem et auctoritatem damus et concedimus per presentes huiusmodi respective sacramenta eisdem thesaurariis singulis annis imposterum tocies quoties novi thesaurarii nominati, electi, deputati et admissi fuerint administrare, et quod post talia sacramenta sic ut prefertur respective prestita et non antea bene liceat et licebit prefato thesaurario sic electo, nominato et prefecto, eligendo, nominando et proficiendo coram maiore et ballivis in curiis de recordo infra burgum predictum tentis et tenendis aliquam personam sive aliquas personas quascunque non existentes scholares vel eorum servientes, ministros vel famulos vel personas per cartas et privilegia cancellarii, magistrorum et scholarium universitatis nostre Cantabrigie predicte concessa privilegiatas in predictis curiis impetere, implacitare et prosequi pro aliqua causa, debito sive denariorum summa aut aliqua alia re, materia sive penalitate, forisfacta seu forisfacienda pro non debita observacione ordinacionum et constitucionum predicti burgi in hiis presentibus inferius mencionatarum, proviso semper quod per hanc licenciam et concessionem nostram dictis thesaurariis aut eorum deputatis

---

[1] MS. *officio.*

successors, within the borough of Cambridge aforesaid, and
the said treasurers of the borough aforesaid we fully and really
incorporate, unite and consolidate for ever by these presents
to be chosen by the mayor, bailiffs and burgesses of the
borough aforesaid or the greater part of them for the time
being, to execute and perform all and singular whatsoever
relates to the aforesaid office of treasurer, having first taken
their oaths on the holy Gospels of God, not only for the
faithful and due execution of their office before the mayor
of our borough aforesaid or his deputy for the time being,
but also for the faithful and full preservation of the liberties
and privileges of our university of Cambridge before the
chancellor or vicechancellor of our university aforesaid or his
deputy being in our university aforesaid, on the same day
at the same place in the same manner and form and words by
which the mayor and bailiffs of our borough aforesaid are
bound every year to take their oaths respectively : To whom,
namely, the chancellor or vicechancellor or his deputy for
the time being and to the mayor of our borough aforesaid or
his deputy for the time being we give and grant by these
presents full power and authority to administer such oaths
respectively to the said treasurers each year for ever so often
as new treasurers have been nominated, elected, deputed and
admitted, and that after such oaths as is aforesaid have been
respectively taken and not before, it may be and shall be
lawful to the aforesaid treasurer so elected, nominated and
appointed, or to be elected, nominated and appointed, to
summon, implead and prosecute before the mayor and
bailiffs in the courts of record held and to be held within
the borough aforesaid any person or persons whomsoever,
not being scholars or their servants, attendants or domestics
or persons privileged in the aforesaid courts by the charters
and privileges of the chancellor, masters and scholars of our
university of Cambridge aforesaid granted, for any cause,
debt or sum of money or any other thing, matter or penalty
forfeited or to be forfeited for not duly observing the ordinances and constitutions of the aforesaid borough below

nullatenus attentent in premissis aut eorum aliquibus impetere, implacitare vel prosequi cancellarium, procancellarium, ministros aut scholares universitatis nostre Cantabrigie aut eorum aliquem, vel aliquos alios persones[1] per dictam universitatem nostram vel per privilegia et immunitates a nobis vel predecessoribus nostris eisdem concessas quovismodo privilegiatas et exemptas dummodo talia debita sive summe, penalitates sive forisfacture non excedant summam quadraginta solidorum: Et ulterius volumus ac per presentes pro nobis heredibus et successoribus nostris concedimus prefatis maiori, ballivis et burgensibus burgi predicti et successoribus suis quod maior, ballivi et burgenses burgi predicti pro tempore existente et successores sui seu eorum maior pars, quorum maiorem burgi predicti pro tempore existente semper unum esse volumus super summonicionem publicam per maiorem eiusdem burgi pro tempore existente inde fiendam ad hoc congregati et assemblati habebit et habebunt plenam potestatem et facultatem condendi, constituendi, obtinendi, faciendi et stabiliendi de tempore in tempus imperpetuum talia et huiusmodi leges, statuta, iura, constituciones, decreta et ordinaciones racionabiliter in scripta quecunque que eis vel maiori parti eorumdem quorum maiorem burgi predicti pro tempore existente unum esse volumus, bona et salubria, utilia, honesta et necessaria iuxta eorum sanas discreciones fore videbuntur pro bono regimine et gubernacione maioris ballivorum et burgensium burgi predicti et omnium et singulorum aliorum burgensium, officiar[ior]um, ministrorum, artificum, et inhabitantium et residentium quorumcumque infra burgum predictum et libertates eiusdem, salvis tamen et semper exceptis personis quibuscunque in dicta universitate nostra vel suburbiis et iurisdiccione eiusdem per privilegia predicta quocunque modo privilegiatis et exemptis, pro uberiori bono publico, communi utilitate ac bono regimine burgi predicti ac eciam pro meliori disposicione, locacione et dimissione terrarum, possessionum,

---

[1] Sic MS.

mentioned in these presents, provided always that by this our licence and grant to the said treasurers or their deputies they shall in no way attempt in the premises or any otherwise to summon implead or prosecute the chancellor, vicechancellor, servants or scholars of our university of Cambridge or any of them or any other persons in any way privileged and exempted by our said university or by privileges and immunities granted to them by us or our predecessors, and provided that such debts, or sums, penalties or forfeits do not exceed the sum of forty shillings: And further we will and by these presents for us our heirs and successors we grant to the aforenamed mayor, bailiffs and burgesses of the borough aforesaid and to their successors that the mayor, bailiffs and burgesses of the borough aforesaid for the time being and their successors or the greater part of them, of whom we will that the mayor of the borough aforesaid for the time being shall always be one, on a public summons to be made thereof by the mayor of the said borough for the time being, gathered and assembled for this purpose, shall have full power and capacity to compose, constitute, obtain, make and establish from time to time for ever such and such kind of laws, statutes, rules, constitutions, decrees and ordinances whatsoever reasonably in writing, which to them or to the greater part of them (of whom we will that the mayor of the borough aforesaid for the time being shall be one) shall appear to be good and salutary, useful, just and necessary according to their sound discretions for the good rule and government of the mayor, bailiffs and burgesses of the borough aforesaid and of all and singular the other burgesses, officers, servants, workmen and inhabitants and residents whomsoever within the borough aforesaid and the liberties of the same (save however and always excepted the persons whomsoever in our said university or the suburbs and jurisdiction of the same by the aforesaid privileges in any manner privileged and exempted) for the ampler public good, the common utility and the good ruling of the borough aforesaid, and also for the better disposition, letting and

revencionum et hereditamentorum prefatorum maioris, ballivorum et burgensium burgi predicti ac rerum et causarum aliarum quarumcunque burgum predictum statum, iura et interesse eiusdem burgi tangencium seu aliquo modo concernencium : Quodque maior, ballivi et burgenses eiusdem burgi pro tempore existente vel eorum maior pars, quorum maiorem pro tempore existente unum esse volumus, quotiescunque huiusmodi leges, statuta, iura, ordinaciones et constituciones condiderint, fecerint, ordinaverint vel stabiliverint in forma predicta huiusmodi et tales penas, puniciones et penalitates per imprisonamentum corporis vel corporum vel per fines et amerciamenta vel per eorum utrumque erga et super omnes delinquentes, non existentes scholares vel personas sic ut prefertur privilegiis universitatis nostre predicte privilegiatos, contra huiusmodi leges, iura, ordinaciones et constituciones sive eorum aliquod vel aliqua qualia et que eisdem maiori, ballivis et burgensibus pro tempore existente vel maiori parti eorum (quorum maiorem pro tempore existente unum esse volumus) necessarie opportune et requisite pro observacione earumdem legum, ordinacionum et constitucionum melius fore videbitur facere, ordinare, limitare et providere : Ac eadem penalitates, fines et amerciamenta per thesaurarios pro tempore existente de tempore in tempus levanda et colligenda et super recusacionem seu denegacionem et non solucionem eorumdem, quod tunc bene liceat et licebit prefatis thesaurariis talem personam sive tales personas sic recusantem vel recusantes, modo non fuerint scholares vel persone sic ut prefertur per privilegia universitatis nostre privilegiati, impetere et secundum legem in eo casu provisam prosequi in curiis de recordo coram maiore et ballivis burgi predicti Cantabrigie et successoribus suis tentis et tenendis, et pro recuperacione huiusmodi finium, forisfacturarum, penalitatum, amerciamentorum, et denariorum summarum constitutarum et constituendarum, ac eadem sic in debita legis forma recuperata ad opus et usum maioris, ballivorum et burgensium burgi Cantabrigie predicte et successorum suorum de tempore in tempus solvere absque

demising of lands, possessions, reversions and hereditaments of the beforenamed mayor, bailiffs and burgesses of the borough aforesaid and of other matters and causes whatsoever touching or in any way concerning the borough aforesaid, the estate, rights and interests of the said borough: And that the mayor, bailiffs and burgesses of the said borough for the time being or the greater part of them, of whom we will that the mayor for the time being shall be one, as often as they shall have ordained, composed, made or established such laws, statutes, rights, ordinances and constitutions in form aforesaid, may make, ordain, limit and provide such and such like pains, punishments and penalties by imprisonment of the body or bodies or by fines and amercements or by either of them for and upon all delinquents, not being scholars or persons as is aforesaid privileged by the privileges of our university aforesaid, against such laws, rights, ordinances and constitutions or any of them or any such like and which to the said mayor, bailiffs and burgesses for the time being or to the greater part of them (of whom we will that the mayor for the time being shall be one) shall appear to be necessary, fit and desirable for the observance of the said laws, ordinances and constitutions: And that the same penalties, fines and amercements shall be levied and collected by the treasurers for the time being from time to time, and upon the refusal or denial and non-payment of the same, that then it may be and shall be fully lawful to the beforenamed treasurers to sue such person or persons so refusing (provided they be not scholars or persons so as is aforesaid privileged by the privileges of our university) and according to the law provided in that case to prosecute in the courts of record held and to be held before the mayor and bailiffs of the aforesaid borough of Cambridge and their successors, and for the recovery of such fines, forfeitures, penalties, amercements and sums of money appointed and to be appointed, and the same when thus recovered in due form of law to pay to the benefit and use of the mayor bailiffs and burgesses of the borough of Cambridge aforesaid and of their

impedimento nostro, heredum vel successorum nostrorum aut alicuius vel aliquorum officiariorum vel ministrorum nostrorum, heredum vel successorum nostrorum, et absque aliquo compoto nobis heredibus seu successoribus nostris inde reddendo : Que omnia et singula leges, ordinaciones, iura et constituciones sic ut prefertur facienda observari volumus sub penis in eisdem continendis : Ita tamen quod leges, ordinaciones, statuta, constituciones, imprisonamenta, fines et amerciamenta huiusmodi sint racionabilia et non repugnancia nec contraria legibus, statutis, consuetudinibus sive iuribus regni nostri Anglie, seu racionabilibus et laudabilibus prescripcionibus et consuetudinibus in eodem burgo antiquo usitatis et consuetis : Et ita tamen quod sint [non] repugnantes vel contraria legibus, statutis, cartis, privilegiis, libertatibus, consuetudinibus, prescripcionibus sive iuribus sic ut prefertur cancellario, magistris et scholaribus dicte universitatis nostre[1] concessis, factis, usitatis vel observatis : Ac pro meliori execucione regie voluntatis nostre in hac parte assignavimus, nominavimus, constituimus et fecimus ac per presentes pro nobis heredibus et successoribus nostris assignamus, nominamus et constitu[i]mus et facimus dilectos nobis Thomam Watson et Ricardum Pottall fore et esse modernos thesaurarios burgi predicti : Proviso semper quod infra triginta dies post datum presencium prestabunt sacramentum per thesaurarios sic ut prefertur respective prestandum : continuandos in eodem officio a dato presencium usque ad festum Sancti Michaelis Archangeli proxime sequentem, et exinde quousque duo alii de burgensibus burgi predicti in officio thesaurarii eiusdem burgi debito modo electi, prefecti et iurati fuerint secundum ordinaciones et constituciones in hiis presentibus superius expressas et declaratas : Et ulterius volumus ac per presentes pro nobis heredibus et successoribus nostris concedimus prefatis maiori, ballivis et burgensibus burgi predicti et successoribus suis quod si contigerit maiorem vel aliquem ballivorum burgi predicti aliquo tempore imposterum infra

---

[1] *nostris* MS.

successors from time to time without impediment of us, our
heirs or successors or any one or more of the officers or
servants of us, our heirs or successors, and without any
reckoning in that matter to be returned to us, our heirs or
successors : Which laws all and singular, ordinances, rights
and constitutions to be made so as aforesaid we will to be
observed under the pains therein to be contained : But so
that such laws, ordinances, statutes, constitutions, imprisonments, fines and amercements be reasonable and not repugnant nor contrary to the laws, statutes, customs or rights of
our realm of England, or the reasonable and laudable prescriptions and customs in the said ancient borough used and
accustomed : And so that they be not repugnant or contrary
to the laws, statutes, charters, privileges, liberties, customs,
prescriptions or rights so as is aforesaid granted to, made,
used or observed by the chancellor, masters and scholars of
our said university : And for the better execution of our
royal will in this behalf we have assigned, named, constituted
and made and by these presents for us our heirs and successors we assign, name, and constitute and make our beloved
Thomas Watson and Richard Pottall to become and to be
the now treasurers of the borough aforesaid : Provided
always that within thirty days after the giving of these
presents they shall each take the oath to be taken by the
treasurers as is aforesaid : to be continued in the same office
from the date of these presents until the feast of Saint
Michael the Archangel next following, and thenceforward
until two other of the burgesses of the borough aforesaid
shall have been elected, appointed and sworn into the office
of treasurer of the same borough in due manner according
to the ordinances and constitutions above expressed and
declared in these presents : And further we will and by these
presents for us our heirs and successors we grant to the
aforenamed mayor, bailiffs and burgesses of the borough
aforesaid and their successors that if it happen that the
mayor or any of the bailiffs of the borough aforesaid at any
time hereafter within one year after he shall have been made

unum annum postquam ad officium maioralitatis vel ballivatis burgi predicti prefectus et iuratus fuerit fore egrotum
et invalidum aut pro aliqua causa necessaria et racionabili
interesse non possit aut possint utpote officium suum in
propria persona sua exequi et intendere nequeat vel nequeant,
quod tunc et tocies in casibus predictis bene liceat et licebit
prefato maiori cum assensu trium aldermannorum pro tempore
existente et prefatis ballivis cum assensu maioris burgi predicti pro tempore existente eligere, appunctuare, nominare
et preficere unum alium probum et idoneum virum de aldermannis burgi predicti qui officium maioris burgi predicti
antetunc gesserit in loco ipsius maioris et unum alium
probum et idoneum virum de burgensibus burgi predicti qui
officium ballivi burgi predicti antetunc gesserit in loco ipsius
ballivi sic languidi, egroti aut absentis in loco maioris et ut
deputatum pro maiore burgi, et in loco ballivi burgi predicti
ut deputatum pro ballivo burgi predicti ad omnia et singula
facienda et agenda durante tempore invalitudinis aut absencie
maioris et ballivi predicti que ad officium maioris et ballivi
burgi predicti realiter pertinebunt seu spectabunt aut devenire
possint et valeant quodque quilibet talis deputatus in loco et
officio maioralitatis vel ballivatis burgi illius sic ut prefertur
nominatus, constitutus et prefectus et constituendus sacramentum corporale in forma predicta prius coram maiore
burgi predicti pro tempore existente necnon coram cancellario
vel procancellario universitatis nostre predicte vel deputato
suo pro tempore existente iuxta modum et formam in ea
parte usitatam pro iuramentis maioris et ballivorum burgi
predicti prestans officium illud habeat et exerceat durante
invalitudine et absencia maioris et ballivi predicti et sic tocies
quoties casus ita accidit : Et ulterius volumus ac per presentes
pro nobis heredibus et successoribus nostris concedimus prefatis maiori, ballivis et burgensibus burgi predicti et successoribus suis, quod maior, ballivi et burgenses burgi predicti
pro tempore existente vel maior pars eorum (quorum
maiorem pro tempore existente unum esse volumus) de
tempore in tempus perpetuis futuris temporibus potestatem

and sworn into the office of the mayoralty or bailiwick of the borough aforesaid shall become sick and weak or for any necessary and reasonable cause may not be able to take part so that he shall be unable to discharge and attend to his office in his own person that then and always in the cases aforesaid it may be and shall be fully lawful to the aforenamed mayor with the assent of three aldermen for the time being and to the aforenamed bailiffs with the assent of the mayor of the borough aforesaid for the time being to choose, appoint, nominate and make another upright and fit man, one of the aldermen of the borough aforesaid who shall formerly have held the office of mayor of the borough aforesaid, in the place of the mayor himself, and another upright and fit man, one of the burgesses of the borough aforesaid who shall formerly have held the office of bailiff of the borough aforesaid, in the place of the bailiff himself thus feeble, sick or absent in place of the mayor and as deputy for the mayor of the borough, and in place of the bailiff of the borough aforesaid as deputy for the bailiff of the borough aforesaid, to do and perform all and singular during the time of the sickness or absence of the mayor and bailiff aforesaid which really shall pertain or relate to the office of mayor and bailiff of the borough aforesaid or may or can happen, and that each such deputy in the place and office of the mayoralty or bailiwick of that borough named, constituted and appointed and to be constituted as is aforesaid taking his corporal oath in the form aforesaid first before the mayor of the borough aforesaid for the time being, and before the chancellor or vicechancellor of our university aforesaid or his deputy for the time being according to the manner and form used on that behalf for the oaths of the mayor and bailiffs of the borough aforesaid, may have and exercise that office during the sickness and absence of the mayor and bailiff aforesaid and so as often as the case thus happens: And further we will and by these presents for us our heirs and successors we grant to the beforenamed mayor, bailiffs and burgesses of the borough aforesaid and to their successors, that the mayor, bailiffs and

et authoritatem habeant et habebunt annuatim et quolibet
anno in die Martis in secunda septimana proxima post festum
pasche comuniter vocatum Hock Tuseday eligendi et nomi-
nandi, et quod eligere et nominare possint et valeant duos de
discretioribus et magis probioribus burgensium burgi predicti
qui erunt thesaurarii burgi predicti pro uno anno integro a
festo Sancti Michaelis Archangeli tunc proximo sequente,
quodque illi postquam sic ut prefertur electi et nominati
fuerint in [officio] thesaurarii burgi predicti antequam[1] ad
officium illud exequendum admittantur sacramentum corporale in die festi Sancti Michaelis tunc proximo sequente
nominacionem et eleccionem predictam in guildhalda burgi
predicti coram cancellario vel procancellario universitatis nostre
predicte, vel deputato suo pro tempore existente, et coram
maiore ville nostre predicte, vel deputato suo pro tempore
existente, sacramentum corporale respective in presentibus
superius expressum, eisdem modo et forma prout prefertur
prestabunt coram maiore eiusdem burgi pro tempore existente, in presencia huiusmodi aldermannorum et ceterorum
de comuni consilio eiusdem burgi qui tunc presentes fuerint
ad officium illud bene, recte et fideliter in omnibus officium
illud tangentibus exequendum prestabunt et eorum alter
prestabit : Et quod post huiusmodi sacramentum prestitum
officii thesaurarii burgi predicti pro uno anno integro tunc
proximo sequente officium thesaurarii burgi predicti exequi
possint et valeant et exinde quousque duo alii de burgensibus
burgi predicti ad officium thesaurarii burgi predicti prefecti
fuerint iuxta ordinaciones in presentibus expressas et declaratas : Et si contigerit predictis thesaurariis burgi predicti
pro tempore existente vel eorum alteri aliquo tempore imposterum infra unum annum postquam ad officium thesaurarii burgi predicti ut prefertur prefecti fuerint obire, quod
tunc et tocies bene liceat et licebit predictis maiori, ballivis
et burgensibus eiusdem burgi pro tempore existente semel
vel maiori parti[2] eorumdem infra quatuordecim dies proxime
subsequentes ipsius vel ipsorum thesaurariorum mortem,

_____

[1] *antiquam* MS.   [2] *maiorem partem* MS.

burgesses of the borough aforesaid for the time being or the greater part of them (of whom we will that the mayor for the time being be one) from time to time in future times may have and shall have power and authority annually and in each year to elect and nominate on the Tuesday in the second week next after the feast of Easter commonly called Hock Tuesday, and that they may and can elect and nominate two of the more discreet and more upright of the burgesses of the borough aforesaid, who shall be treasurers of the borough aforesaid for a whole year from the feast of Saint Michael the Archangel then next following, and that they after that they have been elected and nominated as is aforesaid to the office of treasurer of the borough aforesaid before they be admitted to carry out that office shall take their corporal oath on the day of the feast of Saint Michael then next following the nomination and election aforesaid in the guild-hall of the borough aforesaid before the chancellor or vice-chancellor of our aforesaid university, or his deputy for the time being, and before the mayor of our town aforesaid, or his deputy for the time being, and both of them shall take the corporal oath respectively expressed before in these presents, in the same manner and form as is aforesaid before the mayor of the said borough for the time being, in the presence of such aldermen and others of the common council of the said borough who shall then be present, for the fulfilling of that office well, rightly and faithfully in all things touching that office: And that after such oath taken of the office of treasurer of the borough aforesaid they may and can execute the office of treasurer of the borough aforesaid for one whole year then next following and thenceforward until two others of the burgesses of the borough aforesaid shall have been appointed to the office of treasurer of the borough aforesaid according to the ordinances expressed and declared in these presents: And if it shall happen that the aforesaid treasurers of the borough aforesaid for the time being or either of them at any time hereafter within one year after they have been admitted as aforesaid to the office of treasurer of the

amocionem vel decessum assemblare in guildhalda burgi
predicti seu in aliquo alio loco conveniente infra burgum
predictum et ibidem eligere, nominare et preficere unum
alium vel duos alios probos et idoneos viros de burgensibus
burgi predicti in thesaurarium sive thesaurarios burgi predicti
in loco vel locis ipsius vel ipsorum sic mortui et decedentis
mortuorum et decedentium sicut antehac consueverunt: Et
quod ille sive illi sic electi et prefecti officium illum thesaurarii
burgi predicti habeat et exerceat, habeant et exerceant,
durante residuo eiusdem anni et exinde quousque duo alii de
burgensibus[1] predictis in forma predicta in thesaurarios burgi
predicti electi, prefecti et iurati fuerint, et sic tocies quocies
casus sic acciderit: Ita tamen ut iuramenta respective superius
mencionata coram cancellario vel procancellario dicto universitatis nostre predicte vel deputato suo pro tempore existente
prius prestabunt vel prestabit: Volumus insuper ac ut bonum
regimen, gubernacio civilis et pax et concordia inter inhabitantes et incolas predicti burgi sive limitibus infuturum unita
et stabilita sint[2] concedimus prefatis maiori, ballivis et burgensibus burgi predicti et successoribus suis quod nullus in-
habitans, inhabitantes seu aliqua alia persona sive persone
quecunque infra libertates et precincta eiusdem burgi, modo
non sint scholares aut eorum servientes et ministri aut de
eorum familiis aut alie persone in dicta universitate nostra
predicta vel suburbiis et precinctis eiusdem quovismodo
privilegiate aliqua arte, misterio sive manuali occupacione
utetur sive utentur, exerceat seu exerceant, nisi huiusmodi
persona sive persone pleno tempore septem annorum secundum morem et modum apprenticii et leges statutas regni
nostri Anglie in eo casu provisos inserviet seu inservient, sub
pena et forisfactura viginti solidorum legalis monete Anglie
pro quolibet mense prefatis maiori, ballivis et burgensibus
burgi predicti levanda et solvenda, eadem summa per
thesaurarios burgi predicti pro tempore existente per ac-
cionem debiti in curia de recordo predicta coram maiore
et ballivis burgi de Cantabrigia predicti tenta et tenenda

---

[1] *burgi* MS.   [2] *sit* MS.

borough aforesaid should die, that then and so often it may be and shall be fully lawful to the aforesaid mayor, bailiffs and burgesses of the said borough for the time being at once or the greater part of them within fourteen days next following the death, removal or departure of the said treasurer or treasurers to assemble in the guildhall of the borough aforesaid or in some other convenient place within the borough aforesaid and there to elect, nominate and appoint one other or two other upright and fit men from the burgesses of the borough aforesaid as treasurer or treasurers of the borough aforesaid in the place or places of him or them so dead or departing as heretofore they have been accustomed : And that he or they so elected and appointed may have and exercise that office of treasurer of the borough aforesaid during the rest of the same year and thenceforth until two others of the burgesses aforesaid in form aforesaid shall have been elected, admitted and sworn as treasurers of the borough aforesaid, and so as often as the case shall thus happen : So however that he or they shall first take the oaths respectively mentioned above before the chancellor or vice-chancellor aforesaid of our university aforesaid or his deputy for the time being : We will further and, that good rule, civil government and peace and concord amongst the inhabitants and dwellers of the aforesaid borough or in its limits hereafter may be united and established, we grant to the aforesaid mayor, bailiffs and burgesses of the borough aforesaid and to their successors that no inhabitant, inhabitants or any other person or persons whosoever within the liberties and precincts of the same borough, unless they be scholars or their servants and ministers or of their families or other persons in any way privileged in our said university aforesaid or the suburbs and precincts of the same shall use or exercise any art, mystery or manual occupation, unless such person or persons shall serve for the full term of seven years according to custom and manner of apprenticeship and the statute-laws of our realm of England in that case provided, under the penalty and forfeit of twenty shillings of

recuperanda, nisi pro instruccione pauperum in pannis conficiendis et aliis manufacturis lane, canabis sive lini aut alii materialis: Et ulterius de ampliori gratia nostra speciali ac ex certa sciencia et mero motu nostris damus et concedimus prefatis maiori, ballivis et burgensibus burgi predicti et successoribus suis per presentes quod de tempore in tempus imposterum bene liceat et licebit prefatis maiori, ballivis et burgensibus burgi predicti et successoribus suis racionabiliter et indifferenter taxare, imponere et assidere in et super omnes et singulas personas[1] quascunque inhabitantes sive incolas[2] burgi predicti, non existentes scholares aut eorum servientes et ministros aut de eorum familiis aut alias personas in dicta universitate nostra quoquomodo privilegiatas, tales racionabiles ratas proporciones sive denariorum summam pro, in et circa meliori supportacione et sustentacione onerum et expensarum predicti burgi et manutenacione pontium, altarum [viarum] et aliorum operum necessariorum pro publico et comuni bono eorumdem maioris, ballivorum et burgensium imposterum faciendas quales per ipsos [bonas] et convenientes fore videbitur ac huiusmodi taxacionem, imposicionem et racionabilem denariorum summam sic taxatam et impositam, taxandam et imponendam, levare, colligere et percipere possint ad proprium opus et usum predictorum maioris, ballivorum et burgensium burgi predicti, et pro non solucione eiusdem summe distringere de bonis et cattalis cuiuslibet seu quarumlibet persone sive personarum eandem summam recusantium, aut aliter per sectas, querelas et queremonias huiusmodi personam vel personas recusantem aut recusantes ita solvere in curia de recordo coram prefatis maiore, ballivis et burgensibus burgi predicti tenta et tenenda, impetere, implacitare et prosequi per thesaurarios pro tempore existente, illatam, inferendam et inducendam donec de huiusmodi denariorum summa predicti maior et ballivi burgi predicti plenarie satisfacti[3] et soluti erunt: Et ulterius de ampliori gracia nostra speciali ac ex certa sciencia et mero motu nostris concessimus, approbavimus, ratificavimus et confirmavimus ac per presentes

---

[1] *personis* MS.   [2] *incoles* MS.   [3] *forisfacti* MS.

lawful money of England for each month, to be levied and
paid to the aforesaid mayor, bailiffs and burgesses of the
borough aforesaid, the same sum to be recovered by the
treasurers of the borough aforesaid for the time being by
action of debt in the court of record aforesaid before the
mayor and bailiffs of the borough of Cambridge aforesaid
held and to be held, unless for instruction of the poor in
making cloth and other manufactures of wool, hemp or flax
or other material : And further of our fuller special grace and
from our certain knowledge and mere motion we give and
grant to the beforenamed mayor, bailiffs and burgesses of
the borough aforesaid and to their successors by these
presents that from time to time hereafter it may be and shall
be lawful to the beforenamed mayor, bailiffs and burgesses
of the borough aforesaid and to their successors reasonably and indifferently to tax, impose and assess in and upon
all and singular persons whatsoever, inhabitants or dwellers of
the borough aforesaid, not being scholars or their servants
and ministers or of their families or other persons in any way
privileged in our said university, such reasonable rates, pro-
portions or sum of money for, in and concerning the better
support and sustentation of the burdens and expenses of the
aforesaid borough and the maintenance of the bridges, high-
ways and other works necessary for the public and common
good of the said mayor, bailiffs and burgesses hereafter to
be made as shall be deemed by them to be [good] and
convenient, and such taxation, imposition and reasonable
sum of money so taxed and imposed, or to be taxed and
imposed, they may be able to levy, collect and take to the
proper advantage and use of the aforesaid mayor, bailiffs and
burgesses of the borough aforesaid, and for the non-payment
of the said sum charged, required and incurred, to distrain
upon the goods and chattels of any person or persons refusing
the same sum, or otherwise by suits, pleas and complaints, to
sue, implead and prosecute such person or persons refusing
so to pay, in the court of record held and to be held before
the beforenamed mayor, bailiffs and burgesses of the borough

pro nobis heredibus et successoribus nostris concedimus, approbamus, ratificamus et confirmamus prefatis maiori, ballivis et burgensibus burgi de Cantabrigia predicta et successoribus suis omnia et omnimoda, tot, tanta, talia, eadem, huiusmodi et consimilia concessiones, liberas consuetudines, libertates, privilegia, franchesias, immunitates, quietancias, exempciones, ferias, nundinas, mercatas, theolonea, tolneta, iurisdicciones, commoditates, emolumenta, terras, tenementa et hereditamenta quanta, quot, qualia, et que, maior, ballivi et burgenses burgi de Cantabrigia predicta aut eorum aliqui modo legittimo habent, tenent, gaudent et utuntur aut habere, tenere, uti aut gaudere debent per nomen maioris, ballivorum et burgensium burgi de Cantabrigia aut per nomen ballivorum et burgensium burgi de Cantabrigia aut per nomen burgensium burgi de Cantabrigia sive per quecunque alia nomina sive per quodcunque aliud nomen aut per quamcunque incorporacionem vel corpus politicum seu pretextu cuiuscunque incorporacionis vel corporis politici premissa aut eorum aliqua data seu concessa fuerunt predictis maiori, ballivis et burgensibus aut aliquibus seu alicui predecessorum suorum, racione vel pretextu aliquarum cartarum aut literarum patentium per aliquem progenitorum sive antecessorum nostrorum quoquomodo antehac factarum, confirmatarum vel concessarum, aut racione vel pretextu alicuius legittime prescripcionis, usus seu consuetudinis antehac habite seu usitate seu quocunque alio legali modo iure seu titulo, licet eadem seu eorum aliquod vel aliqua antehac usa non fuerunt vel fuit, aut abusa vel male usa, vel discontinuata fuerunt vel fuit, aut licet eadem aut eorum aliquod vel aliqua deperdita aut forisfacta sint aut fuerint, habendum, tenendum et gaudendum eadem terras et tenementa, libertates, privilegia, franchesias, iurisdicciones, et cetera premissa eisdem maiori, ballivis et burgensibus burgi predicti et successoribus suis imperpetuum : Reddendo inde nobis, heredibus et successoribus nostris talia, huiusmodi et consimilia redditus, servicia, denariorum summas et tenuras qualia proinde nobis antehac debita solubilia et de iure consueta fuerunt:

aforesaid by the treasurers for the time being, until from such sum of money the aforesaid mayor and bailiffs of the borough aforesaid shall have been fully satisfied and paid : And further of our fuller special grace and from our certain knowledge and mere motion we have granted, approved, ratified and confirmed and by these presents for us- our heirs and successors we grant, approve, ratify and confirm to the beforenamed mayor, bailiffs and burgesses of the borough of Cambridge aforesaid and to their successors all and all kinds, so many, so great, such, the same, like and similar grants, free customs, liberties, privileges, franchises, immunities, quittances, exemptions, fairs, feasts, markets, takings, tolls, jurisdictions, commodities, emoluments, lands, tenements and hereditaments, as many, the like, the same and the which the mayor, bailiffs and burgesses of the borough of Cambridge aforesaid or any of them in a lawful manner have, hold, enjoy and use or ought to have, hold, use or enjoy under the name of the mayor, bailiffs and burgesses of the borough of Cambridge or under the name of the bailiffs and burgesses of the borough of Cambridge or under the name of the burgesses of Cambridge or under whatever other names or under whatever other name or under whatever incorporation or body politic or on the pretext of whatever incorporation or body politic the premises or any of them have been given or granted to the aforesaid mayor, bailiffs and burgesses or to any one or more of their predecessors, by reason or pretext of any charters or letters patent by any of our ancestors or predecessors in any way heretofore made, confirmed or granted, or by reason or pretext of any legitimate prescription, usage or custom heretofore had or used or by any other lawful manner, right or title, although the same or any one or more of them heretofore has or have been not used, or abused or badly used, or discontinued, or although the same, or any one or more of them, may or shall have been lost or forfeited : To have, hold and enjoy the same lands and tenements, liberties, privileges, franchises, jurisdictions, and other premises to the said mayor,

Quare volumus et per presentes pro nobis heredibus et
successoribus nostris concedimus prefatis maiori, ballivis et
burgensibus burgi de Cantabrigia predicta et successoribus
suis quod habeant, teneant, utantur et gaudeant ac plene
habere, tenere, uti et gaudere possint et valeant imperpetuum
omnes et omnimoda predicta terras, tenementa, redditus,
reverciones[1], libertates, liberas consuetudines, privilegia, authoritates, quietanceas, et hereditamenta quecunque predicta,
secundum tenorem et effectum harum literarum nostrarum
patencium sine occasione vel impedimento nostri heredum vel
successorum nostrorum quorumcunque: Nolentes quod iidem
maior, ballivi et burgenses burgi predicti vel eorum aliqui vel
aliquis nec aliquis burgensium burgi predicti, racione premissorum sive eorum alicuius per nos, vel per heredes nostros,
iusticiarios, vicecomites, escaetores aut alios ballivos seu
ministros nostros heredum et successorum nostrorum quorumcunque inde occasionentur, molestentur, vexentur seu graventur, molestetur, vexetur, gravetur seu in aliquo perturbetur,
volentes et per presentes firmiter pro nobis heredibus et
successoribus nostris mandantes et precipientes tam Thesaurario, Cancellario et Baronibus Scaccarii nostri heredum et
successorum nostrorum, ac omnibus et singulis aliis iudicibus
et iusticiariis nostris heredum et successorum nostrorum
quam Attornato et Solicitori nostro generali pro tempore
existente et eorum cuilibet et omnibus aliis officiariis et
ministris nostris quibuscunque, quod nec ipsi nec eorum
aliquis sive aliqui aliquod breve seu summonicionem de
quo warranto seu aliquod aliud breve seu brevia vel processum quecunque versus predictos maiorem, ballivos et
burgenses burgi predicti seu eorum aliquos seu homines vel
inhabitantes burgi predicti vel eorum aliquem vel aliquos pro
aliquibus causis, rebus, materiis, offensis, clameis aut usurpacionibus aut eorum aliquo per ipsos sive eorum aliquos
debitis, clamatis, attemptatis, usitatis, habitis seu usurpatis
ante diem confeccionis presencium prosequantur aut con-
tinuantur aut prosequi aut continuari facient et causabunt

[1] *revenciones* MS.

bailiffs and burgesses of the borough aforesaid and to their successors for ever : Rendering thence to us, our heirs and successors such, like and similar rents, services, sums of money and tenures as thence to us heretofore have been due, payable and of right accustomed : Wherefore we will and by these presents for us our heirs and successors we grant to the beforenamed mayor, bailiffs and burgesses of the borough of Cambridge aforesaid and to their successors that they may have, hold, use and enjoy and that they can and may be able fully to have, hold, use and enjoy for ever all and all kinds aforesaid of lands, tenements, rents, reversions, liberties, free customs, privileges, authorities, quittances, and hereditaments whatsoever aforesaid, according to the tenour and effect of these our letters patent without hindrance or impediment of us our heirs or successors whomsoever : We being unwilling that the said mayor, bailiffs and burgesses of the borough aforesaid or any one or more of them or any burgess of the borough aforesaid, by reason of the premises or of any of them by us, or by our heirs, the justices, sheriffs, escheators or other bailiffs or ministers of us our heirs and successors whomsoever should therein be hindered, molested, vexed or aggrieved or in any thing disturbed, willing and by these presents strictly for us our heirs and successors commanding and enjoining as well to the Treasurers, Chancellors and Barons of the Exchequer of us our heirs and successors, and to all and singular the other judges and justices of us our heirs and successors as to our Attorney and Solicitor General for the time being and to each of them and to all others our officers and ministers whomsoever, that neither they nor any one or more of them shall prosecute or continue or shall make or cause to be prosecuted or continued any writ or summons of " Quo Warranto " or any other writ or writs or process whatsoever against the aforesaid mayor, bailiffs and bur-gesses of the borough aforesaid or any of them or the men or inhabitants of the borough aforesaid or any one or more of them for any causes, things, matters, offences, claims or usurpations or any one of them due, claimed, attempted,

seu eorum aliquis faciet aut causabit : Nolentes eciam quod
maior, ballivi et burgenses burgi illius vel eorum aliqui per
aliquem vel aliquos iusticiarios, iudices, officiarios vel ministros
predictos in aut pro debito, usu, clameo, vel abusu libertatum
franchesiarum aut iurisdiccionum infra burgum de Cantabrigia
predicta, suburbia ac precincta eiusdem ante diem confeccionis
harum literarum nostrarum patencium molestentur aut im-
pediantur aut ad ea aut eorum aliquod respondere compellantur : Et ulterius de ampliori gracia nostra speciali ac ex
certa sciencia et mero motu nostris volumus et per presentes
pro nobis heredibus et successoribus nostris concedimus
prefatis maiori, ballivis et burgensibus burgi predicti et
successoribus suis quod he litere nostre patentes vel irrotulamenta earumdem erunt in omnibus et per omnia firme,
valide, bone, sufficientes et effectuales in lege erga et contra
nos heredes et successores nostros tam in omnibus curiis
nostris quam alibi infra regnum nostrum Anglie absque
aliquibus confirmacionibus, licenciis vel tolleracionibus de
nobis heredibus et successoribus nostris imposterum per
predictos maiorem, ballivos et burgenses burgi predicti aut
successores suos procurandis impetrandis aut obtinendis :
Non obstante male nominando vel male recitando aut non
recitando aliquorum premissorum aut alicuius partis vel
parcelle premissorum in hiis literis nostris patentibus men-
cionatis vel recitatis: Et non obstante non inveniendo officium
vel inquisicionem premissorum aut alicuius inde parcelle per
que titulus noster inveniri debuit ante confeccionem harum
literarum nostrarum patencium : Et non obstante statuto in
parliamento domini Henrici nuper regis Anglie sexti antecessoris nostri anno regni sui decimo octavo facto et edito :
Et non obstantibus aliquibus aliis defectibus in non recte
nominando naturam, genera, species, quantitates aut qualitates
premissorum aut alicuius inde parcelle : Proviso semper et
firmiter per presentes pro nobis heredibus et successoribus
nostris prefatis maiori, ballivis et burgensibus burgi predicti
et successoribus suis precipimus et mandamus quod he litere
nostre patentes aut aliquod in eisdem contentum non ali-

used, had or usurped by themselves or any of them before the day of the making of these presents: We being unwilling also that the mayor, bailiffs and burgesses of that borough or any of them by any one or more justices, judges, officers or ministers aforesaid in or for any debt, usage, claim, or abuse of the liberties, franchises or jurisdictions within the borough of Cambridge aforesaid, the suburbs and precincts of the same before the day of confirmation of these our letters patent should be molested or hindered or should be compelled to answer to them or any of them : And further from our fuller special grace and from our certain knowledge and mere motion we will and by these presents for us our heirs and successors we grant to the beforenamed mayor, bailiffs and burgesses of the borough aforesaid and to their successors, that these our letters patent or the enrolment of the same shall be in all things and by all things firm, strong, good, sufficient and effectual in law towards and against us, our heirs and successors, as well in all our courts as elsewhere within our realm of England, without any confirmations, licences or allowances from us, our heirs and successors for ever, to be procured, applied for or obtained by the aforesaid mayor, bailiffs and burgesses of the borough aforesaid or their successors: Notwithstanding the bad naming or bad recital or non-recital of any premises or of any part or parcel of the premises in these our letters patent mentioned or recited : And notwithstanding the not finding the office or inquisition of the premises or of any parcel thereof by which our title ought to be found before the making of these our letters patent: And notwithstanding the statute made and issued in the parliament of the lord Henry sometime King of England the Sixth our predecessor in the eighteenth year of his reign: And notwithstanding any other defects in not rightly naming the nature, kinds, species, quantities or qualities of the premises or of any parcel thereof: Provided always and strictly by these presents we enjoin and command for us our heirs and successors to the beforenamed mayor, bailiffs and burgesses of the borough aforesaid and their successors that

qualiter extendant ad preiudicium, oneracionem seu impedimentum iurisdiccionum, privilegiorum, libertatum, consuetudinum, prescriptorum, composicionum, easiamentorum, finium, forisfacturarum, amerciamentorum, proficuorum seu hereditamentorum quorumcunque cancellario, magistris et scholaribus universitatis nostre Cantabrigie seu alicui seu aliquibus predecessorum suorum per quodcunque nomen incorporacionis seu per quecunque nomina incorporacionum per nos aut aliquos aut aliquem progenitorum aut antecessorum nostrorum nuper Regum seu Reginarum Anglie concessorum seu mencionatorum fore concessorum seu ab iisdem cancellario, magistris et scholaribus vel aliis personis infra universitatem nostram predictam privilegiatis racione vel pretextu alicuius legittime prescripcionis usus seu consuetudinis antehac habitis, factis seu usitatis sed quod iidem cancellarius, magistri et scholares et successores sui omnibus talibus iurisdiccionibus, privilegiis, libertatibus, consuetudinibus, prescripcionibus, composicionibus, seu easiamentis, finibus, forisfacturis, amerciamentis, proficuis et hereditamentis habeant, teneant et gaudeant ac habere, tenere et gaudere valeant et possint, libere, pacifice et quiete hiis presentibus aut aliquo in eisdem contento non obstante: Volumus eciam[1] et per presentes concedimus prefatis maiori, ballivis et burgensibus burgi de Cantabrigia quod habeant et habebunt has literas nostras patentes sub magno sigillo nostro Anglie debito modo factas et sigillatas absque fine in hanaperio cancellario nostro seu alibi ad usum nostrum quoquomodo reddendo seu solvendo: Eo quod expressa mencio de vero valore annuo aut de aliquo alio valore vel certitudine premissorum sive eorum alicuius aut de aliis donis sive concessionibus per nos seu per aliquem progenitorum sive predecessorum nostrorum prefatis maiori, ballivis et burgensibus burgi de Cantabrigia predicta ante hec tempora factis in presentibus minime facta existit aut aliquo statuto, actu, ordinacione, provisione, proclamacione sive restriccione

---

[1] The Patent Roll gives only the opening words of each of these concluding sentences.

these our letters patent or anything contained in the same shall not in any way extend to the prejudice, injury or hindrance of the jurisdictions, privileges, liberties, customs, prescriptions, compositions, easements, fines, forfeitures, amercements, profits or hereditaments whatsoever granted or mentioned to be granted to the chancellor, masters and scholars of our university of Cambridge or to any one or more of their predecessors by whatever name of incorporation or by whatever names of incorporation by us or any one or more of our ancestors or predecessors sometime Kings or Queens of England, or by the same chancellor, masters and scholars or other persons privileged within our university aforesaid, by reason or pretext of any legitimate prescription, usage or custom, heretofore had, made or used, but that the said chancellor, masters and scholars and their successors may have, hold and enjoy all such jurisdictions, privileges, liberties, customs, prescriptions, compositions, or easements, fines, forfeitures, amercements, profits, and hereditaments and may be able to have, hold and enjoy the same freely, peacefully and quietly, these presents or any thing contained in the same notwithstanding : We will also and by these presents we grant to the beforenamed mayor, bailiffs and burgesses of the borough of Cambridge that they may have and shall have these our letters patent under our great seal of England in due manner made and sealed without fine to be rendered or paid into the hanaper to our chancellor or elsewhere to our use in any way : Any omission in these presents of an express mention of the true annual value or of any other value or certitude of the premises or of any of them or of other gifts or grants made by us or by any of our ancestors or predecessors to the beforenamed mayor, bailiffs and burgesses of the borough of Cambridge aforesaid before these times or any statute, act, ordinance, provision, proclamation or restriction heretofore had, made, issued, ordained or provided or any other thing, cause or matter whatsoever in any wise to the contrary hereof notwithstanding : In witness whereof we have caused these our letters to be made patent :

in contrarium inde antehac habito facto edito ordinato sive proviso aut aliqua alia re, causa vel materia quacunque in aliquo non obstante: In cuius rei testimonium has literas nostras fieri fecimus patentes. Teste me ipso apud Westmonasterium sexto die Februarii anno regni nostri Anglie, Scotie, Francie et Hibernie septimo.

per breve de privato sigillo.

XXVIII. Litterae Patentes Caroli Secundi.

1685
Jan. 3.

[1]Carolus Secundus Dei gratia Anglie Scocie Francie et Hibernie Rex, fidei defensor &c. Omnibus ad quos presentes litere pervenerint salutem. Cum maior, ballivi et burgenses corporacionis nostre Cantabrigie in comitatu nostro Cantabrigie omnes potestates, franchesias, libertates, privilegia et authoritates suas de vel concernentes eleccione nominacione constitucione existencia vel appunctuacione aliquarum personarum in, ad vel pro seperalibus et respectivis officiis maioris, capitalis seneschalli, recordatoris, aldermannorum, ballivorum comunis clerici, burgensium de comuni concilio, coronatorum et thesaurariorum dicte corporacionis nobis concessere et sursumreddidere quamquidem concessionem et sursumreddicionem acceptavimus ac per presentes acceptamus

> Here follows a copy[2] of a part of the Letters Patent of Charles I. hereinbefore printed p. 138, l. 7 (Nos igitur publicum &c.) to p. 142, l. 6 (habuerunt et consueverunt :)

Volumus etiam ac per presentes pro nobis heredibus et successoribus nostris concedimus et declaramus quod de cetero imperpetuum sint et erunt[3] infra burgum, libertates vel precincta eiusdem separalia membra et officiaria in forma inferius nominata et constituta, vel mencionata eligenda

---

[1] On five skins. Fine portrait of the King in the initial. Each skin is engraved with a fine border. Great seal cracked and poor impression, appended in a tin box.

[2] With the slight changes indicated in the notes to the Letters Patent of Charles I.

[3] *erint* MS. passim.

Witness: myself at Westminster on the sixth day of February in the seventh year of our reign of England, Scotland, France and Ireland.

by writ of privy seal.

XXVIII. LETTERS PATENT OF CHARLES THE SECOND.

[1]Charles the Second, by the grace of God, of England, Scotland, France and Ireland King, Defender of the Faith &c. to all to whom the present letters shall come greeting. Whereas the mayor, bailiffs and burgesses of our corporation of Cambridge in our county of Cambridge have granted and surrendered to us all their powers, franchises, liberties, privileges and authorities of or concerning the election, nomination, constitution, existence, or appointment of certain persons in, to, or for the separate and respective offices of mayor, high steward, recorder, aldermen, bailiffs, town clerk, burgesses of the common council, coroners and treasurers of the said corporation, which concession and surrender we have accepted and by these presents accept:

> Here follows a copy[2] of a part of the Letters Patent of Charles I. hereinbefore printed p. 139, l. 6 (We therefore graciously &c.) to p. 143, l. 6 (were wont to have:)

We will also and by these presents for us our heirs and successors we grant and declare that henceforth for ever there may be and shall be within the borough, the liberties or precincts of the same, separate members and officers in form below named and constituted or mentioned as to be elected and constituted, namely one upright and discreet man of the burgesses of the borough aforesaid who shall be and shall be called mayor of the borough aforesaid, one upright and

1685
Jan. 3.

---

[1] See Cooper, *Annals*, iii. p. 603.

[2] With the slight changes indicated in the notes to the Letters Patent of Charles I.

et constituenda, videlicet unus probus et discretus vir de
burgensibus burgi predicti qui erit et vocabitur maior burgi
predicti, unus probus et discretus vir de burgensibus burgi
predicti qui erit et vocabitur capitalis senescallus burgi
predicti, unus probus et discretus vir in legibus regni nostri
Anglie eruditus qui erit et vocabitur recordator burgi predicti,
duodecim probi et discreti viri de capitalibus burgensibus
burgi predicti preter maiorem burgi predicti qui erunt et
vocabuntur aldermanni burgi predicti, quatuor probi et discreti viri de burgensibus burgi predicti qui erunt et vocabuntur
ballivi burgi predicti, unus probus et discretus vir de burgensibus burgi predicti qui erit et vocabitur comunis clericus
burgi . predicti, viginti et quatuor probi et discreti viri de
aliis discretioribus burgensibus burgi predicti qui erunt et
vocabuntur de comuni concilio burgi predicti, duo probi et
discreti viri de burgensibus burgi predicti qui erunt et
vocabuntur coronatores burgi predicti et duo probi et discreti
viri de burgensibus burgi predicti qui erunt et vocabuntur
thesaurarii burgi predicti : Ac pro meliori execucione voluntatis nostre in hac parte assignavimus, nominavimus, constituimus et fecimus ac per presentes pro nobis, heredibus et
successoribus nostris assignamus, nominamus, constituimus
et facimus dilectum nobis Nicholaum Eagle generosum fore
et esse primum et modernum maiorem burgi predicti continuandum in eodem officio a data presentium usque festum
sancti Michaelis Archangeli nunc proxime sequens[1] si dictus
Nicholaus Eagle tamdiu vixerit, et exinde quousque unus
alius ad officium maioris burgi predicti electus, prefectus et
iuratus fuerit : Et assignavimus, nominavimus, constituimus
et fecimus ac per presentes pro nobis heredibus et successoribus nostris assignamus, nominamus, constituimus et facimus
dilectum et perquam fidelem conciliarium nostrum Thomasum
Chichley militem, Cancellarium Ducatus nostri Lancastrie
fore et esse primum et modernum capitalem senescallum
burgi predicti, continuandum in eodem officio durante vita
sua : Et assignavimus, nominavimus, constituimus et fecimus

---

[1] *sequent'* MS.

discreet man of the burgesses of the borough aforesaid who shall be and shall be called high steward of the borough aforesaid, one upright and discreet man learned in the laws of our kingdom of England who shall be and shall be called recorder of the borough aforesaid, twelve upright and discreet men of the chief of the burgesses of the borough aforesaid, besides the mayor of the borough aforesaid, who shall be and shall be called aldermen of the borough aforesaid, four upright and discreet men of the burgesses of the borough aforesaid who shall be and shall be called bailiffs of the borough aforesaid, one upright and discreet man of the burgesses of the borough aforesaid, who shall be and shall be called the common clerk of the borough aforesaid, twenty-four upright and discreet men of the other more discreet burgesses of the borough aforesaid, who shall be and shall be called of the common council of the borough aforesaid, two upright and discreet men of the burgesses of the borough aforesaid, who shall be and shall be called coroners of the borough aforesaid, and two upright and discreet men of the burgesses of the borough aforesaid, who shall be and shall be called treasurers of the borough aforesaid : And for the better execution of our will in this behalf, we have assigned, named, constituted and made, and by these presents for us our heirs and successors we assign, name, constitute and make our beloved Nicholas Eagle gentleman to become and to be the first and present mayor of the borough aforesaid, to be continued in the same office from the date of these presents until the feast of Saint Michael the Archangel now next following if the said Nicholas Eagle shall live so long, and thence until another shall have been elected, appointed and sworn to the office of mayor of the borough aforesaid : And we have assigned, named, constituted and made, and by these presents for us our heirs and successors we assign, name, constitute and make our beloved and right faithful councillor Thomas Chicheley knight, Chancellor of our Duchy of Lancaster, to become and to be the first and present high steward of the borough aforesaid, to be continued in the same office during his life :

ac per presentes pro nobis heredibus et successoribus nostris
assignamus, nominamus, constituimus et facimus dilectum et
perquam fidelem Gulielmum dominum Allington, baronem
Allington de Wimondley et Killard Constabularem Turris
nostre London fore et esse primum et modernum recordatorem burgi predicti continuandum in eodem officio durante
vita sua : Et assignavimus, nominavimus, constituimus et
fecimus ac per presentes pro nobis heredibus et successoribus
nostris assignamus, nominamus, constituimus et facimus
dilectos nobis Samuelem Newton, seu Edwinum Mayfeild,
Edwardum Miller, Franciscum Jermin, Thomasum Ewin,
Thomasum Fox, predictum Nicholaum Eagle, Thomasum
Fowle, Matheum Blackley, Thomasum Walker, Carolum
Chambers, Johannem Pepys et Isaacum Watlington generosos
fore et esse primos et modernos aldermannos burgi predicti
continuandos in eodem officio durantibus vitis suis respectivis :
Et assignavimus, nominavimus, constituimus et fecimus ac
per presentes pro nobis heredibus et successoribus nostris
assignamus, nominamus, constituimus et facimus dilectos
nobis Franciscum Harby, Robertum Warne, Christoferum
Oldfield et Thomasum Crabb fore et esse primos et modernos
ballivos burgi predicti continuandos in eodem officio a data
presentium usque ad festum Sancti Michaelis Archangeli
nunc proxime sequens[1] si iidem Franciscus Harby, Robertus
Warne, Christofer Oldfield et Thomasus Crab tamdiu
respective vixerint seu aliquis eorum vixerit et exinde quousque quatuor alii ballivi de burgensibus burgi predicti in
officiis ballivorum burgi predicti de bono modo electi prefecti
et iurati fuerint : Et assignavimus, nominavimus, constituimus
et fecimus et per presentes pro nobis heredibus et successoribus nostris assignamus, nominamus, constituimus et facimus
dilectum nobis Willelmum Baron generosum fore et esse
primum et modernum comunem clericum burgi predicti
continuandum in eodem officio durante vita sua : Et assignavimus, nominavimus, constituimus et fecimus et per presentes
pro nobis heredibus et successoribus nostris assignamus,

[1] *sequent'* MS.

And we have assigned, named, constituted and made and by these presents for us our heirs and successors we assign, name, constitute and make our beloved and right faithful William Lord Allington, Baron Allington of Wymondley and Killard, Constable of our Tower of London, to become and to be the first and present recorder of the borough aforesaid to be continued in the same office during his life: And we have assigned, named, constituted and made and by these presents for us our heirs and successors we assign, name, constitute and make our beloved Samuel Newton or Edwin Mayfield, Edward Miller, Francis Jermin, Thomas Ewin, Thomas Fox, the aforesaid Nicholas Eagle, Thomas Fowle, Matthew Blackley, Thomas Walker, Charles Chambers, John Pepys and Isaac Watlington, gentlemen, to become and to be the first and present aldermen of the borough aforesaid, to be continued in the same office during their respective lives: And we have assigned, named, constituted and made and by these presents for us our heirs and successors we assign, name, constitute and make our beloved Francis Harby, Robert Warne, Christopher Oldfield and Thomas Crabb to become and to be the first and present bailiffs of the borough aforesaid to be continued in the same office from the date of these presents to the feast of Saint Michael the Archangel now next following, if the said Francis Harby, Robert Warne, Christopher Oldfield and Thomas Crabb or any of them shall live so long respectively, and thenceforward until four other bailiffs from the burgesses of the borough aforesaid shall have been elected, appointed and sworn in good manner into the offices of bailiffs of the borough aforesaid: And we have assigned, named, constituted and made and by these presents for us our heirs and successors assign, name, constitute and make our beloved William Baron gentleman to become and to be the first and present common clerk of the borough aforesaid to be continued in the same office during his life: And we have assigned, named, constituted and made and by these presents for us our heirs and successors we assign, name, constitute and make our beloved

nominamus, constituimus et facimus dilectos nobis Thomasum Dickinson, Philippum Hawkins, Johannem Moore, Rogerum Hurst, Josephum Cooper, Johannem Witham, Johannem Sanders, Cornelium Austin, Willelmum Walker, Johannem Walker, Edwardum Chapman, Robertum Smith, Robertum Sanders, Adam Newlin, Johannem Fowkes, Jacobum Mayfeild, Thomasum Silke, Gerardum Herring, Philippum Reynold, Johannem Fage, Josephum Heath, Willelmum Wendy, Nicholaum Apthorp et Henricum Pyke fore et esse primos et modernos burgenses de comuni concilio burgi predicti continuandos in eodem officio durantibus vitis suis respectivis: Et assignavimus, vocavimus, constituimus et fecimus ac per presentes pro nobis heredibus et successoribus nostris assignamus, nominamus, constituimus et facimus dilectos nobis Carolum Chambers et Josephum Cooper generosos fore et esse primos et modernos coronatores burgi predicti continuandos in eodem officio a data presentium usque festum Sancti Michaelis Archangeli nunc proxime sequentem si dicti Carolus Chambers et Josephus Cooper tamdiu vixerint seu aliquis eorum vixerit, et exinde quousque duo alii de burgensibus burgi predicti in officio coronatoris eiusdem burgi de bono modo electi prefecti et iurati fuerint: Et assignavimus, nominavimus, constituimus et fecimus ac per presentes pro nobis heredibus et successoribus nostris assignamus, nominamus, constituimus et facimus dilectos nobis Ricardum Nicholson et Stephanum Hanchet fore et esse primos et modernos thesaurarios Burgi predicti continuandos in eodem officio a data presentium usque festum Sancti Michaelis Archangeli nunc proxime sequens[1], si dicti Ricardus Nicholson et Stephanus Hanchet tamdiu vixerint seu aliquis eorum vixerit et exinde quousque duo alii de burgensibus burgi predicti in officio thesaurarii eiusdem burgi de bono modo electi prefecti et iurati fuerint: Et insuper volumus ac pro nobis heredibus et successoribus nostris concedimus quod predicti maior, capitalis senescallus, recordator, aldermanni, ballivi, comunis clericus, burgenses

[1] *sequent'* MS.

Thomas Dickinson, Philip Hawkins, John Moore, Roger Hurst, Joseph Cooper, John Witham, John Sanders, Cornelius Austin, William Walker, John Walker, Edward Chapman, Robert Smith, Robert Sanders, Adam Newlin, John Fowkes, James Mayfield, Thomas Silke, Gerard Herring, Philip Reynold, John Fage, Joseph Heath, William Wendy, Nicholas Apthorp and Henry Pyke to become and to be the first and present burgesses of the common council of the borough aforesaid to be continued in the same office during their respective lives : And we have assigned, named, contituted and made, and by these presents for us our heirs and successors we assign, name, constitute and make our beloved Charles Chambers and Joseph Cooper gentlemen to become and to be the first and present coroners of the borough aforesaid, to be continued in the same office from the date of these presents until the feast of Saint Michael the Archangel now next following, if the said Charles Chambers and Joseph Cooper or either of them shall live so long, and thenceforward until two others of the burgesses of the borough aforesaid shall have been elected appointed and sworn in good manner into the office of coroner of the same borough : And we have assigned, named, constituted and made and by these presents for us our heirs and successors we assign, name, constitute and make our beloved Richard Nicholson and Stephen Hanchet to become and to be the first and present treasurers of the borough aforesaid to be continued in the same office from the date of these presents until the feast of Saint Michael the Archangel now next following, if the said Richard Nicholson and Stephen Hanchet or either of them shall live so long, and thenceforward until two others of the burgesses of the borough aforesaid shall have been elected, appointed and sworn in good manner in the office of treasurers of the said borough: And further we will and for us our heirs and successors we grant that the aforesaid mayor, high steward, recorder, aldermen, bailiffs, common clerk, burgesses of the common council, coroners and treasurers of the borough aforesaid by these presents named and constituted shall

de comuni concilio, coronatores et thesaurarii burgi predicti
per presentes nominati et constituti officium sive officia,
locum sive loca ad quod vel que sic ut prefertur respective
nominati est et sunt exercebit et exercebunt pro tali tempore et temporibus et in tali modo et forma prout in dicto
burgo antehac usitatum fuit aliquo in presentibus in contrarium
non obstante : Volumus insuper et per presentes firmiter precipimus quod Nicholaus Eagle in presentibus nominatus fore
maior burgi predicti antequam ad seperalia officia maioris
et aldermanni burgi predicti respective infra burgum predictum exequenda admittatur sacramentum corporale super
sanctum dei Evangelium pro fideli et debita execucione officii
maioris et aldermanni prestabit coram dicto Samueli Newton
et Willelmo Baron vel eorum uno quibus quidem Samueli
Newton et Willelmo Baron huiusmodi sacramentum prefatum
Nicholao Eagle dandi et administrandi plenam potestatem
et authoritatem coniunctim et divisim damus et concedimus
per presentes absque aliquo alio warranto vel comissione a
nobis in ea parte procurando et obtinendo : Ac etiam ordinamus ac per presentes firmiter precipimus quod capitalis
senescallus, recordator et aldermanni burgi predicti per
presentes nominati et constituti antequam ad execucionem
officiorum suorum respective admittantur seu aliquis eorum
admittatur seperale sacramentum corporale super sanctum dei
Evangelium pro fideli et debita execucione officiorum suorum
respective prestabunt et eorum quilibet prestabit, ac etiam
ballivi burgi predicti, burgenses de comuni concilio, coronatores et thesaurarii burgi predicti in presentibus nominati
et constituti antequam ad execucionem officiorum suorum admittantur seu eorum aliquis admittatur seperale sacramentum
corporale officia sua respective tangens bene et fideliter
exequenda prestabunt et eorum quilibet prestabit coram
dicto Nicholao Eagle et Willelmo Baron vel uno eorum,
quibus quidem Nicholao Eagle et Willelmo Baron dandi et
administrandi huiusmodi sacramentum dictis officiariis vel personis predictis respective plenam potestatem et authoritatem
coniunctim et divisim damus et concedimus per presentes

perform the office or offices, the place or places, to which as is aforesaid he or they is or are nominated respectively for such time and times and in such manner and form as in the said borough heretofore has been accustomed, anything in these presents to the contrary notwithstanding: We will moreover and by these presents we strictly enjoin that Nicholas Eagle named in these presents to be mayor of the borough aforesaid, before that he shall be admitted to perform the several offices of mayor and alderman of the borough aforesaid respectively, within the borough aforesaid, shall take the corporal oath on the holy Gospel of God for the faithful and due execution of the office of mayor and alderman before the said Samuel Newton and William Baron or one of them, to the which Samuel Newton and William Baron jointly and severally we give and grant by these presents full power and authority to give and administer such oath to the aforesaid Nicholas Eagle and without any other warrant or commission to be procured and obtained from us on that behalf: And also we ordain and by these presents we strictly enjoin that the high steward, recorder and aldermen of the borough aforesaid, named and constituted by these presents, before that they be admitted or any one of them be admitted to the execution of their offices respectively shall take and each of them shall take a several corporal oath on the holy Gospel of God for the faithful and due execution of their offices respectively, and also the bailiffs of the borough aforesaid, the burgesses of the common council, the coroners and treasurers of the borough aforesaid named and constituted in these presents, before that they be admitted or any one of them be admitted to the execution of their offices shall take and each of them shall take a several corporal oath concerning the good and faithful discharge of their offices respectively before the said Nicholas Eagle and William Baron or one of them, to the which Nicholas Eagle and William Baron we give and grant by these presents full power and authority conjointly and severally of giving and administering such oath to the said officers or persons aforesaid respectively and without any other warrant

absque aliquo alio warranto vel comissione a nobis in ea
parte procurando aut obtinendo : Ac etiam ordinamus ac per
presentes firmiter precipimus quod Willelmus Baron comunis
clericus burgi predicti per presentes nominatus et constitutus
antequam ad execucionem officii sui admittatur sacramentum
corporale super sanctum dei Evangelium pro fideli et debita
execucione officii sui prestabit coram prefato Nicholao Eagle
et Samueli Newton vel eorum uno, quibus quidem Nicholao
Eagle et Samueli Newton dandi et administrandi huiusmodi
sacramentum prefato Willelmo Baron plenam potestatem et
authoritatem coniunctim et divisim damus et concedimus
per presentes absque aliquo alio warranto vel comissione a
nobis in ea parte procurando aut obtinendo : Et ulterius
volumus et per presentes pro nobis heredibus et successoribus
nostris concedimus maiori, ballivis et burgensibus burgi predicti pro tempore existente quod servientes ad clavam et
omnes alii inferiores officiarii vel ministri infra burgum predictum qui in presentibus non nominati vel constituti sunt et
qui consueti fuerunt esse infra burgum predictum, libertatem
vel precincta eiusdem de hinc imperpetuum infra conveniens
tempus post datam presentium electi, prefecti et iurati sint et
erunt per et coram tali persona et personis et huiusmodi modo
et forma prout ex antiqua consuetudine in dicto burgo antehac
usitatum fuit, et officium sive officia, locum sive loca ad quod
vel que electi, prefecti et iurati sint et erunt, exercebit et
exercebunt pro tali tempore et temporibus et in tali modo et
forma prout in dicto burgo usitatum fuit aliquo in presentibus
in contrarium non obstante : Et ulterius volumus ac per presentes pro nobis heredibus et successoribus nostris damus
et concedimus prefatis maiori, ballivis et burgensibus burgi
predicti et successoribus suis quod quandocunque acciderit
aliquem maiorem, capitalem senescallum, recordatorem,
comunem clericum et aliquem vel aliquos de aldermannis
et burgensibus de comuni concilio burgi predicti, corona-
torem et thesaurarium burgi predicti pro tempore existente
obire seu ab officio suo vel ab officiis suis amoveri vel
decedere quos et quem pro racionabili causa amobiles esse

or commission to be procured or obtained from us in that behalf: And also we ordain and by these presents strictly enjoin that William Baron the common clerk of the borough aforesaid, named and constituted by these presents, before that he be admitted to the execution of his office shall take the corporal oath on the holy Gospel of God for the faithful and due execution of his office before the aforesaid Nicholas Eagle and Samuel Newton or one of them, to the which Nicholas Eagle and Samuel Newton we give and grant by these presents full power and authority jointly and severally to give and administer such oath to the aforesaid William Baron and without any other warrant or commission to be procured or obtained from us in that behalf: And further we will and by these presents for us our heirs and successors we grant to the mayor, bailiffs and burgesses of the borough aforesaid for the time being, that the sergeants-at-mace and all other inferior officers or servants within the borough aforesaid, who in these presents have not been named or constituted, and have been accustomed to be within the liberty of the borough aforesaid or the precincts of the same, henceforth for ever, within a convenient time after the date of these presents, may be and shall be elected, appointed and sworn by and before such person and persons and in such manner and form as by ancient custom in the said borough heretofore has been accustomed, and the office or offices, place or places to which they may have been or shall have been elected, appointed and sworn, he and they shall perform for such time and times and in such manner and form as in the said borough has been used, anything in these presents to the contrary notwithstanding: And further we will and by these presents for us our heirs and successors we give and grant to the aforesaid mayor, bailiffs and burgesses of the borough aforesaid and to their successors, that whensoever it shall happen that any mayor, high steward, recorder, common clerk and one or more of the aldermen and burgesses of the common council of the borough aforesaid, the coroner and treasurer of the borough aforesaid for the time being shall die

12—2

et amoveri volumus prout antehac in eodem burgo assue-
tum fuit vel in casu vacancie alicuius vel aliquorum officiariorum burgi predicti pro tempore existente, quod tunc et
in quolibet tali casu alia idonea persona vel alie idonee
persone de tempore in tempus ad et in officia illa respective de bono modo eligetur, iurabitur et constituetur,
eligentur, iurabuntur et constituentur per talem personam
et personas in tali loco et modo prout in eodem burgo per
spacium viginti annorum iam ultimum elapsum usitatum
fuit, et officium sive officia, locum sive loca ad quod vel
que sic electus et iuratus fuerit vel fuerint, exercebit et
exercebunt pro tali tempore et temporibus et abinde
amotus erit vel amoti erunt in tali modo prout in huiusmodi casibus in burgo predicto consuetum fuit : Volumus
etiam ac per presentes pro nobis heredibus et successoribus nostris statuimus et ordinamus quod maior, ballivi et
thesaurarii burgi predicti in presentibus nominati et constituti
et maior, ballivi et thesaurarii burgi predicti de cetero
imperpetuum et eorum successores singulis annis respective
prestabunt sacramenta sua pro fideli et plena conservacione
libertatum et privilegiorum universitatis nostre Cantabrigie
coram cancellario vel procancellario universitatis nostre
predicte vel deputato suo in universitate nostra predicta
existente iisdem die, loco, modo et forma ac verbis quibus
nuper maior, ballivi et thesaurarii burgi nostri predicti singulis
annis sacramenta sua respective antehac prestare tenti fuerunt:
Quibus quidem cancellario vel procancellario aut deputato
suo pro tempore existente plenam potestatem et authoritatem
damus et concedimus per presentes huiusmodi respective
sacramentum maiori, ballivis et thesaurariis burgi predicti in
presentibus nominatis et constitutis et maiori, ballivis et
thesaurariis burgi predicti singulis annis imposterum toties
quoties novi maiores, ballivi et thesaurarii nominati, electi,
deputati et admissi fuerint administrare, et quod post tale
sacramentum sic ut prefertur per prefatos thesaurarios respective prestitum et non antea, bene liceat et licebit prefatis
thesaurariis sic electis, nominatis et prefectis, eligendis,

or shall be removed or depart from his or their office, whom we will to be removeable and to be removed for reasonable cause as heretofore in the said borough has been accustomed, or in case of the vacating of any one or more of the officers of the borough aforesaid for the time being, that then and in each such case another fit person or other fit persons from time to time shall be elected, sworn and constituted to and into those offices respectively in good manner by such person and persons, in such place and manner as in the same borough for the space of twenty years now last past has been used, and the office or offices, place or places, to which he or they shall have been elected and sworn, he or they shall execute for such time and times and therefrom he or they shall be removed in such manner as in such cases in the borough aforesaid has been accustomed : We will also and by these presents for us our heirs and successors we order and ordain that the mayor, bailiffs and treasurers of the borough aforesaid, named and constituted in these presents, and the mayor, bailiffs and treasurers of the borough aforesaid hereafter for ever and their successors, in each year respectively shall take their oaths for the faithful and full preservation of the liberties and privileges of our university of Cambridge before the chancellor or vice-chancellor of our university aforesaid or his deputy being in our university aforesaid, on the same day, in the same place, manner and form and words in which formerly the mayor, bailiffs and treasurers of our borough aforesaid in each year have been bound to take their oaths respectively heretofore : To the which chancellor or vice-chancellor or his deputy for the time being we give and grant by these presents full power and authority to administer such oath respectively to the mayor, bailiffs and treasurers of the borough aforesaid named and constituted in these presents, and to the mayor, bailiffs and treasurers of the borough aforesaid in each year hereafter, as often as new mayors, bailiffs and treasurers have been named, elected, deputed and admitted, and that after such oath is taken as is aforesaid by the aforesaid treasurers respectively, and not before, it may be and shall be

nominandis et proficiendis coram maiore et ballivis in curia
de recordo infra burgum predictum tenta et tenenda, aliquam
personam sive aliquas personas quascunque non existentes
scholares vel eorum servientes, ministros vel famulos vel
personas per cartas et privilegia cancellario, magistris[1] et
scholaribus universitatis nostre Cantabrigie predicte concessa
privilegiatas in predicta curia impetere implacitare et prosequi
pro aliqua causa, debito sive denariorum summa aut aliqua
re, materia sive penalitate, forisfacta seu forisfacienda pro non
debita observacione ordinacionum et constitucionum predicti
burgi: Proviso semper quod per licentiam et concessionem
nostram dicti thesaurarii aut eorum deputati nullatenus
attentent in premissis aut eorum aliquibus impetere, implacitare vel prosequi cancellarium, procancellarium, magistros
aut scholares dicte universitatis nostre Cantebrigie aut eorum
aliquem vel aliquas alias personas per dictam universitatem
nostram vel per privilegia et immunitates nobis vel predecessoribus nostris eisdem concessas quovismodo privilegiatas
et exemptas, dummodo talia debita sive summa, penalitates
seu forisfacture non excedant summam quadraginta solidorum: Et ulterius volumus ac per presentes, pro nobis,
heredibus et successoribus nostris concedimus prefatis
maiori, ballivis et burgensibus burgi predicti et successoribus
suis quod si contigerit maiori vel aliqui ballivorum burgi
predicti aliquo tempore imposterum infra unum annum postquam ad officium maioralitatis vel ballivate burgi predicti
prefectus et iuratus fuerit fore egrotum et invalidum aut pro
aliqua causa necessaria et racionabili interesse non possit
aut possint, utpote officium suum in propria persona sua
exequi et intendere nequeat vel nequeant, quod tunc et toties
in casibus predictis bene liceat et licebit prefato maiori cum
assensu trium aldermannorum pro tempore existente et
prefatis ballivis cum assensu maioris burgi predicti pro
tempore existente eligere, appunctare, nominare et proficere
unum alium probum et idoneum virum de aldermannis burgi
predicti qui officium maioris burgi predicti antetunc gesserit

---

[1] *cancellarii, magistri et scholarium* MS.

fully lawful for the aforesaid treasurers so elected, named and appointed, or to be elected, named and appointed, before the mayor and bailiffs, in the court of record held and to be held, within the borough aforesaid, to sue, implead and prosecute any person or persons whatsoever, not being scholars or their servants, officers or domestics or persons privileged by the charters and privileges granted to the chancellor, masters and scholars of our university of Cambridge aforesaid, in the aforesaid court, for any cause, debt or sum of money or for any thing, matter or penalty forfeited or to be forfeited for not duly observing the ordinances and customs of the aforesaid borough: Provided always that by our licence and grant the said treasurers or their deputies shall in no wise try in the premises or any of them to sue, implead or prosecute the chancellor, vice-chancellor, masters or scholars of our said university of Cambridge or any of them or any other persons in any way privileged and exempt by our said university or by the privileges and immunities granted to them by us or our predecessors, and provided that such debts or sum, penalties or forfeitures shall not exceed the sum of forty shillings: And further we will and by these presents, for us, our heirs and successors we grant, to the aforenamed mayor, bailiffs and burgesses of the borough aforesaid and to their successors that if it shall happen that the mayor or any of the bailiffs of the borough aforesaid at any time hereafter within one year after he shall have been admitted and sworn to the office of the mayoralty or bailiwick of the borough aforesaid, shall be sick and infirm or for any necessary and reasonable cause he or they cannot be present, so that he or they cannot perform their office in their proper person that then and so often in the cases aforesaid it may and shall be fully lawful to the aforesaid mayor with the assent of three aldermen for the time being and to the aforesaid bailiffs, with the assent of the mayor of the borough aforesaid for the time being to elect, appoint, nominate and admit another upright and fit man from the aldermen of the borough aforesaid, who heretofore has filled the office of mayor of the borough aforesaid, in the place of the mayor

in loco ipsius maioris, et unum alium probum et idoneum
virum de burgensibus burgi predicti qui officium ballivi
burgi predicti antetunc gesserit in loco ipsius ballivi sic
languidi egroti aut absentis in loco maioris et ut deputatum
pro maiore burgi predicti et in loco ballivi burgi predicti ut
deputatum pro ballivo burgi predicti ad omnia et singula
facienda et agenda durante tempore invaletudinis aut absencie
maioris et ballivi predicti que ad officium maioris et ballivi
burgi predicti realiter pertinebunt seu spectabunt aut devenire
possint et valeant: Quodque quilibet talis deputatus in loco
et officio maioralitatis vel ballivate burgi illius sic ut prefertur
nominatus, constitutus et prefectus et constituendus sacra-
mento corporali in forma predicta prius coram maiore burgi
predicti pro tempore existente necnon coram cancellario vel
procancellario universitatis nostre predicte vel deputato suo
pro tempore existente iuxta modum et formam in ea parte
antehac usitatam pro iuramento maioris et ballivorum burgi
predicti prestando officium illud habeat et exerceat durante
invaletudine et absencia maioris et ballivi predicti et sic toties
quoties casus ita acciderit: Et ulterius volumus ac per presentes pro nobis heredibus et successoribus nostris concedimus
prefatis maiori, ballivis et burgensibus burgi predicti et successoribus suis quod liceat et licebit recordatori burgi predicti
pro tempore existente aliquo tempore imposterum ad libitum
suum postquam ad officium recordatoris burgi predicti prefectus et iuratus fuerit eligere, appunctare, nominare et
preficere unum probum et idoneum virum in legibus regni
nostri Anglie eruditum fore et esse deputatum recordatoris
burgi predicti pro tempore existente, durante bene placito
recordatoris burgi predicti et ad ea omnia et singula facienda
et agenda que ad officium recordatoris burgi predicti realiter
pertinebunt seu spectabunt aut devenire possint aut valeant:
Proviso semper ac plenam potestatem et authoritatem nobis
heredibus et successoribus nostris per presentes reservamus
de tempore in tempus et ad omnia tempora imposterum ad
maiorem, capitalem senescallum, recordatorem, aldermannos,
ballivos, comunem clericum, burgenses de comuni concilio,

himself, and one other upright and fit man from the burgesses
of the borough aforesaid, who heretofore has filled the office
of bailiff of the borough aforesaid, in the place of the bailiff
himself thus ill, sick or absent, in place of the mayor and as
deputy for the mayor of the borough aforesaid, and in place
of the bailiff of the borough aforesaid, as deputy for the
bailiff of the borough aforesaid, to do and perform all and
singular during the time of the sickness or absence of the
mayor and bailiff aforesaid, which really pertain or relate to
the office of mayor and bailiff of the borough aforesaid, or
may or can arise : And that every such deputy so as is aforesaid named, constituted and admitted and to be constituted
in the place and office of the mayoralty or bailiwick of that
borough, having first taken the corporal oath in form aforesaid before the mayor of the borough aforesaid for the time
being and also before the chancellor or vice-chancellor of our
university aforesaid or his deputy for the time being, according to the manner and form in that behalf heretofore used for
the oath of the mayor and bailiffs of the borough aforesaid,
may have and exercise that office during the sickness and
absence of the mayor and bailiff aforesaid and so as often
as the case shall thus happen : And further we will and
by these presents, for us, our heirs and successors, we grant
to the aforenamed mayor, bailiffs and burgesses of the
borough aforesaid and to their successors, that it may and
shall be lawful to the recorder of the borough aforesaid for
the time being at any time hereafter at his pleasure, after that
he shall have been admitted and sworn to the office of
recorder of the borough aforesaid, to elect, appoint, name
and admit an upright and fit man, learned in the laws of
our realm of England, to become and be deputy of the
recorder of the borough aforesaid for the time being during
the pleasure of the recorder of the borough aforesaid and to
do and perform all and singular those things which really
pertain or relate to the office of recorder of the borough aforesaid or may or can arise : Provided always and we reserve by
these presents full power and authority to us our heirs and

coronatores et thesaurarios burgi predicti per presentes
nominatos et constitutos vel imposterum eligendos et nomi-
nandos seu eorum aliquem vel aliquos ad libitum et bene-
placitum nostrum heredum vel successorum nostrorum per
aliquam ordinacionem nostrum heredum aut successorum nostrorum in privato concilio factam et sub sigillo privati concilii
predicti eisdem respective significatam ad amovendum et
amotum et amotos esse declarandum: Et quoties nos,
heredes vel successores nostri, per aliquam talem ordinacionem
in privato concilio factam declarabimus vel declarabunt
huiusmodi maiorem, capitalem senescallum, recordatorem,
comunem clericum aut aliquem vel aliquos de aldermannis,
burgensibus de comuni concilio, coronatoribus vel thesaurariis
burgi predicti pro tempore existente sic amotum vel amotos
esse declaratum sive declarandum ut prefertur, quod tunc
et toties maior, capitalis senescallus, recordator, comunis
clericus et aliquis vel aliqui de aldermannis, burgensibus de
comuni concilio, coronatoribus et thesaurariis burgi predicti
pro tempore existente sic amotus vel amoti esse declara-
tus sive declarandi a seperalibus et respectivis officiis suis
ipso facto et sine aliquo ulteriore processu realiter, et ad
omnes intenciones et proposita quecunque amotus sit et erit,
amoti sint et erunt, et hoc toties quoties casus sic acciderit,
aliquo in contrarium inde non obstante: Et ut maior, ballivi
et burgenses burgi predicti et eorum successores de tempore
in tempus onera et expensas burgi predicti melius sustinere
et supportare possint et valeant de gratia nostra speciali ac
ex certa scientia et mero motu nostris concessimus ac per
presentes pro nobis heredibus et successoribus nostris concedimus licentiam specialem legittimam et licitam facultatem,
potestatem et authoritatem damus prefatis maiori, ballivis et
burgensibus burgi predicti et successoribus suis ad habendum,
perquirendum, recipiendum et retinendum eis et successoribus
suis imperpetuum, tam de nobis, heredibus et successoribus
nostris, quam de quibuscunque subditis et ligeis nostris, aut
de aliis quibuscunque, sive aliqua alia persona sive aliquibus
aliis personis quibuscunque, maneria, mesuagia, terras, tene-

successors from time to time and at all times for ever, to re-
move and declare removed the mayor, high steward, recorder,
aldermen, bailiffs, common clerk, burgesses of the common
council, coroners and treasurers of the borough aforesaid
named and constituted by these presents or hereafter to be
elected and named, or any one or more of them, at the will
and pleasure of us, our heirs and successors, by any ordinance
of us, our heirs or successors made in the Privy Council and
under the seal of the Privy Council aforesaid respectively
signified to them: And as often as we, our heirs and successors,
by any such ordinance made in the Privy Council shall declare
such mayor, high steward, recorder, common clerk, or any
one or more of the aldermen, burgesses of the common
council, coroners or treasurers of the borough aforesaid for
the time being declared or to be declared so removed as
is aforesaid, that then and so often the mayor, high steward,
recorder, common clerk and any one or more of the aldermen, burgesses of the common council, coroners and treasurers
of the borough aforesaid for the time being declared or to be
declared to be removed from their separate and respective
offices *ipso facto* and without any further process really and
to all intents and purposes whatsoever, may be and shall
be so removed, and this so often as the case shall so happen,
anything to the contrary thereof notwithstanding: And that
the mayor, bailiffs and burgesses of the borough aforesaid
and their successors from time to time may and may be able
better to sustain and support the burdens and expenses of
the borough aforesaid, of our special grace and from our
certain knowledge and mere motion we have granted and by
these presents for us, our heirs and successors, we grant
special legitimate licence, and we give lawful faculty, power
and authority to the beforenamed mayor, bailiffs and burgesses of the borough aforesaid and to their successors, to
have, acquire, receive and retain to them and their successors
for ever, as well from us, our heirs and successors, as from any
our subjects and lieges, or from others whomsoever, whether
from any other person or any other persons whomsoever,

menta, rectorias, decimas, redditus, revenciones, servicia et
alia possessiones et hereditamenta quecunque infra burgum
Cantabrigie predicte seu infra suburbia, libertates, limites
aut precincta eiusdem burgi existentes: dummodo eadem
maneria, mesuagia, terre, tenementa, rectorie, decime, redditus,
reverciones[1], servicia et alie possessiones seu hereditamenta
per eosdem maiorem, ballivos et burgenses burgi predicti
et successores suos sic ut prefertur habenda, perquirenda,
recipienda et retinenda in toto non excedant valorem sexaginta librarum per annum, statuto de terris et tenementis
ad manum mortuam non ponendis aut aliquo alio statuto,
actu, ordinacione, provisione seu restriccione in contrarium
inde antehac habito, facto, edito, ordinato seu proviso, aut
aliqua alia causa vel materia quacunque in aliquo non
obstante : Damus etiam ac per presentes pro nobis, heredibus
et successoribus nostris, concedimus cuicunque subdito nostro
et quibuscunque subditis nostris, heredum et successorum
nostrorum, potestatem, licenciam et authoritatem, quod
maneria, mesuagia, terras, tenementa, rectorias, decimas,
redditus, reverciones[1], servicia et alia possessiones et hereditamenta quecunque infra burgum predictum aut infra
suburbia, libertates, limites, seu precincta eiusdem burgi
existentes, prefatis maiori, ballivis et burgensibus burgi
predicti et successoribus suis dare, legare, concedere, alienare
sive convenire[2] possint et valeant: dummodo eadem maneria,
mesuagia, terre, tenementa, rectorie, decime, redditus, revenciones, servitia, et alia possessiones et hereditamenta non
excedant clarum annuum valorem sexaginta librarum per
annum, statuto de terris et tenementis ad manum mortuam
non ponendis aut aliquo alio statuto, actu, ordinacione, provisione seu restriccione inde in contrarium antehac habito,
facto, edito, ordinato seu proviso non obstante: Et ulterius de
ampliori gracia nostra speciali ac ex certa scientia et mero
motu nostris concessimus, approbavimus, dedimus, ratificavimus et confirmavimus ac per presentes pro nobis heredibus
et successoribus nostris concedimus, approbamus, damus,

[1] *revenciones* MS. [2] ? for *convehere.*

manors, messuages, lands, tenements, rectories, tithes, rents, reversions, services and other possessions or hereditaments whatsoever being within the borough of Cambridge aforesaid or within the suburbs, liberties, limits or precincts of the said borough : provided that the said manors, messuages, lands, tenements, rectories, tithes, rents, reversions, services and other possessions or hereditaments to be had, acquired, received and retained, by the said mayor, bailiffs and burgesses of the borough aforesaid and their successors so as is aforesaid, in all do not exceed the value of sixty pounds a year, the statute concerning the not putting of lands and tenements in mortmain, or any other statute, act, ordinance, provision or restriction to the contrary thereof heretofore had, made, promulgated, ordained or provided, or any other cause or matter whatsoever in any wise notwithstanding : We give also and by these presents for us, our heirs and successors, we grant to all and every one or more of the subjects of us, our heirs and successors, power, licence and authority that they may be able to and can give, lease, grant, alienate or convey manors, messuages, lands, tenements, rectories, tithes, rents, reversions, services and other possessions and hereditaments whatsoever, being within the borough aforesaid or within the suburbs, liberties, limits or precincts of the said borough to the aforesaid mayor, bailiffs and burgesses of the borough aforesaid and to their successors : provided that the said manors, messuages, lands, tenements, rectories, tithes, rents, reversions, services and other possessions and hereditaments do not exceed the clear annual value of sixty pounds a year, the statute concerning the not putting of lands and tenements in mortmain, or any other statute, act, ordinance, provision or restriction to the contrary thereof heretofore had, made, promulgated or provided, notwithstanding : And further of our ampler special grace and from our certain knowledge and mere motion, we have granted, approved, given, ratified and confirmed and by these presents for us, our heirs and successors, we grant, approve, give, ratify and confirm to the aforesaid mayor, bailiffs and burgesses of the borough of

ratificamus et confirmamus predictis maiori, ballivis et burgensibus burgi de Cantabrigia predicta et successoribus suis
omnia et omnimoda tot, tanta, talia, eadem, huiusmodi et
consimilia officia, officiarios, concessiones, liberas consuetudines, libertates, privilegia, franchesias, potestates, leges et
constituciones facienda et ordinanda [et] tenenda curias, fines,
amerciamenta, immunitates, quietancias, exempciones, ferias,
nundinas, mercata, theolonea, tolneta, iura, iurisdicciones,
comoditates, emolumenta, maneria, messuagia, terras, tenementa et hereditamenta quecunque quot, quanta, qualia
et que nuper maior, ballivi et burgenses burgi de Cantabrigia
predicta aut eorum aliqui antehac habuere, tenuere, usi vel
gavisi fuerunt aut habere, tenere, uti vel gaudere debuerunt,
per nomen maioris, ballivorum et burgensium burgi de
Cantabrigia aut per nomen ballivorum et burgensium burgi
de Cantabrigia aut per nomen burgensium burgi de Cantabrigia sive per quecunque alia nomina sive per quodcunque
aliud nomen aut per quamcunque incorporacionem vel corpus
politicum seu pretextu cuiuscunque incorporacionis vel corporis politici premissa aut eorum aliqua data seu concessa
fuerunt predictis nuper maiori, ballivis et burgensibus aut
aliquibus seu alicui predecessorum suorum racione vel pretextu aliquarum cartarum aut literarum patentium per nos
vel per aliquem progenitorum sive antecessorum nostrorum
quoquomodo antehac factarum, confirmatarum vel concessarum, aut racione vel pretextu alicuius legittime prescripcionis, usus seu consuetudinis antehac habite seu usitate, seu
quocunque alio legali modo, iure seu titulo, licet eadem seu
eorum aliquod vel aliqua antehac usi non fuerunt vel fuit, aut
abusi vel male usi, vel discontinuati fuere vel fuit, aut licet
eadem aut eorum aliquod vel aliqua deperdita aut forisfacta
sint aut fuerint, tamen sub limitacionibus et provisionibus
predictis, habendum, tenendum, occupandum, possidendum
et gaudendum eadem maneria, mesuagia, terras et tenementa,
libertates, privilegia, franchesias, iurisdicciones et cetera
premissa eisdem maiori, ballivis et burgensibus burgi predicti
et successoribus suis imperpetuum : Reddendo inde nobis,

Cambridge aforesaid and to their successors, to make and ordain all and all sorts, so many, so great, such, the same, like and similar offices, officers, grants, free customs, liberties, privileges, franchises, powers, laws and customs and to hold courts, fines, amercements, immunities, acquittances, exemptions, feasts, fairs, markets, takings, tolls, rights, jurisdictions, commodities, emoluments, manors, messuages, lands, tenements and hereditaments whatsoever, as, so many, such like and which formerly the mayor, bailiffs and burgesses of the borough of Cambridge aforesaid or any of them heretofore have had, held, used or enjoyed or ought to have had, held, used or enjoyed under the name of the mayor, bailiffs and burgesses of the borough of Cambridge, or under the name of the bailiffs and burgesses of the borough of Cambridge, or under the name of the burgesses of the borough of Cambridge or under whatever other names, or under whatever other name, or under whatever incorporation or body politic, or by pretext of whatever incorporation or body politic the premises or any of them have been given or granted to the aforesaid late mayor and bailiffs, or any one or more of their predecessors, by reason or pretext of any charters or letters patent heretofore in any way made, confirmed or granted by us or by any of our ancestors or predecessors, or by reason or pretext of any legitimate prescription, use or custom heretofore had or used, or by any other lawful manner, right or title, although the same or any one or more of them heretofore has or have been not used, or has or have been abused, or badly used, or discontinued, and although the same or any one or more of them have been lost or forfeited under the aforesaid limitations and provisions, to have, hold, occupy, possess and enjoy the said manors, messuages, lands and tenements, liberties, privileges, franchises, jurisdictions and other the premises to the said mayor, bailiffs and burgesses of the borough aforesaid and to their successors for ever : Rendering thence to us, our heirs and successors, such, like and similar rents, services, sums of money and tenures as thence heretofore were due, payable and of right accustomed to us :

heredibus et successoribus nostris, talia, huiusmodi et consimilia redditus, servicia, denariorum summas et tenuras
qualia proinde nobis antehac debita solubilia et de iure
consueta fuerunt : Quare volumus et per presentes pro nobis,
heredibus et successoribus nostris concedimus prefatis maiori,
ballivis et burgensibus burgi de Cantabrigia predicta et
successoribus suis quod habeant, teneant, utantur et gaudeant
ac plene habere tenere uti et gaudere possint et valeant imperpetuum omnia et omnimoda predicta maneria, mesuagia,
terras et tenementa, redditus, reverciones, libertates, privilegia,
potestates, franchesias, liberas consuetudines, authoritates,
consuetudines, exempciones, iurisdicciones, quietancias, hereditamenta et cetera premissa quecunque predicta secundum
tenorem et effectum harum literarum nostrarum patentium
sine occasione vel impedimento nostri heredum vel successorum
nostrorum quorumcunque : Nolentes quod iidem maior,
ballivi et burgenses burgi predicti vel eorum aliqui vel
aliquis nec aliquis burgensis burgi predicti racione premissorum sive eorum alicuius per nos vel per heredes vel
successores nostros iusticiarios, vicecomites aut alios ballivos
seu ministros nostros heredum seu successorum nostrorum
quorumcunque inde occasionentur, molestentur, vexentur seu
graventur, molestetur, vexetur, gravetur seu in aliquo perturbetur : Proviso semper et firmiter per presentes pro nobis
heredibus et successoribus nostris prefatis maiori, ballivis et
burgensibus burgi predicti et successoribus suis precipimus et
mandamus quod he litere nostre patentes aut aliquid in
eisdem contentum non aliqualiter extendat ad preiudicium,
oneracionem seu impedimentum iurisdiccionum, privilegiorum,
libertatum, consuetudinum, prescriptionum, composicionum,
easiamentorum, finium, forisfacturarum, amerciamentorum,
proficuorum seu hereditamentorum quorumcunque cancellario,
magistris et scholaribus universitatis nostre Cantabrigie seu
alicui seu aliquibus predecessorum suorum per quodcunque
nomen incorporacionis seu per quecunque nomina incorporacionum per nos aut aliquos aut aliquem progenitorum aut
antecessorum nostrorum nuper regum seu reginarum Anglie

Wherefore we will and by these presents for us, our heirs and successors, we grant to the aforenamed mayor, bailiffs and burgesses of the borough of Cambridge aforesaid and to their successors that they may have, hold, use and enjoy and can and may be able to have, hold, use and enjoy fully for ever all and all kinds of the aforesaid manors, messuages, lands and tenements, rents, reversions, liberties, privileges, powers, franchises, free customs, authorities, customs, exemptions, jurisdictions, acquittances, hereditaments and other premises aforesaid whatsoever, according to the tenour and effect of these our letters patent, without let or hindrance of us, our heirs or successors whomsoever: Being unwilling that the said mayor, bailiffs and burgesses of the borough aforesaid or any one or more of them, or any burgess of the borough aforesaid by reason of the premises or any of them should herein be let, molested, vexed or impeded or in any way disturbed by us or by our heirs or successors, justices, sheriffs or other bailiffs or servants of us or of our heirs or successors whomsoever: Provided always and we strictly enjoin and command by these presents for us, our heirs and successors, to the mayor, bailiffs and burgesses of the borough aforesaid and to their successors, that these our letters patent or anything contained in the same shall not in any way extend to the prejudice, injury or hindrance of the jurisdictions, privileges, liberties, customs, prescriptions, compositions, easements, fines, forfeitures, amercements, profits or hereditaments whatsoever granted or mentioned to be granted to the chancellor, masters and scholars of our university of Cambridge or any one or more of their predecessors, under whatever name of incorporation or under whatever names of incorporation by us or any one or more of our ancestors or predecessors sometime Kings or Queens of England, or by the said chancellor, masters and scholars, or to other persons privileged within our university aforesaid by reason or pretext of any legitimate prescription, use or custom heretofore had, made or used, but that the said chancellor, masters and scholars and their successors may have, hold

concessorum seu mencionatorum fore concessorum seu ab iisdem cancellario magistris et scholaribus vel [ad] alias personas infra universitatem nostram predictam privilegiatas, racione vel pretextu alicuius legittime prescripcionis, usus seu consuetudinis antehac habite, facte seu usitate, sed quod iidem cancellarius, magistri et scholares et successores sui omnibus talibus iurisdiccionibus, privilegiis, libertatibus, consuetudinibus, prescripcionibus, composicionibus seu easiamentis, finibus, forisfacturis, amerciamentis, proficuis et hereditamentis habeant, teneant et gaudeant ac habere, tenere et gaudere valeant et possint, libere, pacifice et quiete, hiis presentibus aut aliquo in eisdem contento non obstante : Eo quod expressa mencio de vero valore annuo vel certitudine premissorum seu eorum alicuius aut de aliis donis sive concessionibus per nos seu per aliquem progenitorum sive predecessorum nostrorum prefatis maiori, ballivis et burgensibus burgi de Cantabrigia ante hec tempora factis in presentibus minime facta existit, aut aliquo statuto, actu, ordinacione, provisione, proclamacione sive restriccione in contrarium inde antehac habito, facto, edito, ordinato sive proviso, aut aliqua alia re, causa vel materia quacunque in aliquo non obstante : In cuius rei testimonium has literas nostras fieri fecimus patentes : Teste me ipso apud Westmonasterium tertio die Januarii, anno regni nostri tricesimo sexto.

Per breve de privato sigillo.

PIGOTT.

Pro fine in Hanaperio iij*li.* vj*s.* viij*d.*

GUILFORD, C. S.

Irrotulate in Memorandis scaccarii ciii Rotulo apud Westmonasterium scilicet inter commissiones et litteras patentes de termino Pasche anno tertio regni regis Jacobi secundi ex parte Rememoratoris Thesaurarii.

JO. TAYLEURE.

and enjoy and may be able to and can have, hold and enjoy freely, peacefully and quietly, all such jurisdictions, privileges, liberties, customs, prescriptions, compositions or easements, fines, forfeitures, amercements, profits and hereditaments, these presents or anything contained in the same notwithstanding : Any omission in these presents of an express mention of the true annual value or certainty of the premises or of any of them, or of the other gifts or grants made by us or by any of our ancestors or predecessors to the aforenamed mayor, bailiffs and burgesses of the borough of Cambridge before these times or any statute, act, ordinance, provision, proclamation or restriction heretofore had, made, promulgated, ordained, or provided, or any other fact, cause or matter whatsoever in any wise to the contrary thereof notwithstanding : In witness whereof we have caused these our letters to be made patent : Witness myself at Westminster on the third day of January in the thirty-sixth year of our reign.

By writ of Privy Seal.

PIGOTT.

For fine into the Hanaper £3. 6s. 8d.

GUILFORD, C. S.

Enrolled in the Memoranda of the Exchequer in Roll 103 at Westminster to wit amongst the commissions and the letters patent of Easter Term of the third year of the reign of King James the Second on behalf of the Treasurer's Remembrancer.

JOHN TAYLOR.

APPENDIX.

I. Littere Exemplificatorie Regis Edwardi Tertii.

1365
Nov. 20 [1]Edwardus dei gracia Rex Anglie Dominus Hibernie et Aquitannie omnibus ad quos presentes litere pervenerint salutem.   Inspeximus placitum et processum habitos coram baronibus de scaccario nostro in hec verba : Placita coram baronibus de scaccario de octabis sancti Martini anno regni Regis Edwardi tercii post conquestum quadragesimo.   Prior de Caldewelle venit coram baronibus xviij die Novembris hoc termino per Iohannem de Roderham attornatum suum et queritur per billam de Edmundo Litester ballivo ville Cantebrigie presente super compoto suo de debitis domini Regis levabilibus intra libertatem eiusdem ville reddito hic (*sic*) modo in octabis sancti Martini pro hominibus ville predicte de eo quod cum maior et ballivi predicte ville Cantebrigie qui pro tempore erunt reddent prefato priori annuatim xii marcas x solidos pro tercio denario firme ville predicte quos quidem xii marcas x solidos dominus Iohannes dudum Rex Anglie progenitor domini Regis nunc assignavit comiti David et licet idem ballivus integram firmam ville predicte levaverit et idem prior ipsum ballivum solvendi ei redditum illum sepius requisierit, idem tamen ballivus colore officii sui redditum predictum de duobus annis proxime preteritis videlicet quolibet anno xii marcas x solidos penes ipsum detinet et inde nichil predicto priori solvere voluit set solucionem redditi illius contradixit et adhuc contradicit unde deterioratur et dampnum habet ad valenciam xl librarum : Et hec offert &c.: Et predictus ballivus presens &c.: Et super premissis per barones allocutus defendit dampnum et quicquid &c.: Et petit diem inde loquendi usque in crastinum et habet eundem diem : Et predictus prior similiter : Ad quem diem predictus prior venit per dictum attornatum suum : Et Iohannes de Londonia maior dicte ville Cantebrigie et predictus ballivus veniunt similiter in

---

[1] Original in Borough Archives.   Exchequer seal appended, not by silk strings but by parchment queue.

APPENDIX.

I. LETTERS EXEMPLIFICATORY OF KING EDWARD THE THIRD.

[1]Edward by the grace of God King of England, Lord of Ireland and of Aquitaine, to all to whom the present letters shall come greeting. We have inspected the plea and the process held before the Barons of our Exchequer in these words:—Pleas before the Barons of the Exchequer in the octave of Saint Martin in the fortieth year of the reign of King Edward the Third since the conquest. The Prior of Caldwell comes before the Barons on the 18th day of November in this term by John of Rotherham his attorney and complains by a bill concerning Edmund Litster[2] bailiff of the town of Cambridge now present on his account of the debts of the lord King leviable within the liberty of the said town, rendered in this manner within the octave of Saint Martin for the men of the said town, inasmuch as that whereas the mayor and bailiffs of the said town of Cambridge for the time being render to the said Prior yearly 12 marks and 10 shillings on account of the third penny of the farm of the said town, which 12 marks and 10 shillings the lord John formerly King of England, ancestor of our present lord the King, assigned to Earl David and although the said bailiff has levied the whole farm of the said town and the said Prior has often called upon the said bailiff to pay him that rent, nevertheless the said bailiff under colour of his office keeps the aforesaid rent for the two years last past, namely for each year 12 marks and 10 shillings in his own hands, and would not pay anything thereof to the said prior but has refused the payment of that rent and still refuses, whereby he is defrauded and suffers damage to the value of 40 pounds : And this he offers &c.: And the aforesaid bailiff being present &c.: And being called upon by the Barons concerning the premises he defends the damage and whatever &c. : And he asks for a day for pleading thereon, until the morrow and has the said day :

---

[1] See Cooper, *Annals*, i. 109.
[2] Dyer.

propriis personis suis: Et bene cognoscunt quod maior et ballivi
predicte ville Cantebrigie qui pro tempore erunt reddent prefato
priori annuatim xii marcas x solidos prout predictus prior per billam
suam predictam supponit et quod dictus redditus aretro est predicto
priori per duos annos proxime preteritos: Et predictus prior petit
iudicium de cognicione &c.: Ideo consideratum est quod predictus
prior recuperet redditum predictum versus predictum ballivum videlicet xvij libras pro duobus annis predictis et dampna sua taxata per
barones ad xl solidos: Et idem ballivus pro iniusta detencione in
misericordia &c.: Et predictus prior remittit dampna &c.: et
concessit predicto ballivo diem solvendi ei denarios predictos in
festo concepcionis beate Marie virginis proxime futuro quem diem
solucionis dictus ballivus admisit &c.: Nos autem tenorem placiti et
processus predictorum ad requisicionem predicti prioris sub sigillo
de scaccario nostro duximus exemplificandum.   In cuius rei testimonium has literas nostras fieri fecimus patentes.   Teste T. de Bodelowe
apud Westmonasterium xx die Novembris anno regni nostri tricesimo
nono.

per rotulum placitorum de anno xl termini sancti Michaelis.

II.   Littere Patentes Regis Henrici Sexti.

1455
March 15

[1] Henricus dei gracia Rex Anglie et Francie et dominus Hibernie
omnibus ad quos presentes litere pervenerint salutem.   Sciatis quod
cum prior prioratus de Anglesey et eiusdem loci conventus die
veneris in vigilia Apostolorum Petri et Pauli anno regni nostri
vicesimo sexto per quandam cartam suam dederint, concesserint et
carta illa confirmaverint nobis quoddam gardinum vocatum Henablay
iacens in villa Cantebrigie inter aulam Sancte Trinitatis ex parte
australi et hospicium vocatum Garet hostelle ex parte boriali et

---

[1] Original in Borough Archives.   Great seal in yellow wax appended by
parchment queue.

And the aforesaid prior likewise : On which day the aforesaid prior comes by his said attorney : And John of London the mayor of the said town of Cambridge and the aforesaid bailiff come likewise in their own persons : And they fully acknowledge that the mayor and bailiffs of the aforesaid town of Cambridge for the time being should render yearly to the aforesaid prior 12 marks and 10 shillings, as the aforesaid prior by his aforesaid bill alleges, and that the said payment is in arrears to the said prior for the two years last past : And the aforesaid prior asks for judgment on the acknowledgment &c. : Therefore it is considered that the aforesaid prior shall recover the aforesaid payment from the aforesaid bailiff, namely 17 pounds for the two years aforesaid and his damages assessed by the Barons at 40 shillings : And the said bailiff for unjust detinue in mercy &c. : And the aforesaid prior remits the damages &c. and granted to the aforesaid bailiff a day for payment to him of the aforesaid money on the feast of the conception of the Blessed Virgin Mary next ensuing which day of payment the said bailiff agreed to &c. : We therefore at the request of the aforesaid prior have caused the tenour of the aforesaid plea and process to be exemplified under the seal of our Exchequer. In witness whereof we have caused these our letters to be made patent. Witness T. de Bodelowe at Westminster the 20th day of November in the thirty-ninth year of our reign.

By the roll of Pleas of the 40th year for the Michaelmas term.

II.   LETTERS PATENT OF KING HENRY THE SIXTH.

[1]Henry by the grace of God King of England and France and Lord of Ireland to all to whom the present letters shall come greeting.   Know ye that whereas the prior of the priory of Anglesey and the convent of the same place on the Friday in the Vigil of the Apostles Peter and Paul in the twenty-sixth year of our reign by a certain charter of theirs have given, granted and by that charter have confirmed to us a certain garden called Henablay lying in the town of Cambridge between the hall called Trinity Hall on the South side and the inn called Garret Hostel on the North side and abuts at the

1455
March 15

---

[1] See Cooper, *Annals,* i. 206.

abuttat ad caput orientale super le Mylnestrete et ad caput occidentale super fossam vocatam Kingesdiche, habendum et tenendum gardinum predictum cum suis pertinenciis nobis, heredibus et assignatis nostris imperpetuum, prout in carta predicta plenius continetur, nos de gracia nostra speciali et in recompensacione inter alia cuiusdam fundi sive soli vocati strawlane sive Salthithelane nobis pro elargacione situs collegii nostri Regalis beate Marie et Sancti Nicholai de Cantebrigia per dilectos nobis maiorem, burgenses et comunitatem dicte ville Cantebrigie nuper dati et concessi dedimus et concessimus et per presentes confirmavimus eisdem maiori, burgensibus et comunitati eiusdem ville predictum gardinum cum suis pertinenciis pro comuni transitu sive via inde fiendo et habendo pro comunitate eiusdem ville a dicto vico vocato Milnestrete usque aquam vocatam le Ree habendum et tenendum sibi heredibus et successoribus suis absque aliquo nobis vel heredibus nostris inde reddendo imperpetuum : eo quod expressa mencio de vero valore annuo gardini predicti aut de aliis donis et concessionibus per nos vel aliquem progenitorum nostrorum prefatis maiori et burgensibus aut aliquibus predecessorum suorum ante hec tempora factis in presentibus minime facta existit aut aliquibus statutis sive ordinacionibus editis, factis sive ordinatis non obstantibus. In cuius rei testimonium has literas nostras fieri fecimus patentes. Teste me ipso apud Westmonasterium quintodecimo die Marcii anno regni nostri tricesimo tertio.

per bieve de privato sigillo et de data predicta auctoritate parliamenti.

KYRKEHAM.

Irrotulatur.

East end on the Mylnestrete and at the West end on the ditch called
Kingesdiche to have and to hold the garden aforesaid with its
appurtenances to us, our heirs and assigns for ever, as in the charter
aforesaid is more fully contained, of our special grace and in com-
pensation amongst other things for a certain plot or piece of ground
called Strawlane or Salthithelane lately given and granted to us
for the enlargement of the site of our Royal College of the blessed
Mary and Saint Nicholas at Cambridge by our beloved mayor,
burgesses and commonalty of the said town of Cambridge, we have
given and granted and by these presents we have confirmed to the
said mayor, burgesses and commonalty of the said town the aforesaid
garden with its appurtenances for a common passage or way thence
to be made and to be had for the commonalty of the said town
from the said street called Milnestrete as far as the water called "le
Ree" to have and to hold to them, their heirs and successors, without
any payment to be rendered thence to us or our heirs for ever : any
omission in these presents of an express mention of the true annual
value of the garden aforesaid or of the other gifts and grants made
by us or any of our progenitors to the aforesaid mayor and burgesses or to any of their predecessors before these times or any
statutes or ordinances issued, made or ordained, notwithstanding.
In witness whereof we have caused these our letters to be made
patent. Witness myself at Westminster on the fifteenth day of
March in the thirty-third year of our reign.

By writ of the private seal and of the date aforesaid by authority of
parliament.

KYRKEHAM.

Enrolled.

III. AWARD ON THE TOLL OF NORTHAMPTON BURGESSES.

[1]To all true cristen people to whome this present wrightyng in-
dented of award shall come unto, Richard Ellyott knyght, and Lewes
Pollard knyght, too of the Kynges Justices of his comon bank, send
gretyng in our Lord God everlastyng. Where variance and debates
hath been dependyng between the mayar, beyliffs and burgesses of
the town of Cambrigge on that oon partie and the mayar, beyliffs
and the comburgesses of the town of Northamton on that other
partie, of, for and upon certeyn tolle and custome cleymed and
asked by the said mayar, beyliffs and burgesses of Cambrigge of
the said mayar, beyliffs, ffranchesed, ffremen and comburgesses of
Northampton for fysshys and barells and all other stuffe and merchaundizes by them particularly bought in Stirbrigge ffeyre and all other
maner of passages and carriages thurgh and by the said town of
Cambrigge all tymes of the yere, which the seid parties have compro-
mitted them selffs to abyde and stond to the arbitrament, ordinaunce
and iuggement of us the said Richard Elyott and Lewes Pollard, and
we the said Richard and Lewes heryng and seyng aswell the tytles
and cleyme made by the said mayar, beyliffs and burgesses of
Cambrigge as the aunswers and allegyngs of the said mayar, beyliffs
and comburgesses of Northamton and also rypely perceyvyng the
same upon good deliberacyon and advysament by the assent of both
the seid parties have awarded in fourme folowying, that is to sey, ffirst,
where the said mayar, beyliffs and burgesses of Cambrigg have
certeyn plegges for tolle by them cleymed and asked of the said
mayar, beyliffs and comburgesses of Northamton by them taken at
Stirbrigge ffayre last holden, that the said mayar, beyliffs and burgesses
of Cambrigge or oon of them shall before the ffest of the exaltacion
of the holy Crosse next comyng upon request made, redelyver the
said gages to the ownar therof or to his deputie or deputies peying
so moche money, tolle and custome as the said gages ys leyd for,
and that the said mayar, beyliffs and comburgesses of Northamton
or oon of them shall paye yerly for ever for them and for all the
comburgesses and ffranchesed and fremen of the same town of
Northamton and ther successours to the said mayar, beyliffs and

---

[1] See Cooper, *Annals*, i. 301. In the Borough Archives.

burgesses of Cambrigge and to ther successours or to ony of them for all maner of stuffe, barelled ware and other merchaundizes bought in the same feyre and all other passages and carriages thurgh and by the seid town of Cambrigge at all tymes of the year only x^s by yere in full recompence and satisfaccion of all maner of tolle or custome hereafter to be due to the said mayar, beyliffs and burgesses of Cambrigge and to ther successours and the same some of x^s to be payd yerly in the tolle-both or ellswher within the said fayre in the vigill of the exaltacion of the holy Crosse aforesaid to the seid mayar, beyliffs and burgesses of Cambrigge aforesaid or to ony of them over and besides for every cart that goeth loden owt of the said ffayre with ther stuffe, the said cartar to paye to the said mayar, beyliffs and burgesses of Cambrigge or to ther assynes for ever ij^d. And also it ys awarded between the seid arbitratours that all fforeners that be no comburgesses nor ffranchesed men nor freemen of the said town of Northamton shall not be discharged by this present arbitrament but to be contributours to the said mayar, beyliffs and burgesses of Cambrigge accordyng to right and custome of the seid ffayre this award not withstondyng. Also we the seid arbitratours award that for further suarte of this owr award that the seid parties before the ffest of All Saynts next commyng shall make indentures eche to other concernyng this our award sealed with ther comon sealles and after the same indentures be so sealed and delyvered that the seid parties or ony of them shall delyver suche obligacyons as they stond bounden in eche to other for the perfourmaunce of this award. In witnesse wherof we the said arbitratours to every parte of this present award have sette our sealles; yoven the iiijth daye of the moneth of June in the xith yere of the reign of king Henry the viijth.

IV. Littere Patentes Philippi et Marie.

1557
June 3

[1]Philippus et Maria Dei gracia Rex et Regina Anglie, Hispaniarum, Francie, utriusque Sicilie, Jerusalem et Hibernie, Fidei Defensores, Archiduces Austrie, Duces Burgundie, Mediolani et Brabantie, Comites Haspurgi, Flandrie et Tirolis, omnibus ad quos presentes littere pervenerint salutem. Cum quidam annualis redditus octo librarum quindecim solidorum et duorum denariorum annuatim exeundus et soluendus de certis Shopis et lez Bowthes in Sturbridge in comitatu nostro Cantebrige in tenura maioris, ballivorum et burgensium ville nostre Cantebrige ad sustentacionem et manutencionem certorum obituum, anniversariorum et annualis cuiusdam elemosine erga pauperes infra predictam villam annuatim fiende ratione cuiusdam actus parliamenti apud Westmonasterium anno regni precharissimi fratris nostri Edwardi Sexti nuper Regis Anglie secundo tenti ac ratione cuiusdam presentacionis secundum tenorem eiusdem actus habite et facte in manus dicti nuper fratris nostri devenit ac eciam in manibus nostris iam existit, et cum dictus precharissimus frater noster a tempore eiusdem parliamenti annuatim durante vita sua soluerit et dederit ac nos similiter a regno nostro inchoato hucusque annuatim solverimus et dederimus prefatis maiori, ballivis et burgensibus ville nostre predicte quendam alium annualem redditum sex librarum decem solidorum et sex denariorum parcellam suprascripti annualis redditus octo librarum quindecim solidorum et duorum denariorum, ea intencione quod iidem maior, ballivi et burgenses annuatim et de tempore in tempus predictum annualem redditum sex librarum decem solidorum et sex denariorum per nos ut prefertur eisdem datum et solutum erogarent et distribuerent ac erogari et distribui facerent pauperibus et egenis infra predictam villam nostram Cantebrige inhabitantibus commorantibus ad tempora et loca usitata iuxta pias et laudabiles donatorum voluntates ac modo et forma prout iidem maior, ballivi et burgenses semper antea usi ac facere soliti fuissent : Sciatis igitur quod nos tam pro causis et consideracionibus predictis ac intuitu pietatis quam habemus ad pios ecclesie ritus et ceremonias secundum catholicam fidem et donatorum voluntates infra predictam villam nostram Cantebrige annuatim imperpetuum de cetero fiendas et observandas, ac eciam pro eo quod

---

[1] Original in Borough Archives with a portion of the great seal in brown wax appendant. Initials elaborately adorned with portraits of the King and Queen, Tudor arms, &c.

IV. LETTERS PATENT OF PHILIP AND MARY.

[1]Philip and Mary, by the grace of God, King and Queen of England, Spain, France, the two Sicilies, Jerusalem, and Ireland, Defenders of the Faith, Archdukes of Austria, Dukes of Burgundy, Milan and Brabant, Counts of Hapsburg, Flanders, and Tyrol, to all to whom the present letters shall come, greeting. Whereas a certain yearly rent of eight pounds, fifteen shillings and twopence, yearly issuing and to be paid from certain shops and booths in Sturbridge in our county of Cambridge in the tenure of the mayor, bailiffs and burgesses of our town of Cambridge, for the support and maintenance of certain obits, anniversaries and of a certain annual alms to be made to the poor within the aforesaid town yearly, by reason of a certain act of a parliament held at Westminster in the second year of the reign of our dearest brother Edward the Sixth late King of England, and by reason of a certain presentment had and made according to the tenour of the said act, fell into the hands of our said late brother and is also now in our hands, and whereas our said dearest brother, from the time of the said parliament yearly during his life, paid and gave, and we likewise from the beginning of our reign till now yearly paid and gave to the aforesaid mayor, bailiffs and burgesses of our town aforesaid a certain other yearly rent of six pounds, ten shillings and sixpence, parcel of the aforesaid annual rent of eight pounds, fifteen shillings and twopence, with the intention that the said mayor, bailiffs and burgesses yearly and from time to time should levy and distribute and cause to be levied and distributed the aforesaid annual rent of six pounds, ten shillings and sixpence given and paid by us to them as is aforesaid for the poor and needy dwelling and staying within our aforesaid town of Cambridge, at the times and places accustomed, according to the pious and praiseworthy wills of the donors and in manner and form as the said mayor, bailiffs and burgesses ever before were used and wont to make it : Know ye therefore that we, both for the causes and considerations aforesaid, and by the prompting of the piety which we feel towards the pious rites and ceremonies of the church according to the catholic faith and towards the wills of donors henceforth to be carried out and observed yearly for ever within our aforesaid town of Cambridge, and also because the aforesaid shops

[1] See Cooper, *Annals*, ii. 132.

predicte shope et lez bowthes in Sturbridge predicta sunt et tempore
sessionis parliamenti predicti fuerunt terre custumarie et non de
nobis aut de aliquo manerio nostro tente ac proinde supradictus
annualis redditus octo librarum quindecim solidorum et duorum
denariorum de eisdem shopis et lez bowthes exeundus ac ut prefertur
annuatim soluendus iuxta puram simplicem legittimam intencionem
predicti actus parliamenti ac ratione et vigore eiusdem aliquo legittimo
modo in manus predicti precharissimi fratris nostri devenire non
debuisset et in manibus nostris iam existit aut existere potest quam
pro fidelitate, industria ac acceptabili servicio nobis per predictos
maiorem, ballivos et burgenses antehac habitis factis et impensis ac
imposterum habendis fiendis et impendendis de gracia nostra speciali
ac ex certa sciencia et mero motu nostris dedimus et concessimus ac
per presentes damus et concedimus prefatis maiori, ballivis et burgensibus predicte ville nostre Cantabrigie, supradictum annualem
redditum octo librarum, quindecim solidorum et duorum denariorum
de predictis shopis et lez bowthes in Sturbridge annuatim exeundum
et soluendum adeo plene libere et integre ac in tam amplis modo et
forma prout iidem maior, ballivi et burgenses predicti postremo reci-
tatum annualem redditum vnquam habuerunt, usi vel gavisi fuerunt,
aut habere, vti vel gaudere debuerunt, aut potuerunt, si idem annualis
redditus nunquam in manus predicti precharissimi fratris nostri aut
nostras devenisset, et adeo plene, libere et integre ac in tam amplis
modo et forma prout idem annualis redditus ad manus dicti precharissimi fratris nostri ratione vel pretextu predicti actus parliamenti
vel aliter quocumque modo devenit seu devenire debuit devenerunt
seu devenire debuerunt ac in manibus nostris iam existit vel extite-
runt seu existere debet vel debuerunt: Habendum, tenendum,
gaudendum et retinendum predictum annualem redditum octo
librarum quindecim solidorum et duorum denariorum per nos per
presentes preconcessum eisdem maiori, ballivis et burgensibus et
eorum successoribus imperpetuum ad opus, usus et intenciones
supradictas annuatim imperpetuum ut prefertur [ut] observarent
perimplendo: Mandantes enim et per presentes firmiter iniungentes,
precipientes tam Thesaurario et Baronibus Scaccarii nostri quam
omnibus et singulis receptoribus, auditoribus et aliis officiariis et
ministris nostris heredum et successorum nostre prefate Regine
quibuscumque et eorum cuilibet quod ipsi et eorum quilibet [per]
solam demonstracionem harum litterarum nostrarum patentium aut

and booths in Sturbridge aforesaid are and at the time of the session of the parliament aforesaid were customary lands and not held of us or of any manor of ours, and therefore the aforesaid annual rent of eight pounds, fifteen shillings and twopence issuing from the said shops and booths and to be paid yearly as is aforesaid, according to the pure, simple, lawful intention of the aforesaid act of parliament, and by reason and by force of the same, could not come into the hands of our aforesaid dearest brother and is not and cannot be in our hands now in any lawful manner, and further for the fealty, zeal and acceptable service hitherto had, done and rendered to us by the aforesaid mayor, bailiffs and burgesses and henceforth to be had, done and rendered, of our special grace and from our certain knowledge and mere motion we have given and granted and by these presents we give and grant to the aforesaid mayor, bailiffs and burgesses of our aforesaid town of Cambridge the aforesaid annual rent of eight pounds, fifteen shillings and twopence, issuing and to be paid from the aforesaid shops and booths in Sturbridge yearly, as fully, freely and wholly and in as ample a manner and form as the said mayor, bailiffs and burgesses ever had the last-named yearly rent or were wont to use or enjoy or ought to or could have, use or enjoy the same, if the said yearly rent had never fallen into the hands of our aforesaid dearest brother or our own, and as fully, freely and wholly and in as ample a manner and form as the said yearly rent came or ought to come to the hands of our said dearest brother by reason or pretext of the aforesaid act of parliament or otherwise in any way, and now is or ought to be in our hands: To have, hold, enjoy and keep the aforesaid yearly rent of eight pounds, fifteen shillings and twopence by these presents above granted by us to the said mayor, bailiffs and burgesses and their successors for ever, that as is aforesaid they may see to the fulfilling of the use, purpose and intents above named yearly for ever: Ordering and by these presents firmly enjoining and command-ing both the Treasurer and the Barons of our Exchequer, and all and singular the receivers, auditors and other officers and ministers of us and of the heirs of our aforesaid Queen, whomsoever and to each of them, that they and each of them make and cause to be made on a single exhibition of these our letters patent or of the enrolment of the same, without asking, seeking or prosecuting any other writ or warrant from us or the heirs or successors of our

super irrotulamentum earundem, absque alio breui seu warrento
a nobis vel heredibus aut successoribus nostre prefate Regine quoquo
modo impetrando obtinendo seu prosequendo, plenam, integram,
debitamque allocacionem, defalcacionem, deduccionem et exonera-
cionem manifestam prefatis maiori, ballivis et burgensibus et eorum
successoribus de omni predicto annuali redditu octo librarum quindecim solidorum et duorum denariorum per nos per presentes
preconcesso facient et fieri causabunt: Et hec littere nostre patentes
aut irrotulamentum earumdem erunt annuatim et de tempore in
tempus tam dictis Thesaurario et Baronibus Scaccarii nostri quam
omnibus et singulis predictis receptoribus, auditoribus et aliis officiariis et ministris nostris heredum et successorum nostre prefate
Regine quibuscumque et eorum cuilibet sufficiens warrantia et exone-
racio in hac parte: Ac ulterius damus pro consideracione predicta ac
ex certa sciencia et mero motu nostris, [et] per presentes concedimus
prefatis maiori, ballivis et burgensibus totum illum predictum redditum octo librarum quindecim solidorum et duorum denariorum et
proficua eiusdem a festo Sancti Michaelis archangeli ultimo preterito
hucusque proveniencia siue crescencia: Habendum eisdem maiori,
ballivis et burgensibus ex dono nostro absque compoto seu aliquo alio
proinde nobis et heredibus vel successoribus nostre prefate Regine
quoquomodo reddendo, solvendo vel faciendo: Ac eciam volumus
pro consideracione predicta ac ex certa sciencia et mero motu nostris
per presentes concedimus prefatis maiori, ballivis et burgensibus quod
habeant et habebunt has litteras nostras patentes sub magno sigillo
nostro Anglie debito modo factas et sigillatas absque fine seu feodo
magno vel parvo nobis in hanaperio nostro seu alibi ad usus nostros
quoquo modo reddendo, solvendo vel faciendo: Eo quod expressa
mentio de vero valore annuo aut de certitudine premissorum sive
eorum alicuius aut de aliis donis sive concessionibus per nos vel per
aliquem progenitorum nostre prefate Regine prefatis maiori et ballivis
et burgensibus ante hec tempora factis in presentibus minime facta
existit aut aliquo statuto, actu, ordinacione, provisione sive restriccione inde incontrarium facto, edito, ordinato, seu proviso, aut
aliqua alia re, causa vel materia quacumque in aliquo non obstante:
In cuius rei testimonium has litteras nostras fieri fecimus patentes.
Testibus nobis ipsis apud Westmonasterium vicesimo tercio die
Junii annis regnorum nostrorum tercio et quarto.

per breve de priuato sigillo &c.

NAYLOUR.

aforesaid Queen in any way, full, entire and due allowance, exemption, deduction and open exoneration to the aforesaid mayor, bailiffs and burgesses and their successors, of all the aforesaid annual rent of eight pounds, fifteen shillings and twopence granted above by us by these presents: And these our letters patent or the enrolment of the same shall be yearly and from time to time a sufficient warrant and excuse in this behalf both to the said Treasurer and Barons of our Exchequer and to all and singular the aforesaid receivers, auditors and other officers and ministers whomsoever of us and of the heirs and successors of our aforesaid Queen and to each of them: And further we give for the consideration aforesaid and from our certain knowledge and mere motion and by these presents we grant to the aforesaid mayor, bailiffs and burgesses all that aforesaid rent of eight pounds, fifteen shillings and twopence and the profits of the same from the feast of St Michael the Archangel last past arising or accruing till now: To have to the said mayor, bailiffs and burgesses of our gift without rendering, paying or making any account or anything else therefor to us and the heirs or successors of our aforesaid Queen in any way: And also we will for the aforesaid reason and from our certain knowledge and mere motion by these presents we grant to the aforesaid mayor, bailiffs and burgesses that they may and shall have these our letters patent under our great seal of England, made and sealed in due manner without fine or fee, large or small, to be rendered, paid or made to us into our hanaper or elsewhere for our use in any way: Any omission in these presents of an express mention of the true annual value or of any other value or certitude of the premises, or of any of them, or of other gifts or grants made by us or by any of the ancestors or predecessors of our aforesaid Queen before these times to the beforenamed mayor, and bailiffs and burgesses, or any statute, act, ordinance, provision or restriction, made, issued, ordained or provided to the contrary hereof or any other fact, cause or matter in any wise notwithstanding: In witness whereof we have caused these our letters to be made patent. Witness ourselves at Westminster, the twenty-third day of June in the third and fourth years of our reigns.

By writ of privy seal &c.

NAYLOUR.

B. C.   14

Cambridge:

PRINTED BY J. AND C. F. CLAY,
AT THE UNIVERSITY PRESS.

For EU product safety concerns, contact us at Calle de José Abascal, 56–1°, 28003 Madrid, Spain or eugpsr@cambridge.org.

www.ingramcontent.com/pod-product-compliance
Ingram Content Group UK Ltd.
Pitfield, Milton Keynes, MK11 3LW, UK
UKHW010341140625
459647UK00010B/733